SMOKY POKERSHIP

VERLAG *für* MODERNE KUNST

IMPRINT
Editing and Concept
Sibylle Omlin

Layout
Bonbon – Valeria Bonin, Diego Bontognali,
and Pierrick Brégeon, Zürich

Texts
Sally De Kunst, Barnaby Drabble, Katya
García-Antón, Federica Martini, Sibylle
Omlin, Dorothee Richter, Gavin Wade

Translation
Michael Turnbull (German › English),
Nikolaus G. Schneider (English › German)

Proofreading
Ines Gebetsroither, Silvia Jaklitsch, Sibylle
Omlin, Katharina Sacken (German),
Michaela Alex, Helmut Gutbrunner, Steve
Tomlin, Michael Turnbull (English)

Production
DZA Druckerei zu Altenburg GmbH
© 2013, Sibylle Omlin, Verlag für moderne
Kunst Nürnberg, the artists and authors

Photo Credits (Artists)
Evelyn Bermann (Simon Kindle / Sophie Hofer),
Christian Glaus (Dorothea Rust), Ingrid
Kaeser (Davor Ljubičić), Davor Ljubičić
(Janusz Baldyga, Katrin Keller, Pe Lang, Davor
Ljubičić, Denis Romanovski, Dorothea Rust),
Valerian Maly (Klara Schilliger / Valerian
Maly), Sibylle Omlin (Janusz Baldyga, Boris
Nieslony, Christophe Fellay, Victorine Müller,
Katja Schenker, Stuart Sherman), Stefan Postius
(Janusz Baldyga, Berclaz de Sierre), Michael
Zanghellini (Victorine Müller).

Photo Credits (Texts)
Thomas Hirschhorn (p. 14), Christoph
Schlingensief (pp. 16, 57), Santiago Sierra
(p. 24), Dexter Sinister (p. 27), Charles
Filch (p. 29), Spartacus Chetwynd (p. 58),
Belluard Bollwerk International Fribourg
(pp. 64, 65, 67, 69, 70), Sylviane Tille (p. 66),
Wrigth & Sites (p. 68), Christian Hasucha
(p. 71), Kosi Hidama & Gosie Vervloessem
International Fribourg (p. 72), Reggie Watts
(p. 73), Eastside Projects Birmingham (pp. 76,
77), Heather & Ivan Morison (p. 78), Peter
Fend & Lawrence Weiner (p. 79)

ISBN 978-3-86984-413-8
Printed in Germany. All rights reserved.

Published by
Verlag für moderne Kunst Nürnberg GmbH
Königstrasse 73, D-90402 Nürnberg
www.vfmk.de

Bibliographic information published by
Die Deutsche Nationalbibliothek. Die Deutsche
Nationalbibliothek lists this publication
in the Deutsche Nationalbibliografie; detailed
bibliographic data is available on the Internet
at http://dnb.ddb.de.

Distributed in the United Kingdom
Cornerhouse Publications
70 Oxford Street, Manchester M1 5 NH, UK
Phone +44-161-200 15 03,
Fax +44-161-200 15 04

Distributed outside Europe
D.A.P. Distributed Art Publishers, Inc.
155 Sixth Avenue, 2nd Floor, New York, NY
10013, USA
Phone +1-212-627 19 99,
Fax +1-212-627 94 84

ACKNOWLEDGEMENTS
Artists and Authors
Federica Martini, Barnaby Drabble (Co-Orga-
nizer of the symposium in April 2011)

Partner and Financial Support
Kunstraum Engländerbau, Vaduz (Evelyn
Bermann); K3, Zürich (Sandi Paucic); Marks
Blond Bern (Daniel Suter); Kunstverein
Konstanz e.V., Konstanz (Michael Günther);
Fondation Château Mercier, Sierre (René-
Pierre Antille); Pro Helvetia; Ernst Goehner
Stiftung; Ecole cantonale d'art du Valais,
Sierre; HES-SO, fonds stratégique; Loterie
Romande; Jubiläumsstiftung Raiffeisen;
Migros-Kulturprozent; Ernst und Olga Gubler-
Hablützel Stiftung; Kanton Bern/Swisslos
Kultur (Valerian Maly/Klara Schilliger);
Stadt Bern, Bürgergemeinde Bern (the Marks
Blond Project, Bern); Kanton Wallis (Berclaz
de Sierre, Christoph Fellay); Kulturstiftung
Liechtenstein (Victorine Müller);
Liechtensteinische Landesbank Vaduz (Simon
Kindle and Sophie Hofer); Stiftung Fürstlicher
Kommerzienrat Guido Feger, Vaduz (Simon
Kindle and Katrin Keller); Kanton Solothurn
(Victorine Müller); Kanton Zürich Fachstelle
Kultur (K3); Regierungspräsidium Freiburg
(Kunstverein Konstanz); Kulturförderung
Kanton St.Gallen (Katja Schenker); Stiftung
Ostschweizer Kunstschaffen (Katja Schenker);
Freunde und Förderer des Kulturzentrums am
Münster e.V.; Sappi Schweiz AG; Kunstgiesserei,
Stadt Gossau (Katja Schenker)

Project Assistance
Ingrid Kaeser (Assistance)
Jérôme Lanon (web)

prohelvetia

RAIFFEISEN
Raiffeisen Jubiläumsstiftung

ERNST GÖHNER STIFTUNG

SMOKY POKERSHIP

Perform
the Exhibition
Space

Sibylle Omlin
(Ed.)

Introduction

This book brings together contributions from an international group of art practitioners, curators and theorists exploring the relationship between performance and installation in the context of the contemporary art exhibition. Key concern of the book is the possibility of rethinking the static model of installation and exhibition and exploring the way in which 'performative' approaches, adopted by artists and curators alike, can reframe the exhibition and its work exposed as an environment undergoing formal, temporal or relational transformation.

The notion of the performance installation or installAction itself implies an element of 'live performance' issued from a spatial installative setting, and in these particular surroundings the performance will be the act of a transformation. The performer performs a selected process that alters an installation/spatial setting during an exhibition. This process of exhibiting/organising installations and performances itself could be seen as a process of meta-representation of the live performance as later elements of an installation, as the contribution of Sibylle Omlin points out. The objects and relicts of a performance in such a context are reflected by the contribution of Federica Martini.

With reference to history, theory and examples of contemporary projects, these texts reflect upon the way that diverse artistic and curatorial practices can be seen addressing several linked questions: If allowed to transform and evolve its surroundings, how might performance reprogram the exhibition format? To what extent do experiments between performance and installation describe a new role for exhibition audiences? Theses two questions are followed in the contributions of Katya Garcia Anton, reflecting on the possibilities of relational art, and of Dorothea Richter, who in her contribution develops the relation between performing arts in post-dramatic theatre and installations in a visual art context. In Barnaby Drabble's text the relation between art work and public within an exhibition follows the interpretation as a play of voices and dialogues.

With a renewed focus on the participatory and process-based possibilities of the exhibition, one main thesis of all contributors was to what extent has curating itself become a performative activity. The texts of Gavin Wade and Sally De Kunst, reflecting their own practice as curators in a contemporary art space in Birmingham and as a director of a Performance Festival in the public space in the city of Fribourg, CH, try to develop this thesis as artistic palimpsest practice in the exhibition space and conceptual in situ art work for public spaces.

These texts represent the content of a symposium about this issue, held in April 2011, at Château Mercier in Sierre (organised by ECAV, the Ecole cantonal d'art du Valais). The symposium marked the end of a performative exhibition project that linked 5 different spots/organisations and 17 different artists in the field of performance and installation art, called *Belly of the Whale*, organised and curated by Sibylle Omlin (www.installaction.com). The contributions of the symposium at the historical and mannerist late 19th century castle consisted not only of texts and lectures, but also of performances, installations and lectures of respondents to the conferences. The images in the central part of the book suggest a possible story of this exhibition project, *Belly of the Whale*.

The editor

TRANSFORM THE EXHIBITION SPACE

Performance Art Practice between Performance and Installation

Sibylle Omlin

The practice of the installation in performance art has become increasingly interesting for contemporary art over the past two decades, especially the dovetailing of performance and installation. Diverse curatorial formats have been explored in this context in art spaces, festivals, museums and public spaces. With museums such as the Museum of Modern Art in New York,[1] the MOCA in Los Angeles[2], the Museum for Contemporary Art in Frankfort, the Villa Arson in Nice and the Migros Museum in Zurich[3], to name only a few examples, addressing performance art, the recording of the performance as space and object, apart from the moment of the live event, has become a specific theme.

As a form of activity and physical action, performance art is not only closely connected to the pictorial invention of visual art and theatrical performance but also to music, dance, spoken word and process-oriented art.[4] New performance-specific forms such as interactions in public space, performative installations in alternative spaces and long-duration performances increasingly demand new formats in the exhibition world.

Theoretical reflection on the transformation of performance into spatial installation and vice versa is, however, still available only in its incipient stages. That is why this essay focuses on research into this transformation, in theory and in artistic practice. I take performance as the point of departure for an exhibition apparatus that oscillates between event/performance and installation in the exhibition context and contains temporal and spatial aspects. Thus it revolves less around the symbiosis of action, event and installation in the exhibition space than around the question of transformation and temporal duration of exhibition formats and the artistic works involved.

How can something emerge from the performance, from the event or the action, from the material, that is more enduring than a photograph of a performance? How is a performance transformed into an installation and how can it leave behind spatial relationships?

I will start from the following theses/observations which where also important to start the project *Belly of the Whale:*

1. The integration of objects or materials into a performance is already structured in a way that the object can lead its own life even apart from the performance.
2. The installation as a form of thematic or political event tied to space lends itself to the spatial expansion of performance. The transformation or metamorphose of the performance plays an especially crucial role here.
3. The extent of the performativity of an installation in relation to its appearance and intensity cannot be completely predictable and controllable (cf. especially Thomas Hirschhorn's and Christoph Schlingensief's concepts of installation). That turns the installation into an appropriate artistic medium for transforming the performance into spatial presence and duration.

4. The transformation of ephemere materials like language or weather phenomena into space can be linked to sculptural-installative elements.

The concept of installAction, coined by the Swiss performers Valerian Maly (*1959) and Klara Schilliger (*1953), is also interesting in this context. The Maly/Schilliger duo locates its work above all in the space between performance and installation, since their performances and installations are often, but not always, site-specific interventions, which are preceded by research related to the project. Still powerful as well are the concepts of 'living sculpture', used by the British artists Gilbert and George, and of 'performative sculpture', used by Victorine Müller (*1961), which also applies to exhibitions of relicts and performance materials in the context of space.

From Speech Act Theory
to the Aesthetic of Installation

The central theory concealed behind the performance action is speech act theory, which attributes to every element of the performance in its execution of the performative character that is in fact the essence of an authentic execution of performance.[5] In her interpretation of this theory, Judith Butler later emphasised as well that the performative character of a linguistic action, or any action, can only be determined from the constantly renewed execution of that action. Some people today, such as Philip Auslander, are considering whether it might not be the case that performance is always already structured towards deferred action – that is, planned and executed for a document or fixing visual medium.[6] The narration of the event, the discourse about it, also represents an essential component of the artistic performance.

Over the past ten years in the history of contemporary performance art, there has thus been a shift in interest away from the body of the performer to the relational space and context of the performance. This concern with the space intended for the performance – stage, public space, exhibition format – calls for new forms in the evolution of performance, for example, the environment or the action, politically committed projects, or art actions in social space.

The concepts of the event and the installation have become central to the development of contemporary performance art. Let us look somewhat more intently at the second term: the installation.

The installation stands for a construction of a space within the space of art that is defined by the artist. The performance stands for the enlivening, inhabiting and occupation of this space by the artist's body. Both forms of art began during the period of political upheaval around 1968, when conventions and institutions that had previously been considered valid were called into question.

Both installation and performance are no longer satisfied with the accustomed space for art – the museum or exhibition space. Both forms of art tend to expand into public space, to inhabit a space of social intervention. Both performance and installation have thus extended and scrutinised the context of art. The position of the beholder/viewer has also been affected. The beholder in the museum, walking along the walls and looking at paintings or photographs, becomes a 'flâneur' moving freely within the space of the installation or performance, seeking her or his own perspective and standpoint. The relationship between the work and the viewer in art forms based on the installation and performance is conceived as part of space in the life-world.

The Transformation
of the Installation

The term 'installation' – first used by Dan Flavin in 1967 for a work with fluorescent lights – already referred at that time to this space of the life-world that became relevant for artistic questions. Dan Flavin integrated everyday fluorescent lights, electrical lighting, electrical wiring and installation elements from building technology into his artistic works. The context of life-world and everyday life lend a corresponding significance to the term 'installation'. Flavin used the term because 'environment' sounded too sociological to him.[7] Using everyday elements such as electrical lighting for simple perceptions of space was, in his eyes, a radically simple artistic activity. This simplicity and radicalness subsequently became significant both for installation and performance art. The dramatic quality associated with such aesthetic questions is also central to both media. The term 'installation' was also submitted to a form of deconstruction in the works of Gordon Matta Clark – his *anarchitectures* were direct interventions in abandoned buildings and industrial sites – although the deconstructing gesture left something transformed behind. Transformation is thus inherent in both contexts – performance and installation.

"What is created under the term 'installation' are not so much works as models of their possibilities." With this observation, Juliane Rebentisch legitimises, in her *Ästhetik der Installation*, an indeterminacy factor that is fundamental to installation art; the continual transgression of genre boundaries and definitions can be seen as the main characteristic of this artistic phenomenon. According to Rebentisch, the installation fundamentally calls into question the given context of aesthetic expectations.[8]

The nature of the concretisation at work in the case of an installation is characterised by the process-based character of reception and its uniqueness in relation to the body of the active observer. That means a primary subjectivisation of aesthetic reflection. In that context, installation art certainly has similarities to other time-related and performative art forms, which can be included under the keywords action, happening, performance and body art. As Paul Schimmel demonstrated in his influential 1998 study, these art forms imply a changed understanding of the perceiving audience.[9] The viewer is no longer the passive recipient of content represented by artistic media.[10] On the contrary, the reactions of the viewer are an integral component of performative forms of art, just like the actions of the artist-protagonist and the props used.

These reactions are activities related to the presence of the body, and they drive the event and thus create discursive situations that can be experienced in time and as real. Such works of art do not lay claim to the audience's contemplative reflection and perception but rather involve "the whole physical polysensuality and the viewer's active relationships that are constitutive of the work." [11]

If we compare the viewer's involvement in time-related, performative art forms with the relation of the observer within installation art, it becomes clear that the physicality of the viewer is also involved as an active constituent of the work in spatial installation art and provides the foundation for shaping his or her experience when perceiving an installation. But as the specific technique for provoking an experience does not go back to the action of the artist/performer (performance) or to his or her instructions (happening) but rather to the spatial arrangement itself, it is referred to as 'situative'.

Studies of situation- and site-specificity in art in turn do not take the spatial localising of the installation as their point of reference, but rather its performative potential.[12] If we consider the process of perception that takes place when aesthetically opening up an installation, it becomes clear that installations are time-dependent art forms.[13] In an installation, a very precise function is assigned to time in the dependence on perception that is generally necessary for aesthetic experience. It is the time a viewer needs to walk through the installation. This simple fact also determines the make-up and installation organisation of the given exhibition space, which is also a space of perception.

The design of an installation space is dictated by the idea of prescribing as far as possible the viewer's movement and visual perspectives. But this is precisely what makes it possible to describe this movement as narrative or even cinematic in nature. The opening up of the installation space is determined by a space-time, before-and-after perspective that dictates the observer's movement and their supposedly free wandering through space. If we consider, under these premises, the way an installation space is perceived, we can speak of the establishment of a rhythm of the excerpts of reality, perceived as a succession of impressions.

One important example in the area of installation, one that above all integrates performative and narrative elements into the space of the installation, is the work of Thomas Hirschhorn (*1957 in Bern, Switzerland; lives in Paris).

The Swiss artist defamiliarises forms of presentation in the area of the installation. Using wood, Plexiglas, cling wrap, aluminium foil, wrapping paper and tape, he builds chaotic-seeming, inscrutable structures where a spectator easily can feel lost. They are connected with research on a specific kind of historical event or philosophical thought, which finds expression in a performative interaction with the audience.

Not content with the imposed definitions and limitations of a capitalist, multinational rhetoric of globalisation, Thomas Hirschhorn makes use of the communicative potential of thinking. His work, which ignores material value, comprises various models of the installation, primarily composed of the cheap product packaging materials of the consumer industry – aluminium foil, plastic, cardboard and plywood – and thus converts the desires of capitalism into a state of enduring creative anarchy. Hirschhorn's temporary monuments for Benedict de Spinoza (1999 and 2009, Amsterdam), Gilles Deleuze (2000, Avignon) and Georges Bataille (2002, *dOCUMENTA*, Kassel), which address community commitment and the 'quality of inner beauty' (Hirschhorn), follow a logic of ephemerality, accretion and potential openness.

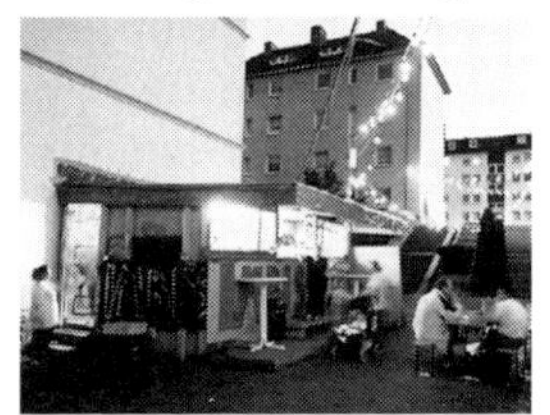

For his *Bataille Monument* Hirschhorn mapped the city for more than a year, from personal and social perspectives, eventually integrating the work into the life of a marginalised community in the Friedrich Wöhler-Siedlung for the duration of *dOCUMENTA11*.[14] Dispensing with the traditional categories of knowledge production, the work takes the collecting and exhibiting functions of the museum, which have become formalised into a ritual, and brings them back into public space. The philosophical recourse to Georges Bataille is deliberate. Thomas Hirschhorn writes: 'I am a fan of Georges Bataille; he is at once a role model and pretext. Bataille explored and developed the principles of loss, of overexertion, of the gift, and of excess. I admire him for his book *La part maudite* and his text *La notion de dépense*. Choosing Bataille means opening up a broad and complex force field between economy, politics, literature, art, erotica, and archaeology.[15]
The *Bataille Monument* consisted of eight related elements:
— A sculpture out of wood, cardboard, tape, and plastic.
— A Georges Bataille Library, with books that refer to Bataille's oeuvre, arranged according to categories of word, image, art, sports, and sex – a collaboration with Uwe Fleckner.
— A Bataille exhibition with the topography of his oeuvre, a map, and books on and by Georges Bataille – a collaboration with Christophe Fiat.

— Various workshops through the duration of the exhibition (8 June to 15 September 2002) – a collaboration with Manuel Joseph, Jean-Charles Massera, Marcus Steinweg, et al.
— A stand with food and drinks.
— A television studio that broadcasts daily a brief show from the *Bataille Monument* on the public-access channel Offener Kanal Kassel.
— A shuttle service that brings the visitors from *dOCUMENTA11* to the *Bataille Monument* (and back) and residents of the neighbourhood to *dOCUMENTA11*.
— A website with webcams from the *Bataille Monument* (24 hours, 7 days).[16]

The monument was intended not only to call the concept of the monument into question, through its location, its materials and the duration of its exhibition, but also to provide a special place and time for discussion and ideas. Hirschhorn's monuments emphasise the view from below, the view of the mobile, social and non-representative. The *Bataille Monument* was thus also a social project, which permitted connections to a non-exclusive audience and created relationships that would not have been possible otherwise in this neighbourhood. The installation was also the pretext or occasion in this project to go through performative actions with a group of visitors, to transform events medially and to convey content.

Performance as Visual Event and Presentation

In parallel with the development of the exhibition apparatus forming the performance as an image, its repeatability as visual activity and the exhibiting of relicts of the performance have opened up the path to the museum, to the classical exhibition situation, for this medium.[17] Exhibitions on performance art with installations, dance performances in the white cube and monographic exhibitions on individual performance artists reveal a transformation in this art form. The audience continues to be direct observers of and accomplices in a live action, but increasingly the performers choose spatial displays to anchor their action specifically in the exhibition space.

In the late 1990s, cultural theorists re-launched the discussion of the terms 'presentation', 'performance', and 'performativity' in the arts, beginning in Germany with the theatre studies scholars Erika Fischer-Lichte and Hans-Thies Lehmann.[18] Starting with reflections on the 'linguistic turn' in the 1950s in the United States and the United Kingdom (J. L. Austin's *How to Do Things with Words*), in view of the 'iconic turn' in the 1990s the discussion was expanded to 'how to do things with images/art'. The use of images and visual activities seemed attractive for theatre and dance performances; socially active art's grab of public space and the space of classical cultural institutions was on the programme. The notion of performance in the visual arts as conspiratorial and taking place in the seclusion of insider festivals, where it was seen only 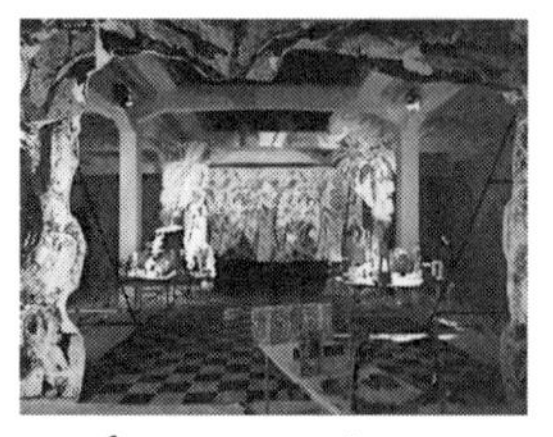 by the initiated, was over. Today, performance is presented in large-scale dramatisation on institutional stages. With his work, Christoph Schlingensief, who was then still known primarily as a man of the theatre, swept through the Biennials and the museums. Conversely, the artist Jonathan Meese staged large-scale performances such as *Jonathan Meese ist Mutter Parzival* at the Staatsoper in Berlin.

The performative turn even began to influence the view of knowledge in cultural studies. The view of knowledge as drama – that is, the change from a model of knowledge to one of presentation in its (self-)description – became a paradigmatic role model for the interpretation of performance in theatre and art studies at the end of the twentieth century.[19] Analogously to the theoretical discussions of space in the 1970s by Henri Lefebvre *(La Production de l'espace)* and Michel de Certeau *(L'Art du quotidien/L'Art d'agir)*, performance underwent a transformation into space, which included the space of society as well.

The Combination of Performance and Installation

One important exhibition for this discussion was *Mise en Scène: Theater und Kunst* at the Grazer Kunstverein in 1998, which was dedicated to the combination of presentation and stage elements. The theme was taken up by Andreas Baur and Stephan Berg in 2002, organising the exhibition *On Stage* at their institutions in Esslingen and Hanover (Kunstverein Hannover), respectively, in 2002/2003. Udo Kittelmann was likewise concerned with issues of the life world and of performance in the museum context, as demonstrated by the exhibition *Das lebendige Museum* at the Museum für Gegenwartskunst in Frankfurt in 2003 (no catalogue), where he was head curator at the time.

Also in 2003, a team of curators led by Angelika Nollert (now head of the Neues Museum für Kunst und Design Nürnberg) organised an exhibition on 'performative installation', conceived for various art spaces in Germany and Austria.[20] The five-part exhibition series *Performative Installation* at the Galerie im Taxispalais in Innsbruck (2003), the Ludwig Museum in Cologne (2003–2004), the Museum für Gegenwartskunst Siegen (2003–2004), the Secession in Vienna (2004), and the Galerie für zeitgenössische Kunst Leipzig (2004) took place at the initiative of and in cooperation with the Siemens Arts Program. Each exhibition was autonomous and took up one possible aspect of the theme. The concept of 'performative installation' was coined for this series of exhibitions and understood to mean a concrete artistic work with the character of an event.[21]

The exhibition series *Performative Installation* explored very distinct concepts of performative installation. Ranging from constructed situations of reality in the exhibition space to participatory media installations in which the audience was invited to participate, and *Body Display*, which thematised the exhibition space of the Vienna Secession as a stage and showed bodies acting on it in its quality as a projection screen for public identities. The works thus demonstrated performative, installational, referential and communicative processes. The exhibition as 'display' standing for a spatial form of presentation that attempted to integrate the audience directly and actively into the events.

The subject matter of performativity as an aspect of action and of the character of an event in relationship to the present was achieved through the concept of the installation and the end product of the installation's qualities, characterised with the adjective 'performative'. That also meant that performance as the singular execution of an action in Judith Butler's and Peggy Phelan's sense was not the focus of the exhibition's investigations. 'The performative installation is not about breaking down the work in the event, but rather about the event as constitutive power of the installation, about the symbiosis of event and work.'[22]

This exhibition project was thus about launching a concept, while defining it only tentatively. The focus of interest was on the concept of performative installation, which has to organise the theatrical quality of the presentation in a different way than common to a stage space, where the temporal formats of the audience's presence are predefined. The concept of the installation has become a universal concept. It subsumes many forms of artistic expression that escape more precise definition. Based on its etymology, the word means first and foremost the submitting and inserting of objects as process and result. Installation introduces one thing to another and seeks to take the viewer into this space of relationships. It can incorporate and fit together everything. Above all, 'installation' is also an evaluative concept that, in addition to its quality of space and experience, possesses the ability to create an original, singular, and individual context similar to that of performance. The concept of the installation would thus appear to be in a position to create a unique context for art that is able to address in a special way the intrinsic context of the system of art.

Summary

Performance art thus remains a field for situational and site-specific activities, one that can figure into all the areas and contexts of life. One of the great challenges for this medium is that the context – that is, the venue, the space and the audience – directly influences the performance. By 'directly' I mean more quickly, more reactively, more relentlessly than in other forms of art such as painting, composed music or theatre. This demonstrates that the broad field of performance makes it necessary to differentiate. Historical, media and contextual relationships are becoming increasingly important when positioning oneself clearly within the mass of offerings and interpretations. 'Whether it is a spontaneous initiative of artists in temporary spaces or a performance from established institutions such as theatres or theatre festivals influences how they are perceived and in turn reflects back on the works', emphasises the performance artist Dorothea Rust, who is also active as an organiser of performances.[23]

Performance art continues to be an artistic strategy with which performers trigger surprises, densely packed moments, astonishment and confusion, even to the point of a lack of understanding. That also affects not least the aesthetic of the performative installation.

1   Marina *Abramovič, The Artist Is Present,* Museum of Modern Art, 14 March – 31 May 2010. In this context the artist showed her longest long-duration performance conceived for a museum context.

2   See Paul Schimmel's exhibitions since 1998, such as *Out of Actions: Between Performance and Object, 1949–1979,* conceived and curated by Paul Schimmel for MOCA Los Angeles in 1998.

3   *While Bodies Get Mirrored: An Exhibition about Movement, Formalism and Space,* 6 March 2010–30 May 2010; Christoph Schlingensief, *Querverstümmelung,* 3 November 2007 – 3 February 2008, among others.

4   See Sibylle Omlin, ed., *Performativ! Performance-Künste in der Schweiz; ein Reader* (Zurich: Pro Helvetia, 2004).

5   J. L. Austin, *How to Do Things with Words* (Oxford: Clarendon Press, 1962)

6   Philip Auslander, *Liveness: Performance in a Mediatised Culture* (London and New York: Routledge, 1999), esp. 'Against Onthology', pp. 38–45.

7   Johannes Stahl, *Installation,* in Hubertus Butin, ed., *DuMonts Begriffslexikon zur zeitgenössischen Kunst* (Cologne: DuMont, 2002), pp. 122–126, esp. p. 124.

8   Juliane Rebentisch, *Ästhetik der Installation* (Frankfurt am Main: Suhrkamp, 2003), p. 103.

9   Paul Schimmel, ed., *Out of Actions: Aktionismus, Body Art und Performance, 1949–1979,* (Ostfildern-Ruit: Hatje Cantz, 1998).

10   Lea Vergine, *Body, Art and Performance: The Body as Language* (Milan: Skira, 2000; orig. pub. 1974).

11   *Gerhard Graulich, Die leibliche Selbsterfahrung des Rezipienten: Ein Thema transmodernen Kunstwollens* (Essen: Verlag Die Blaue Eule, 1989), p. 17.

12   For a critical discussion of the state of research in English on this subject, see Peter Osborne, *Review on Recent Literature on Installation,* in Caroline Arscott, ed., *On Installation,* special issue of *Oxford Art Journal,* vol. 24, no. 2 (2002), pp. 145–154.

13   See Rebentisch, *Ästhetik der Installation* (see note 8), pp. 146–162.

14   The artist worked with young people from the Philippinenhof boxing camp to construct the monument; they were paid for the work they did.

15   See www.bataillemonument.de (accessed 20 June 2011).

16   Benjamin Buchloh, Alison M. Gingeras, Carlos Basualdo. *Thomas Hirschhorn,* (London; New York: Phaidon, 2004).

17   The performer Boris Nieslony considers that performance art in the 1970s was actually produced in the gallery space, and hence always worked with the spatial apparatus. The development of the performance with the culture of festivals is primarily a Francophone and European phenomenon. Discussion with the artist, 8 April 2011.

18   Erika Fischer-Lichte, Clemens Risi and Jens Roselt, eds., *Kunst der Aufführung, Aufführung der Kunst,* Recherchen 18 (Berlin: Theater der Zeit, 2004); Erika Fischer-Lichte and Christoph Wulf, eds., *Theorien des Performativen,* special issue of *Paragrana* 10, no. 1 (Berlin: Akademie-Verlag, 2001); Erika Fischer-Lichte, (2004): *Ästhetik des Performativen* (Frankfurt am Main: Suhrkamp Verlag, 2004); Erika Fischer-Lichte and Christoph Wulf, eds., *Praktiken des Performativen,* special issue of *Paragrana* 13, no. 1 (Berlin: Akademie-Verlag, 2004); Uwe Wirth, *Performanz: Zwischen Sprachphilosophie und Kulturwissenschaften* (Frankfurt am Main: Suhrkamp, 2002). Hans-Thies Lehmann, *Postdramatisches Theater* (Frankfurt am Main: Verlag der Autoren, 2005); Erika Fischer-Lichte and Doris Kolesch, eds., *Kulturen des Performativen,* special issue of *Paragrana* 7, no. 1 (Berlin: Akademie-Verlag, 1998).

19   See Christoph Wulf and Jörg Zirfas, eds., *Die Kultur des Rituals: Inszenierungen, Praktiken, Symbole* (Paderborn: Wilhelm Fink Verlag, 2004); Doris Bachmann-Medick, *Performative Turn,* in D.B.-M., *Cultural Turns: Neuorientierungen in den Kulturwissenschaften,* 3rd rev. ed. (Reinbek: Rowohlt, 2009), pp. 104–143; and Jacques Derrida, 'Signature Event Context', trans. Samuel Weber and Jeffrey Mehlman, in Derrida, *Limited Inc.* (Evanston, IL: Northwestern Univ. Press, 1988), pp. 1–23.

20   Angelika Nollert, ed., *Performative Installation,* exh. cat. (Cologne: Snoeck, 2003).

21   This series of exhibitions was also a central point of departure for my reflections and curatorial experiences in the project *Im Bauch des Wals.* See www.installaction.com.

22   Nollert, *Performative Installation* (see note 20), p. 14.

23   Dorothea Rust, e-mail to the author, 8 July 2011.

SLAVES TO THE RHYTHM

Performing Sociability in the Exhibitionary Complex

Katya García-Antón

Just what is it that has made performativity in the exhibitory complex of the last fifteen years so appealing, so attractive?[1] Has the unpredictable, and fruitful, dynamic of performativity been condensed into aesthetic forms of ambiguous sociability and superfluous experience? How did the 1960s and 1970s' conceptual drive to extend aesthetic process over time and location, from the studio to the gallery space and beyond, result in the congealment of process and its commodification into a performative event? These questions and more are at the core of an intense internal debate taking place amongst curators regarding the limits of performativity in today's exhibition making.

The spell of performativity that has infiltrated the tissue of the exhibitory complex has transformed the relation between artist, curator and audience. This trend goes beyond exhibitions featuring performances or performative installations to span curatorial and artistic projects defined by multiple orchestrations of conferences, dialogues, interviews, debates, conversations, performed publications as well as educational projects and learning events. It seems that performativity has become an art of encounter, privileging a space for sociability amongst audiences (including art professionals, funders and collectors). Indeed there is much common ground between the performative and what has become known in recent years as the discursive and the educational turn in curatorial practice. Within which context are these developments operating? Undoubtedly the correlation between the notion of the society of the spectacle and the emergence of 'the experiential' drives the wave of performativity in the arts today. Moreover, one cannot ignore the impact on creative practice of a society led by the dynamics of consumption, where art works suffer from the pressure to be suitably easy to consume and ready to entertain. Furthermore, curators exposed to the increasing demands of the capitalisation of knowledge find themselves having to perform as discursive brokers of their reputation, in order to territorialise their intellectual capital and compete in an experiential terrain.

In a society where the state is gradually withdrawing from its cultural and social responsibilities, and in a period of radicalisation between the 'haves and have-nots', how have the original dynamics of performativity been transformed? Is this related to an art world where creative value is increasingly defined by market players; an art world politically manoeuvred by government's populist and democratic agenda, and socially hijacked by the wealthy to serve as their private playground? Has performativity ceased, to a large extent, to operate as a radical agent: producer of aesthetic knowledge and a transgressor of aesthetic boundaries? Has it been infiltrated by the dynamics of consensus-making and camouflaged by the false promise of a democratic art? This text will highlight how shifts in the triangulation 'curator, artist and audience' in recent performative exhibition making has rendered the practice problematic; and point to a number of ways to explore spaces of resistance to this impasse.

Three Models for an Art of Encounter

One of the most commonly observed hallmarks of a performative art project today is the notion of 'participation'. Nowhere has this been more prevalent in recent times than in Nicolas Bourriaud's 1998 theorisation of a group of artists whose work came to be known under the aegis of 'relational aesthetics'.[2] Posited as an art form of social exchange, Bourriaud also considered that relational aesthetics offered a way to overcome "the utopianism of the historical avant-garde, not by simply abandoning it, but by realising it, through the localised and momentary formation of alternative ways of living"[3]. The French critic's thoughts have often been referred to as a theory of art for the 1990s; and they certainly became a mantra for many an exhibition in the following decade. According to Bourriaud, relational artworks were being produced by a panoply of artists, amongst them Rikrit Tiravanija, Pierre Huyghe, Philippe Parreno, and Carsten Holler, with the aim of enacting deep social transformation of the conditions and conception of art. Bourriaud's introduction to his text on the subject reads as follows: "Rikrit Tiravanija organises a dinner in a collector's home, and leaves him all the ingredients required to make a Thai soup. Philippe Parreno invites a few people to pursue their favourite hobbies on May Day on a factory assembly line… Christine Hill works as a checkout assistant in a supermarket and organizes a weekly gym workshop in a gallery". However, as we shall see, this focus on the theatricalisation of experience has turned out to be one of the weaknesses in Bourriaud's argument.

There is a sense in Bourriaud's ideas whereby relational artworks are conceived as autonomous communes, even if they are actualised only for a moment. For example, Rikrit Tiravanija's project *The Land,* which he co-founded in 1998 in rice fields outside of Chiang Mai in Thailand, was described by the artist as a lab for sustainable environment and artistic projects, a sort of eco-aesthetic community. The realised utopianism of such a relational project made it resonate with the formation of various anti-capitalist movements since the 1990s. Indeed the series of articles brought together in Bourriaud's book *Relational Aesthetics* could be read as a manifesto, in his own words "for a new political art, a micro-political disengagement from the capitalist exchange, creating a trading community that eludes the capitalist economic context."[4] Such a declaration resonated reassuringly with much of the activist background behind performance in the 1960s and 1970s, giving it gravitas and pedigree.

In the last six years, however, various critics have explored, on the one side, the darker side of the relational coin; and on the other, the wider socio-economic factors that have contextualised its seamless ubiquity in curatorial practice. Stewart Martin and Claire Bishop sought in two different articles, *Critique of Relational Aesthetics* and *Antagonism and Relational Aesthetics* respectively (both from 2006), to draw attention to the profound limits in Bourriaud's problematic proposal.[5] They discuss the need to reclaim history and reconstruct the idea of relational aesthetics as a 'critical' art of social exchange. Stewart observes that the anaesthetisation of novel forms of capitalist exploitation, in the works mentioned by Bourriaud, become "helplessly reversed into an aestheticisation of capitalist exchange."[6] Both authors point to the exclusion of relational artists whose work challenges Bourriaud's model, and hence highlight the need to reassess this history. In particular Bishop proposes the notion of 'antagonism' as a form of relational resistance, whereby relational art functions as an immanent critique of the commodity of form. A prime example for both critics is the work of Santiago Sierra who, along with other artists engaged in arguably relational work, is not discussed in *Relational Aesthetics*. Sierra sets up simple situations in which on the one hand, people are employed (with contractual remuneration) to operate the art work in a manner that highlights their commodification and instrumentalisation, whilst simultaneously embroiling the gallery visitor within the very ethics of such processes. Such was the case of *Three people paid to lay still inside three boxes during a party* staged during the Havana Biennial in 2000. Three young women were hired and paid 30 dollars each to remain inside a wooden box during a biennial art party. Invited guests were not informed about the content of the boxes they were using as seats. Si-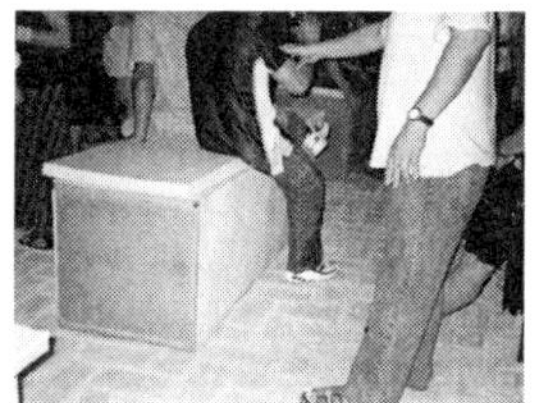erra literally bought the time of those young women; and the guest was caught in the artist's web, their presence being the motivation for the piece to be created in the first place. This type of work is an anomaly for Bourriaud's theory; a relational art which doesn't posit a social space apart from commodification, but rather highlights the social exchange as being mediated by money, building on the traditions of institutional critique of the 1970s.

Bishop and Stewart's central arguments are similar, both maintaining that Bourriaud's convivial encounters are not adequately antagonistic to count as democratic, and in doing so they push for a corrective to Bourriaud's ethics of inter-subjectivity. This opens up questions regarding the political substance of relational art by asking for an antagonistic (political) rather than convivial (ethical) account of art's social relations. But it is also true that within this alternative theory of the relational, the presumption is that the politics of encounter have to be resolved within the work. The problem is that in establishing this as the main parameter of the work, one neglects other options, in which hegemony could also be challenged.

In relation to Bourriaud's conviviality and the more conflictual relations favoured by Bishop and Stewart, Grant Kester offers a third model to this debate, one which neither limits social encounters to convivial ones nor restricts its political antagonisms to the ones overtly present in the work. In his book *Conversation Pieces, Community and Communication in Modern Art*, Kester provides a robust account of the relationship between participatory cultural processes and the turn to discursive practices. He tracks a reflection that operates, in his own words, "between art and the broader social and political world."[7] This model is politically spiced up: a "new genre of public art", which develops an ethics for artists out of the contrast between a "patronising form of tourism", and "a more reciprocal process of dialogue and mutual education."[8] As an introduction to his ideas, Kester proposes that the traditional aesthetic strategies and categories of both modernism and postmodernism converged on "a general consensus that the work of art must question and undermine shared discursive conventions."[9] He lists the common features of these avant-garde frameworks as follows: on the one hand, "they favoured a reductive model of discursive interaction based on the traditional opposition between somatic and cognitive experience"; on the other hand, they tended "to restrict the definition of aesthetic experience to moments of immediate visceral insight"; and finally, they were "based on an essential solitary interaction between the viewer and a physical object, which disallows a comprehension of collective processes in the moments of production and reception within the creative practices."[10]

In opposition to this, Kester looks towards a different view of the artist, one interested in an emancipatory model of "dialogical interaction". Indeed we could consider that by extension his thoughts inevitably could also form our understanding of a performative curatorial practice. The directive proposed is one for an open, listening and vulnerable artist, in relation to the viewer or collaborator. The social models and techniques that Kester's dialogical artists use tend to be derived from political contexts. Kester traces his argument within existing practices including the work of Stephen Willats whose practice is conducted as an open work, based on agreement and open agreement. Willats' work encompasses the polemics and issues of our contemporary culture and society as a means of consciously examining the function and meaning of art in society. This necessarily takes it beyond the norms and conventions of an object-based art world, rather seeing it as a function of his work to transform peoples' perceptions of a deterministic culture of objects and monuments, into the possibilities inherent in the community between people, the richness of its complexity and self-organisation; the artwork having a dynamic, interactive social function. For Willats these concepts have remained a constant, as he wrote in the 1960s:

"A work of art can itself constitute a societal state, a model of human relationships.

A work of art can consist of a process in time, a learning system through which the concepts of the social view forwarded in the work are accessed and internalised.

A work of art must acknowledge the relativism inherent in perception and the transience of experience, there being no right or wrong, it taking the form of an open-ended process.

A work of art can engage anyone meaningfully, being available to whoever wishes to enter its domain, only through embodying in its presentation the means by which people are able to acquire the necessary language and procedures to receive and internalise its meaning.

My work engages the audience in a new way of encountering art in society. I am not talking about a compliance, but something more active, a mutual understanding, an interaction between people – similar to the dynamic image of the Homeostat where all the parts of the network are equal and equally linked."[11]

More recently the German group WochenKlausur have developed projects that intervene directly in the social fabric providing medium term infrastructural, institutional, strategic solutions to perennial social problems like prostitution, elderly care, medical provision for the homeless, classroom design, voting systems, immigration, and social barriers, amongst others. In their own words, "on invitation from different art institutions, the artist group WochenKlausur develops concrete proposals aimed at small but nevertheless effective improvements to socio-political deficiencies. Proceeding even further and invariably translating these proposals into action, artistic creativity is no longer seen as a formal act but as an intervention into society."[12]

The problem is that Kester's argument, and the examples of artistic practice cited (consider the use of the term 'socio-political deficiencies' in the web-site introduction by WochenKlausur), can default into being a moralising one, due to its focus on the conduct of the artist in relation to a given community. This raises the question of whether such thinking limits the art of the encounter (the social in art) to the political field, and this problematic aspect is left unresolved by Kester.

Having now looked at three models of sociability within the art of encounter, let us consider the wider conditions under which they operate. It is a context, let us not forget, in which curators are increasingly under pressure to literally perform spaces of communality in their projects; a context to which audiences (or, more influentially, funders both private and public?) appear increasingly addicted.

A Contextual Critique
of Sociability in Art

Jan Verwoert's text, *Exhaustion and Exuberance. Ways to Defy the Pressure to Perform,* looks at the sinister turn that faces the labours of contemporary art workers, in particular the pressures to 'excessively' perform. The text was written by Verwoert during a performative printing project initiated by Dexter Sinister in 2007 at the Centre d'Art Contemporain in Geneva, where they compiled and printed issue 15 of the publication Dot Dot Dot [13]. The issue investigated the nature of contemporary production, overproduction and exhaustion. Dexter Sinister forced Verwoert to work within the conditions he had called into question in an earlier text that year entitled *Use Me Up* [14]. As Dexter Sinister observe in their introduction: "Quite literally to force the producer to produce in the immediate space of his imminent deadline, symbolised by the brooding presence of a waiting printing press. Over a compressed fortnight the rest of the issue then emerges in realtime around this premise." [15]

As Verwoert explains in his performative text: "After the disappearance of manual labour from the lives of most people we have entered into a culture where we no longer just work, we perform. Being an ever expanding group of creative types, who invent jobs for ourselves, by exploring and exploiting our talents to perform small artistic and intellectual miracles on a daily basis. It is we, the socially engaged – who create communal spaces for others and ourselves by performing as instigators of social exchange. When we perform we generate communication and thereby build forms of communality. When we perform we develop ideas and thereby provide the content for an economy based on the circulation of a different currency: information." [16]

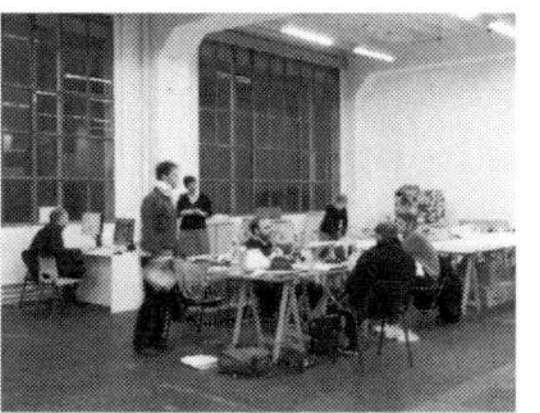

Verwoert concludes that in a high performance culture, 'we' are the avant–garde but 'we' are also the job-slaves. Being part of that 'we', one cannot help sympathising at this stage with Verwoert's further description of the similarities of the world of art workers and that of sex workers. 'We' are always ready to perform, any time, any place in the world, thinking new and creative ways to augment the satisfaction of the experience for our clients, and hopefully achieve a new commission.

Indeed 'experience' does seem to be the leitmotif of our times. Lars Bang Larssen has made this patently clear in a recent text entitled *Zombies of Immaterial Labour: The Modern Monster and the Death of Death* regarding the pressure that the capitalisation of creativity has exerted on artistic practice and thinking in the last decade; pushing it towards the terrain of the experiential and consensual. For Bang Larssen art has become a norm, and within the current 'experience economy' arts normative power consists in commodifying a conventional idea or art's mythical otherness with a view to the reproduction of subjectivity and economy. Bang Larssen goes on to present the thinking of James H. Gilmore and B. Joseph Pine II, who ten years ago launched the concept of the experience economy with their book *The Experience Economy: Work is Theatre and Every Business has a Stage*.[17] This proposal describes an economy where experience is a new source of profit to be obtained through staging the memorable.

"What is being produced is the experience of the audience, and experience is generated by 'authenticity effects'. In the experience economy it is often art, and its markers of authenticity – creativity, innovation, provocation – that ensure economic status to experience … The psychological premise of being able to alter the consumers' sense of reality is central. Gilmore and Pine highlight the profitability of simulated situations … It is clear how the consequences of the experience economy can have an effect on dismantling of artistic and institutional signification as well as social connections."[18]

In the same article Bang Larssen points to the evocative notion of self-doping imagined by fellow critic Diedrich Diederichsen, in his article *Eigenblutdoping: Selbstverwertung, Kunstlerromatik, Partizipation*, in 2008.[19] In this Diederichsen goes one step further than Bang Larssen by looking at the addiction in audiences drawn to projects whose experiential promise is one in which there is actually nothing new to inscribe, no unique identity to contribute or craft towards construction of something new, but rather the space of inscription is one of predictability, consensuality. Diederichsen posits that the traditional power of the cultural institution is displaced when audiences are invited to play and participate, in an ostensible democratisation of art. Within this false premise audiences lose the possibility of inscribing their subjectivities on anything beside themselves, and are robbed of an important opportunity to respond to the institution and the exhibitionary complex where art is presented.

The thinking of Bourriaud, Bishop, Stewart, Verwoert, Bang Larssen and Diederichsen, amongst others, constitutes a revealing discussion regarding the factors that create and problematise the notion of performativity today. It is vital, however, not to limit the debate to critique; let us also attempt to imagine a space for a practice of resistance for art workers within the performative scenario. What indeed might be these other ways to perform? Could we imagine an aesthetic experience that operates within a field of collective agency, where workable forms of resistance can be devised?

Mining the Social through Conflict, Laxity and Crime

One way to enter this discussion is by imagining how to challenge the role of the audience within a performative field. Indeed if so far we heard calls to reconstitute the history of artistic practice, or a repossession of the energy expenditure within the furnaces of the art world, it is also essential to consider the operative space of the audience within this debate. In the final series of the trilogy *The Nightmare of Participation*, Markus Miessen imagines a new type of participant, one not subservient to predefined codes of practice and production, but an uncontrollable irritant.[20] The idea leads Miessen to go as far as advocating the possibility of a 'conflictual participant'. He argues that over the last decade, the term 'participation' has become increasingly overused. When everyone has been turned into a participant, the often uncritical, innocent and romantic use of the term becomes frighteningly vacuous. Supported by a repeatedly nostalgic veneer of worthiness, phony solidarity and political correctness, participation has become the default of politicians withdrawing from social and cultural responsibility. Similar to the notion of an independent politician dissociated from a specific party, this third part of Miessen's *Participation* trilogy encourages the role of what he calls the 'crossbench practitioner,' an 'uninterested outsider' and 'uncalled participator' who is not limited by existing protocols, and who enters the arena with nothing but creative intellect and the will to generate change.

It is perhaps the kind of participant that Charles Filch seeks. Filch, 'the beggar', is the secondary and marginal character that artist Dora Garcia asks to sporadically 'escape' (re-cast by professional actors) from Bertolt Brecht's *Three Penny Opera*. Filch's first invitation by the artist was to spend the summer in the *Munster Sculpture Project* (2007) and keep a diary of his encounters with the locals and the international art scene there (www.beggarsopera.org). His latest escapade was to the Spanish Pavilion in the Venice Biennial 2011, appearing on stage in the project *L'Inadeguato, Lo Inadecuado, The Inadequate*. The pro-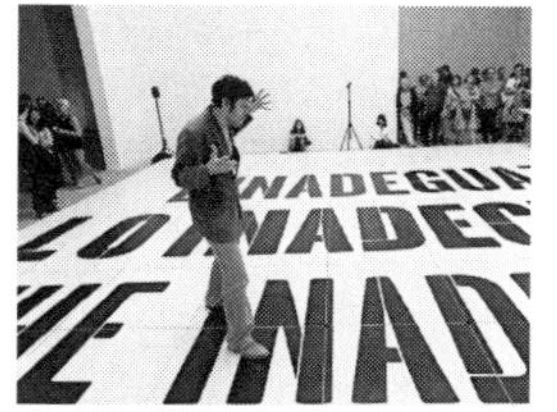ject gives us a reason to discuss on the one hand, the different kind of space for the audience, an aspect sympathetic to Miessen's conflictual participant, and on the other, a model for a processual type of performativity which avoids the congealment of the event.[21]

In a discursive, extended performance broaching the notions of deviation, radicality, the outsider, exclusion, censorship and marginality, actors Samir Kandil and Peter Aers, who developed the role, were given few directives by Garcia. Whilst in Venice they inevitably fed from their experiences in Munster, they also called on the internal logic of their own work. The performance fed too from the lax, occasional member of the audience who made the decision to engage or whom they attempted to engage with, or disengage from or ignore. For this space of dis/engagement there was no predetermined protocol, no task to complete and no groups of participants, previously sought out by a mediator, to make the work possible. Indeed Filch doesn't exist for the public specifically, his presence and actions take place whether or not an audience is present. Indeed none of the usual 'facilities' were offered to the audience to participate within the project, it was an inadequate forum ambiguous towards participation as such. The spectator was not conceived of as an essential part of the work, but as a casual passerby. And yet the engagement with different moments of Filch's process, or indeed of *The Inadequate's* dynamics, could take forward the internal structure of the work, furthering in an immaterial manner its creative density.

And yet whilst the parameters of *The Inadequate* were rigorously elaborated, an openness of form remained in each of its moments. In the case of Filch this freedom provoked us into unearthing and questioning the dichotomies that Garcia inserted into a situation, and which characterise so much of her practice. With Filch, the artist sidesteps the concept of participation as understood in *Relational Aesthetics*. She operates beyond modes of consensus, and opens up a space for Miessen's notion of conflictual participation – no longer a process by which others are invited 'in', but a means of acting without mandate, as an uninvited irritant: a forced entry into fields of knowledge that arguably benefit from exterior thinking. If participatory art has been fetishised as the conduit of a democratic art, then sometimes, democracy has to be avoided at all costs. Indeed the promise of participation today in performative exhibitions can also be experienced as a default space from which politicians can withdraw responsibility. The democratisation of art may indeed bear the pungent whiff of its privatisation. Rather than breeding the next generation of consensual facilitators and mediators, one could argue for irritation as a creative force. If, in *The Inadequate,* processual discursivity liberated the audience from the confinement of participation, the project *A Crime against Art* scripted the audience into the performance, thereafter giving them freedom of action. A hybrid project, somewhere between a conference, collective workshop and performance, it fundamentally employed discursivity as a means to explore the triangulation between performativity – spectacle – participation. *A Crime against Art* explored the inherent contradictions and complexities within the figure of the curator, the artist, the critic and the spectator within such a performative setup.

Conceived as a staged conceptual trial within the environment of the ARCO art fair, Madrid, in 2007, *A Crime against Art* was inspired by the mock trials organised by avant-garde movements (André Breton) in the 1920s and 1930s, which theatrically raised a number of polemical issues in the world of contemporary art.[22] The project, set as a television courtroom drama and filmed by four camera crews, began with the assumption that a crime had been committed. The process took place in real time and was not scripted, this openness being a key factor in the performative discussion held. The potential perpetrators of the crime, the defendants, had handed themselves in, yet the nature and evidence around the crime were allusive and no victims had come forward. Within this open-ended theatrical discussion the testimonies and cross-examinations became an attempt to unravel the nature of the puzzling 'crime against art'.

The accusations summarised the problematics of performance that concern this essay, that is the dichotomy between the creation of a space for agency, set off against the collusion with the gargantuan machine of spectacle and consumption that typify an art fair (or biennial, amongst other platforms) as places in which to produce performative art. In other words it asked the question of how to accept the invitation to create a performative project within a space such as an art fair, and still maintain a space of independence that questioned the morals of participation within the system. *A Crime against Art* incorporated a questioning discourse into its remit in an attempt to avoid becoming a wasted possibility of critical artistic agency; another moment of entertainment contributing to the further reduction of the little space left for contemporary art as a vector of enquiry. Such an impasse was eloquently targeted by Expert Witness and curator Maria Lind, who presented excerpts from an art report regarding the art world of the future which foresaw that 'In 2015, artists' … (we could say here that this applies to all art workers) … "who refuse to take part in the entertainment industry will inevitably live under deteriorating conditions."[23]

The result of the trial in *A Crime against Art* – the issue of whether the defendants were ruled innocent or guilty – was not really the point. The purpose rather was a discussion and enactment of the use and abuse of performative structures, within the eroticised and spectacularised space of an art fair. *A Crime against Art* attempted to reconfigure performance as a potential value for change, and so unveil several points of controversy in the contemporary art scene. Furthermore, the project questioned the notion of responsibility within an art work, especially where performance and participation are concerned, and experimented with ways of negotiating the performative creation of art discourse.

A rhythmic NO

What the performances of *Charles Filch* and *A Crime against Art* point to is the importance of discursivity on various fronts. On the one hand, in problematising performance's natural good fit with public entertainment in today's consumer based society, and on the other, in creating a different dynamic for the public's engagement with, and construction of, the work of art. Finally these works also highlight the value of discursivity as an internal mode of critique for art workers and thinkers.

Perhaps out of this heterogeneous genealogy of objectives we might understand the strange complementarity and synchronicity between the ascendancy of the curatorial gesture (evermore creator of discourse) and the advocacy of language exchange as a paradigm of practice. Added to which is the ubiquitous appeal of the term 'discourse' as a word to conjure and perform power. In short the discursive turn that predominates the art world (curators and artists) … and therefore the quandary of performativity today.

There is nothing novel in this discursive turn however, at least in the case of artistic discursivity. Let us think back to Conceptualism's reception of J. L. Austin's *How to Do Things with Words*, first published in 1962.[24] Austin's notions, coupled with the failure of criticism at the time, prompted artists to fill the discursive gap between self-representation in interviews and other formats. Carl Andre, Donald Judd and Robert Morris, for example, took the explanation of the work into their own hands and employed published conversation as a genre to achieve this. These artists and others coupled the productive powers of language within the stock-assumptions of their experimental art practices and attendant commentary.

More recently, the literalised realisations of conversation have exceeded their precedents in anglophone conceptualism of the late 1960s and early 1970s. Indeed during these decades, the turn to language in Conceptual Art was not straightforwardly an injection of language into art, but a militant assertion of art's implication in its own distributive and promotional structures, and of its adjacency to and involvement in text. Thus the turn to the discursive is presented as a reflexive attending to the conditions of possibility reproduced, in and as the art system. In the late 1980s and 1990s one observes a subsequent correlation between the turn to the discursive and the explicit thematisation of the infrastructural processes and roles of the art world. This is evidenced in a very diverse range of practices, from Hans Haacke's social surveys to, more recently, Tino Sehgal's theatrical gamesmanship with art market processes and Dora Garcia's problematisation of the role of institution and spectator in the artwork. What is more novel, however, is the ever-growing discursive role of the curator, as in artistic projects such as *A Crime against Art*. A shift due in part to similar circumstances as those recounted above – that is, the failure of the critic in providing a sufficiently strong discourse. But the shift is also related to the new dynamics of territorialisation and knowledge trading current in our times, and the pitfalls lying within the commodification of process and knowledge have been recently underlined by Carolyn Christov-Bakargiev. In her booklet for *dOCUMENTA13* she comments that in the "obsolete twentieth century object, the exhibition, a form of mannerism of the exhibition has evolved", so that at times, specific contents have become disembodied, and specific artworks have become almost translucent in their lack of transcendence.[25] Christov-Barkagiev goes on to affirm that "procedural questions are as meaningful as, if not more than, the so-called thematic content or subject matter of an art project – how one exercises agency and relates to others, how one proceeds as an artist, or how one acts as a member of the audience for example." In particular she goes on to highlight the dangers of attempting to package the process of artistic creativity. "Although the process through which one reaches a result might be 'creative' it is important to not turn that process itself into a new kind of product and as a consequence I am not fully in favour of the emerging, uncritical, dominant ideology of creativity ... The problem we both need to consider is how to proceed as artists, makers of culture, and intellectuals in the emerging economy and hegemony based on the exchange of knowledge products."[26]

Whatever one may make of this reading of cross-relations, it is clear that the discursive in the performative artwork or curatorial endeavour has entailed, as one of its many moments, a move to reformulate the various relationships of practitioners, audiences and institutional processes. Projects such as Dora Garcia's *Charles Filch* and *A Crime against Art* remind us of this militancy, pointing to and problematising the potential of falling into a form of gestural, crystallised performativity rather than processual, mercurial performativity.

While the creative processes of performance and performativity have become singularly congealed into packages of entertainment and audiences herded into pre-established formats of vacuous participation, the question today is how to alleviate the practice and its audiences from these burdening imperatives. Over a century ago, Robert Walser chose to become a 'charming round zero', in order to escape similar pressures in his literary career as those we have been describing. Having been a successful writer in Berlin, Walser returned to his native Switzerland to duck beneath the 'accepted' level of language of the time. His 'ducking' involved occupying his pen through a series of microscripts, unintelligible to the normal eye and seemingly the fruit of non-sensical behaviour. Walser's NO was viewed by society as a form of marginalisation, antithetically heroic in its slightness. Today, even such small-but-big gestures would be absorbed by markets and discourse.

Since we are on the subject of words, it is perhaps fitting to consider another literary figure, and master of the NO, as an open window to our impasse, and as a temporary ending to this discussion. I had in mind the many apparitions of Bartleby recounted by Enrique Vila-Matas in his masterful novel *Bartleby & Co.* [27] This compilation of footnotes, eschewing the traditional narrative structure and progression, takes up Herman Melville's original Bartleby who leads the epitomy of a negated existence, and whose standard reply to any request was 'I would prefer not to'. Vila-Matas goes on to recount the many incarnations of Bartleby in modern culture, in particular in literature. As the writer tells us, "Only from the negative impulse, from the labyrinth of the No, can the writing of the future appear." [28] With this spirit in mind, escaping the enslaving rhythm of our performative times involves a consideration of practice (artistic or curatorial) as a way of preferring not to, a sort of practitioners side-step, which doesn't attempt to take on the system head on, but creates a space alongside it; a form of open-ended indeterminateness sufficiently distant from an absorbable reality. Whether this position is then developed through the many channels of lateral action available to us, such as insidious charlatanry, trickstery deception, or smokey poker-ship, in order not to disclose the creative process, is up to our collective imaginarium to conceive. Indeed, what is being called for here is what has been described (in a different context; a recent philosophical text by Chus Martinez, which I nevertheless find particularly relevant to the field of performativity) as the creation of "a language capable of dealing with a secret or embodying it… the possibility of creating different kinds of thinking; logics capable of merging us with the substance of art, instead of placing us at a critical (I would add consumable) distance." [29]

1   This refers to the poster *Just what is it that makes Today's Homes so Different, so Appealing* designed by Richard Hamilton for the exhibition *this is tomorrow* at the Whitechapel Gallery, London, 1956. The work was destined to become emblematic of 1950s American consumer society.

2   Nicolas Bourriaud, *Relational Aesthetics* (1998), Les Presses du Réel, Dijon: Les Presses du Réel 2002.

3   Stewart Martin, *Critique of Relational Aesthetics*, third text, Vol. 21, No. 4, July 2007, pp. 371.

4   Bourriaud, cit., p. 42.

5   Martin, cit.; Claire Bishop, *Antagonism and Relational Aesthetics*, october, No. 110, Fall 2004, pp. 51–79.

6   Martin, cit., p. 371.

7   Grant Kester, *Conversation Pieces: Community and Communication in Modern Art*, Berkeley – Los Angeles – London: University of California Press, 2004.

8   ibid., p. 151.

9   ibid., p. 88.

10   ibid., pp. 88–89.

11   Steven Willats. Accessed 7.05.2012. http://stephen willats.com/context

12   WochenKlausur. Accessed 7.05.2012. http://www.wochenklausur.at/projekte/menu_en.htm

13   Jan Verwoert, *Exhaustion and Exuberance, Ways to Defy the Pressure to Perform*, Dot Dot Dot 15, 15 December 2007, produced at the Centre d'Art Contemporain, Geneva for Dot Dot Dot Magazine, New York, 2007. *Dot Dot Dot Issue 15*, was produced on location at the Centre d'Art Contemporain Genève, Switzerland, between 24 October and 7 November 2007 by Mai Abu ElDahab, Stuart Bailey, Walead Beshty, Sarah Crowner, Joyce Guley, Will Holder, Anthony Huberman, Polona Kuzman, David Reinfurt, Joke Robaard, Jan Verwoert and Jan Dirk de Wilde, printed on Ricoh TC2, Ricoh JP 8500, and Riso V8000 stencil printing machines in an edition of 3000. This project was part of the exhibition *Wouldn't it be Nice... Wishful Thinking in Art and Design*, Centre d'art Contemporain, Genève, Switzerland, 2007 (curated by Emily King and Katya García-Antón).

14   Jan Verwoert, *Use Me Up* in metropoLIS M, No. 1, February 2007.

15   Dexter Sinister, accessed 7.5.2012. http://www.dexter sinister.org/index. html?id=123

16   Jan Verwoert, *Exhaustion and Exuberance...*, cit., p. 90.

17   James H. Gilmore and B. Joseph Pine II, *The Experience Economy: Work Is Theatre and Every Business a Stage*, Cambridge –Ma.: Harvard Business School, 1999.

18   Lars Bang Larssen, *Zombies of Immaterial Labor: The Modern Monster and the Death of Death*, in e-flux journal *Are You Working too Much? Post Fordisms, Precarity, and the Labor of Art*, London: Sternberg Press, 2001, p. 86.

19   Diedrich Diederichsen, *Eigenblutdoping: Selbstverwertung, Künstlerromantik, Partizipation*, Cologne: Kiepenheuer & Witsch, 2008.

20   Markus Miessen, *The Nightmare of Participation (Crossbench Praxis as a Mode of Criticality)*, London: Sternberg Press, 2010.

21   The expanded performance *L'Inadeguato, Lo Inadecuado, The Inadequate* occupied the Spanish Pavilion in the 54th edition of the Venice Biennial. I was the curator of the Pavilion. The project can be viewed in detail on www.theinadequate.net. Versions of the publication in Spanish, English and Italian are available for download at this site.

22   Based on *The Trial* organised in Madrid in February 2007 by Anton Vidokle and Tirdad Zolgdhar, *A Crime against Art* was edited into a video by Eric Menard and Hila Peleg, and produced by Bureau des vidéos, Paris, 2007.

23   Maria Lind. 2005. *European Cultural Policies 2015. A Report with Scenarios on the Future of Public Funding for Contemporary Art in Europe*. European Institute for progressive Cultural policies, http://eipcp.netpolicies/2015lind/en. Accessed 13.5.2012.

24   J.L. Austin, *How to Do Things with Words*, Oxford: Clarendon Press, 1962

25   Carolyn Christov Barkagiev, *Letter to a Friend*, in *100 Notes – 100 Thoughts*, Ostfildern Ruit: Hatje Cantz, 2011

26   ibid., p. 4.

27   Enrique Vila-Matas, *Bartleby & Co* (2000), Vintage, London: Vintage 2005.

28   ibid., p. 2.

29   Chus Martinez, *As little time on the ground as possible. First attempt on the possibility of artistic significance beyond philosophy of history*, mousse magazine, No. 30, Milan October–November 2011, p. 102.

DETECTION, LEFTOVERS, 'DEAD THINGS' AND THE TIME IN-BETWEEN

Notes on Exhibiting Performance

Federica Martini

Between 1970 and 1986, Joseph Beuys regularly paid visits to the Hessisches Landesmuseum Darmstadt to re-arrange and manipulate the seven-room installation of works, objects from his life and props from his performances known as the *Beuys-Block*. After his death, the installation has stayed unchanged in the museum galleries, as an aging trace of past actions. Frozen under the spell of museum conservation standards for more than twenty years, the *Beuys-Block* has recently been at the centre of a lively debate following the renovation plans of the Landesmuseum Darmstadt: will the Beuys-Block be the same once the floor and walls of this site-specific originally-performative but today static installation have changed? What was the artist's intention? Hasn't the artist's gesture turned into documentation or a significant collection, once the regular re-arrangement of the rooms performed by the artist is over?

> "It is very curious but the detective story which is you might say the only really modern novel form that has come into existence gets rid of human nature by having the man dead to begin with the hero is dead to begin with and so you have so to speak got rid of the event before the book begins."
>
> Gertrude Stein[1]

Beuys' early experiment in translating performance props and ephemera into a museum space points to one of the main issues in the exhibition of performance, that is the loss and inaccessibility of the live act.

To this loss, the exhibition traditionally responds by presenting performance through its evidence and objects, such as photographs, videos, props, notes, sketches and oral interviews that try to reconstruct the artists' intention as well as historical and aesthetic contexts.[2] A mediated view of performance partially based on the assumption that in the live act, the audience has 'direct, unmediated access' to information through the artist's presence.[3]

As Thomas MacEvilley highlights in a text on James Lee Byars, for many performance artists in the 1960s and 1970s, the direct, unmediated access to information in exhibitions about performances was guaranteed by self-exhibition.[4] Invited to show in the Antwerp gallery Wide White Space in 1969, Byars "seated in a white suit, mask and hat in a chair-like arrangement which draped him in red velvet, in an otherwise empty white gallery", engaged in conversations with visitors, based on questions. Byars' presence and his work were supposed to be inseparable, as implied by a declaration he made in 1978: "Death cancels all my works, never show them again".

Still, today Byars' performances are shown through what remains of the historical acts, as it happened in the retrospective *I'm Full of Byars*, organised in 2009 in Detroit, Milton Keynes and Bern, where objects, texts and videos were put together to illustrate his work. While it is understandable from an art historical point of view to try and reconstruct the context and reception of past performances, the attempt to install the documents as a substitute for 'the real work', the performance, is more questionable. In this latter perspective, performance acts the way a corpse does in detective stories that start when the event is over, and the crime is already committed. Still, between mourning and investigation, as Gertrude Stein wittingly suggests, the death of the hero at the beginning of the story may be the most productive modern narrative source if we consider leftovers of the crime – the act – not only as evidence of an unattainable past but as tools for performing the novel's present.[5]

Translated into terms of exhibiting performance, this 'detection attitude' influences our way of considering the status of the performance document. As art historian Sophie Delpeux writes, the photograph of a performance is not necessarily only a document or 'mise-en-image' of a gesture, but *is* an autonomous image.[6] Delpeux traces back this position to 1966, when Allan Kaprow's performance photographs were published not as 'documents of events', but as tools for enhancing viewers' imagination.[7]

Furthermore, documentation of performance also implies 'staging', as film-maker Babette Mangolte observes regarding her collaboration with dancer Trisha Brown: "As a filmmaker I knew that dance doesn't work with cutting and that an unbroken camera movement was the way to film the four-minute solo. I had learned it by watching Fred Astaire and Gene Kelly's dance numbers. Somehow the film camera has to evoke the hypnotic look and total concentration of the mesmerised spectator and fragmenting the solo in small pieces taken from different camera positions would break the spectator's concentration and awe." [8]

Which implies that photographs of performances may be "produced *as* (or perhaps *by*) the performance (rather than *of* the performance)".[9] This concern animated Vito Acconci's *Photo-Piece* (1969), consisting of a linear walk in the city, holding a camera and shooting an image every time his eyes blinked, thus producing images that are at the same time evidence of the act and the act itself.[10]

Both Mangolte's hypnotic camera movements and Acconci's shots as a response to his blinking gaze go beyond the simple chronicle of a gesture, as the recording media and the positions they take towards the act provide a somehow unfaithful translation of it. They show 'almost the same thing', almost the same act, but in this fracture between the original gesture and its restitution through video and photography, they produce new, autonomous images.

In *Playing with Dead Things* (1993, Arnhem; re-staged in 2004, at Tate Modern, London) curated by artist Mike Kelley, this feeling of glimpsing recognition and ambiguous status was condensed in the idea of the uncanny, which implies past memories being triggered by a present encounter and the uncertainty about the object being animate or inanimate. A similar uncertainty, as arisen by objects and images documenting performances, was tested in 2008 by the show *Not to Play with Dead Things* at Villa Arson, Nice, which challenged the dependence of props from the performative acts through decontextualising them in an exhibition space.[11] The curatorial strategy focused on the rereading of John Bock's solo show at FRAC Provence-Alpes-Côte d'Azur

(2005), where the staging and the content of the exhibition were determined by the leftovers of the performance held during the opening in the art centre. Based on the assumption that performance implies a certain degree of 'updating, rewriting and re-staging',[12] *Not to Play with Dead Things* aimed at discussing the aesthetic position of performance objects 'after the act': "Are they meaningless ghosts?", asks co-curator Eric Mangion; are they bound to "restore the energy of the action that gave birth to them?"; do they contradict the immediacy of the performance?[13]

Along with the hypotheses of performance objects being autonomous or being something in between performance and objects, as was the case for Fluxus artist Georges Brecht, *Not to play with dead things* also worked on "the mis-appropriation of performance historical documents as a creative process." As art historian Amelia Jones observes, performances are always also looked at "through the memory screen", the limited access to the live act implying two forms of knowledge, participation, for the witness, and eventually interpretation through documents and oral history, for the historian.[14] The witness and the historian knowledge are, in Jones' view, equally legitimate also because of the way performance traces are preserved, that is, writes Jessica Santone, as "something that must be replayed, reread or reinterpreted in order to be experienced." [15] In reading performance not only as a unique live act but as an event inviting repetition and re-presentation, artists such as Tania Bruguera and Catherine Sullivan proposed works based on the displacement of historical documentation in different time- and site-specific situations.[16]

This position became a curatorial statement in the exhibition *A Little Bit of History Repeated*, curated by Jens Hoffman at Kunst-Werke Berlin in 2001, including performances from the 1960s and 1970s reenacted as copies of historical presentations, re-interpreted by artists from younger generations or used as source of inspiration for new works.[17] Concentrated over a few days, the project did not historicise the selected performances, but chose a way of performing the exhibition space such as once experimented in the *Between* series at the Kunsthalle Düsseldorf in 1969–1973.[18] Conceived and directed by Karl Ruhrberg and Jürgen Harten, the Kunsthalle's project consisted of a series of invitations to artists such as Tony Morgan to occupy the exhibition space between the exhibitions officially included in the institution's programme.

While Jens Hoffman's show was based on juxtaposing documents and their performative interpretations, the *Between* series was questioning the possibility to create a space for performance by disrupting the spatial institutional discourse and time frame. What happens with *Between* is that, when considered as a form of cultural production and inscribed in a curatorial perspective, performance brings up questions about the temporality of the exhibition, beyond the mere positioning of gestures, objects and images in a historical before and after the act, and beyond duration. The habit of showing performance retrospectively is here counteracted by the idea of constructing performance actual presence in the exhibition space.

One response to this is the increasing dissemination of the festival format in exhibition spaces, in order to create a platform where the audience can participate in the live act and the performative gesture can be enacted or re-enacted in a site-specific situation. Nonetheless, this way the performance scene and the exhibition of documents mainly stay separated. Two recent exhibition projects tried to go beyond this distinction, focusing on the connection between documenting and curatorial practice within the exhibition space.

In 2011, Mamco (Musée d'art moderne et contemporain de Genève) presented *Hotel Sarkis*, a 'paradoxical retrospective exhibition' showing a selection of Sarkis' works paying homage, evoking or openly drawing inspiration from writers, painters, musicians and other cultural figures from the past.[19] Most of them are posthumous interpretations, called upon by Sarkis' disappointment facing the exhibitions of artists such as Marcel Broodthaers and Joseph Beuys after their deaths. This inspired him the idea to have curator and Mamco director Christian Bernard practice the retrospective interpretation of his work in his absence to discover his exhibition only the day before the opening.[20] Imagining his museum to be a hotel or shelter for works previously installed internationally in different exhibition contexts, Christian Bernard had the pieces emerge in the show in a similar fashion to Sarkis' process of "evoking, rewriting, up dating and re-staging". Meant as a possible execution of Sarkis' original score, the exhibition redraws the museum walls with sudden bumping of colours sampled from paintings referenced in Sarkis' works. A red thread traversed and organised the chromatic space of the exhibition, the main curatorial strategy of which develops from a careful handling of back- and forward looks through the use of repetition and synchronicity, a choice that both actualises the memorial aspect of the works and summons the works and their different temporalities through the exhibition lens. Instead of documenting loss, like many retrospectives do, *Hotel Sarkis* worked on the idea of memory being performative and ended up producing (curatorial) knowledge instead of commemorating. Another way is to 'connect archival research to practice', such as in *If I can't dance I don't want to be part of your revolution*, a platform founded in 2005 by curators Frédérique Bergholtz, Annie Fletcher and Tanja Elstgeest to explore "the evolution and typology of performance and performativity in contemporary art".[21] Taking on Hannah Darboven's definition of her work as "contemplation interrupted by action", *If I can't dance* is based on a combination of research and production of two-year programmes presented in public situations, which develop "through their very enactment, at each event and at each location". All stages in the programme, research, the act of setting the scene, the involvement of the audience and the production of knowledge are equally on the agenda of the artists, researchers and curators. The focus is no longer on the status of live acts, connected documents and objects, but on the circumstances that enable a curatorial project to become a platform for cultural production.[22] The translation of visual poetry, an act negotiating the transposition of the text in terms of form and meaning, also demands this kind of positioning between respecting the visual format (how to translate) and selecting the meanings underlying both words and forms (what to translate) that inform the presentation of performance in an exhibition context. Both poetry translation and performance exhibitions deal with this idea of how much loss the original artistic or poetic gesture can take in order to bear witness to the past event.

The other option, as the project *If I can't dance* proposes, is one of imagining the performance exhibition as a situation to participate in. In this respect, documentation becomes one of the elements in the exhibition/situation where knowledge is not merely represented but produced.

This echoes, somehow, Marshal McLuhan's belief that recorded jazz is as stale as yesterday's newspapers.[23] The statement accounts for the difficult conciliation of retrospective and prospective gazes in a unique topicality. Still, yesterday's newspapers produce, by definition, a time-specific knowledge that is supposed to last for the duration of a day. In this particular time frame, the main goal is not historicising, but performing history in a limited present, within an ongoing, non-linear discourse that is bound to negotiate its format again the day after.

1   Gertrude Stein, *What Are Masterpieces and Why Are There So Few of Them* (1940), in *Modernism: An Anthology*, ed. Lawrence S. Rainey (London: Blackwell Publishing, 2005), p. 413.

2   See Barbara Clausen, ed., *After the Act: The (Re)presentation of Performance Art.* (Vienna: MUMOK, Vienna, 2005).

3   Amelia Jones, *Presence in Absentia: Experiencing Performance as Documentation*, in *Art Journal*, Vol. 56, No. 4, 1997, 11–18.

4   Thomas MacEvilley, *James Lee Byars – A Study of Posterity*, in *I'm Full of Byars – A Homage*, exh. cat., eds. Susanne Friedli, Matthias Frehner (Bielefeld: Kerber Verlag, 2009), p. 105

5   Gertrude Stein, cit.

6   Sophie Delpeux, *Le corps-caméra. Le performer et son image.* (Paris: Editions Textuel, 2010), p. 17.

7   Ibid.; see also Allan Kaprow, *Assemblages, Environments and Happenings,* (New York: Harry N. Abrams, Inc., 1966).

8   Babette Mangolte, *On the Making of Water Motor, A Dance by Trisha Brown filmed by Babette Mangolte,* unpublished paper, 2003.

9   Philip Auslander, *The Performativity of Performance Documentation*, in *Performance Art Journal*, No. 84, 2006, pp. 1–10.

10   See also Sophie Delpeux , cit.

11   *Not to Play with Dead Things*, exh. cat., eds. Eric Mangion, Marie de Brugerolle (Zurich: JRP Ringier, 2009).

12   Richard, Martel, *Performance*, in: Eric Magnion, Marie de Brugerolle, cit. p. 14.

13   Ibid.

14   Amelia Jones, cit.

15   Jessica Santone, *Marina Abramovic's Seven Easy Pieces: Critical Documentation Strategies for Preserving Art History*, in *Leonardo*, Vol. 41, No. 2, 2008, pp. 147–152.

16   See Tania Bruguera, *Tribute to Ana Mendieta* (1985–1996); Catherine Sullivan, '*Tis a Pity She's a Fluxus Whore* (2003).

17   *A Little Bit of History Repeated*, exh. cat., ed. Jens Hoffman, (Paris: Editions Valerio, 2001).

18   *Chronik Einer Nicht-Austellung Between 1969–73 in der Kunsthalle Düsseldorf*, ed. Renate Buschmann (Berlin: Dietrich Reimer Verlag, 2007).

19   See Christian Bernard, *Hôtel Sarkis*, 2011, http://www.mamco.ch

20   Samuel Schellenberg, *Sarkis. Chambre avec vue*, in *Le Courrier*, February 19, 2011, www.lecourrier.ch

21   http://www.ificantdance.org/

22   See Barnaby Drabble, p. 43ff.

23   Marshall McLuhan, *Understanding Media*, (New York: McGraw-Hill, 1964).

VOICES IN THE EXHIBITION

Barnaby Drabble

In a scene from the film *Play It Again Sam*[1], the main character Allan, played by Woody Allen, visits an art gallery in a desperate attempt to pick up girls. He pauses in front of a painting by Jackson Pollock and nervously makes conversation with the young woman standing in front of it.

Allan: That's quite a lovely Jackson Pollock, isn't it?

Young woman: Yes it is.

Allan: What does it say to you?

Young woman: It restates the negativeness of the universe, the hideous, lonely emptiness of existence. Nothingness. The predicament of man forced to live in a barren, godless eternity like a tiny flame flickering in an immense void with nothing but waste, horror and degradation forming a useless, bleak straitjacket in a black, absurd cosmos.

Allan: What are you doing Saturday night?

Young woman: Committing suicide.

Allan: What about Friday night?

In some ways the question 'What does it say to you?' can be seen as a central motif in over 200 years of thought about the relationship between art and its viewers, and the supposed grounds for visiting exhibitions remain bound to this central premise that artworks speak to us. The history of art variously documents how art experiences have, in various ways, been defined as different from other parts of our everyday lives. Yet, although this man-made differentiation lies at the heart of our exchanges with art, and points towards a specific function of the exhibition, the highly subjective nature of the sphere it produces is often wilfully overlooked.

However, if we want to analyse the idea of the speaking object, we need to take a few steps back from analysing art as art and note the importance of this designation in and of itself. [...] Art objects and experiences, are inseparably bonded to the expectation of meaning and understanding, and for much of the last two centuries these characteristics have been understood as inherent, insofar as particular formal, referential, pictorial or narrative qualities in the work can suggest ways in which it might be 'correctly' understood, or what it ultimately might mean.

Although the above understanding of the work as the site of some kind of inherent meaning can broadly be described as tied to the development of European modernism in the arts, pragmatically speaking it would be wrong to see the intervention of postmodern thought as anything more than a caesura in the still popular idea that the work itself 'holds the keys' to its own meaning, or that good work 'speaks for itself'. However, this idea is necessarily challenged by common sense; because, taken literally, objects cannot speak. So, we can ascertain that the context for observing and experiencing artworks has a great influence on any speculation on their content. The art exhibition has a transformative character, although it cannot actively make mute objects speak, by presenting them 'as art' it creates a space of expectation. In short, the exhibition is a site where we, as visitors, are encouraged to enter into a mental game – one in which we *imagine* that objects speak to us. To complicate this we can observe that the dominant art-historical view of the art experience favours content over context and upholds the myth that the works are the primary source of meaning. But, if we look more closely we realise that the aspect of conjecture involved in listening to imaginary voices is essentially far more speculative in nature than art history would have us believe. When we visit an exhibition and listen carefully to what the works have to say, we are essentially improvising around a few set parameters in the exhibition space. What we choose to hear there is as likely to be influenced by our concerns about where we parked the car as it is by our concerns about formal or structural elements in the work. Add to this the fact that our behaviour in the exhibition is often in response to others who we find ourselves sharing the space with and we realise that meaning is not latent, but emergent, understanding is effectively performed by the visitors, together. If we can say that a voice emerges, it does so at a tangent to the works, rather than from within them.

It is easy to see why dominant opinion continues to uphold the historical idea that artworks are the primary source of meaning in a professionalised art world context where the terms of power, economy and knowledge have been built around that very assumption. Whether talking to an artist, art historian, gallerist, museum curator, collector, critic or art student, the centrality of 'the work' in what they do is unavoidable; works are, after all, the things stacking up in the studio, the things bought and sold, the things selected, transported, hung, written about and collected. These activities describe, and prescribe, an attitude that takes us back to the earlier points about differentiation and expectation. With all this activity going on around them, these objects *become* special, and with this status comes a responsibility to mean something. Nowhere are works more exposed to this responsibility than in the exhibition and over the last half-century in particular, the physical attributes of the exhibition space have been designed to support the idea that the works are fiercely, predominantly meaningful. The ritualised characteristics of the exhibition (a bright, quiet, white space with things separated out from one another on the walls and floor) set the stage for a silent transfer. This is what Brian O'Doherty observed in the forms adopted by commercial galleries in the early 1970s[2]. The *white cube,* he argues, is designed primarily to stress the individual value of discrete auratic objects. Its interior-architectural characteristics also block out temporal and contextual factors that might confuse a reading of the work that, it is understood, should mean something in and of itself. The featureless walls and plinths privilege the formal and the objective, and once the public is familiar with what is signalled by such rituals the entire environment raises by implication all its contents to the status of art, even as O'Doherty wryly observes the fire hose in the museum.

It is revealing that a painting by Jackson Pollock forms the central prop for the art gallery scene in Woody Allan's Film *Play It Again Sam*.

In the debate about who speaks in the exhibition, the phenomenon of abstract expressionism proves interesting, as the critics of this painterly development in what is now regarded as late modernism became increasingly divided on the grounds for defence of these works. It was famously Clement Greenberg who promoted Pollock as the most important artist of his generation, supporting his claim with a strictly formal rationale in relation to the composition of his paintings[3] and linking him to a longer tradition of painters engaged with abstraction. For him, Pollock's physical approach to producing his work, dripping paint onto the prone canvasses and actively stepping on and into the image, was interesting, but not valid in any assessment of the work as work. His nemesis at the time, Harold Rosenberg, was convinced that the gestural approach to painting was a break with tradition, and represented an attempt to recuperate more expressive elements of the activity of painting from overly theoretical or academic impulses. He termed the approach that interested him 'action painting' and stressed the fact that the canvasses could no longer be judged in terms of their surface or formal qualities, instead they had to be understood as "an arena in which to act"[4], a site where an event had taken place[5]. This moment in criticism reflects a widening of the parameters by which work could be assessed, from the position that the value of work was purely intrinsic to one where its relation with its maker could contribute to its meaning and understanding. Despite the fact that these two positions, as held by Greenberg and Rosenberg, were acrimoniously opposite, the emerging field of popular culture was to find fewer problems with this shift. The attributes of the work and its creator were simply merged, the maker becoming as much object as subject, and the voices in the exhibition understood as *per se* those of the artists, speaking through their works.

In 1996 Bruce Ferguson published the essay *Exhibition Rhetorics*[6], in which he put forward the idea that exhibitions can be understood as the speech act of an institution. Introducing a linguistic model for analysing exhibitions, he suggested that first and foremost the voices we hear in the exhibition are neither those of the artworks, nor those of the artists, but those of the institution. The exhibition, he argues, is full of voices, but these are synthesised into a predominant institutional voice, which in turn speaks through them. The 'rhetorics' of the essay's title relate to his belief that this voice is continually communicating an identity, telling and retelling an institutionalised story. For the critical audience member, listening becomes important here, because recognising the 'institutional voice' radically reframes the question 'What does it say to you?' The 'it' becomes tied up in the question of institutional power, and the possibility is raised that, as visitors, we are willingly signing up to our own normalisation or indoctrination. Ferguson's linguistic analogy appears as a precursor to a new kind of listening in the exhibition; a tool for affording distance, from which we can see who is speaking, who is being spoken to and on what terms the conversation is taking place. Rather depressingly he concludes that when listened to in these terms, too many institutional exhibitions sound like "a loud monologue followed by a long silence." [7] In place of this Ferguson imagines what a more conversational institutional voice might sound like, arguing that such a conversation could only take place when the pedagogue's booming tones are replaced by a more hesitant, uncertain and questioning voice. The resultant engagement with what he terms an institution's 'slips of tongue and anxious parapraxes [8] might allow visitors to get a word in edge-ways, to intervene in the affirmative institutional narrative with less dominant narratives of their own.

This lack of variety in exhibition speech, and the institution's propensity for specific approaches to pedagogy, is also the focus of Oliver Marchart in his more recent essay *The Institution Speaks, Art Education as a Strategy of Domination or Emancipation.* [9] Like Ferguson before him, Marchart examines the ways in which institutions voice themselves, noting that the growth in interpretation, outreach and gallery education departments effectively distracts attention away from the fact that the public art institution itself is a giant interpretative machine; its abiding logic is one of informing and educating 'through' art and not solely 'about' it. A decade after Ferguson, he notes that the monologue remains the predominant form of institutional expression, and discusses a similar necessity for break or rupture. Helpfully he calls on an example to illustrate this concept, and describes his own role in the education project of the *dOCUMEN-TA11* and the conscious wish of the team, headed by Okwui Enwezor, to design a structure for extending the project in an educational direction, without recourse to dominant methods of pedagogy. Convinced that this direction had to be initiated and developed by the learners themselves, Marchart describes how the team set about making a series of 'slots', or empty spaces for activity of this kind. Marchart discusses how the quality of experience suggested in this 'education project' differed from that more familiar idea of an education programme. The project logic is one of initiation without expectation of specific goal-oriented learning, whereas the programme already suggests more structure, for if it wishes to function it cannot avoid being programmatic. These ideas and observations suggest how we might see all exhibitions as potential non-programmatic knowledge experiences, were it not for their enduring wish to be perceived as complete, discrete and authoritative. Just as reflections on the work of Jackson Pollock describe the impossibility of isolating the voice of the work from that of the artist, the ideas of Ferguson and Marchart recognise that those of the work, the exhibition and the institution are similarly inseparable.

With all the above in mind, the question of whose voice we hear when we visit the exhibition is hard to answer. Exhibitions, it becomes clear, are polyphonous constructions. Here, not only the objects but also their surroundings speak, and artists' voices are joined by those of the curators and the institutions they work within. As such, exhibitions can be harmonious or discordant in tone and judging their merits entails careful listening – an ear for how the various voices sound together and how they supplement, extend or oppose one another. If we listen carefully enough we start to perceive an ongoing series of overlapping debates. An artist's sensitivity to the voice of the institution may result in a critical contradiction, or a playful echo. Curatorial decisions can bring artistic positions into dialogue with one another, or reveal the process behind the objects by way of a parallel commentary. Yet, there is a very real danger here that in analysing what we hear, we allow ourselves to imagine too great a critical distance from the voices in the exhibition. After all, the question 'What does it say to *you*?' reminds us that we too are present as speaking subjects. If we choose to answer the question, even quietly in our own minds, one of the voices in the exhibition is our own. Whether visiting exhibitions alone or in company, the conversations that accompany or follow these have a specific quality, as we attempt to unlock what leads us to our conclusions about what we have seen. When arguing our point of view about art, even to ourselves, we find ourselves addressing a far greater topic through the vehicle of our aesthetic taste. We start to rehearse our subjectivity – constructing and defending a personal and particular role for ourselves in relation to what we have witnessed in the gallery [10].

The voice of the audience is currently the least discussed of the many in the exhibition. Yet, if the last decade appears to be the golden age of the curator, the next may well belong to the visitor. This prediction might appear to be a further step away from recognition of the artist's key role in exhibitions, or be mistaken for a call for populism. These risks are very present but do not exclude the fact that a genuine recognition of the audience's ability to speak, and not just to listen, is more radical than it might appear. Far from detracting from the importance of artists, it actually strengthens the argument for the importance of their work. The artwork remains central to the quality of both the exhibition and the conversation it provokes, precisely because the best work, though professing to say something and introducing new languages in which to say it, deliberately refuses to entirely reveal itself and make its meaning transparent. It is this very fact that so frequently raises questions of elitism and obscurity in relation to contemporary art, but it is one built on a fundamental misunderstanding. Because although it is understandable that people like to have things explained to them, art can sometimes provoke the frustration of not knowing what something is *supposed* to mean. This should only be seen as a critique of an exhibition if a programmatic acquisition of knowledge or expertise is the kind of understanding they are trying to promote. This observation might serve to point back to the primacy of the game we agree to play in the museum or gallery environment – we *imagine* that objects speak to us. To play this game well, it is primarily investment in feeling, idea association and a willingness to speculate on meaning that prove useful and ultimately instructive.

It is interesting to end with a consideration of the curatorial in the light of these gathered thoughts and references. On the one hand, the exhibition functions inevitably as a meta-artwork. As such, it presents a whole ranWge of interesting parameters within which the game of speaking objects can be developed and experimented with. That said, on the other, there is an implicit danger in the curator as author construct that this implies – because the idea that the curatorial concept is a tool for understanding the exhibition is as questionable as the premise that the artist's intention explains the work. Theirs are all voices in the exhibition, but the full breadth of meaning is restricted when one claims to be more authoritative than the others. So, recognising the audience's voice as well has the potential to be quite the opposite of dumbing-down the art experience – it *per se* demands recognition of the complexity of the art experience and the need to avoid pre-empting meaning. As such, in relation to exhibitions, interpretation[11] might be best understood as the job of validating the audience's voice.

Short version. Original version in spanish as 'Voces de la exposición', in: *Casa N°2*. Revista del Museo Nacional de Arte Reina Sofia, Madrid, Primavera–Verano 2011.

First edition: *Swiss Exhibition Award 2009*. Hg. Bundesamt für Kultur /Julius Bär Stiftung, Bern 2010.

1   Ross, H. *Play It Again Sam*. Paramount Pictures, 1972.

2   O'Doherty, B. *Inside the White Cube: the Ideology of the Gallery Space*. 2nd ed. Santa Monica: Lapis Press 1976.

3   Greenberg, C. *American-type Painting*, Partisan Review, No. 22, Spring, 1955.

4   Rosenberg, H. *The American Action Painters*, Art News, no. 6, 1952.

5   Rosenberg's ideas in *The American Action Painters* later influenced Allan Kaprow to write about Jackson Pollock as an inspiration for the new genre of performative art emerging in the late 1950s in the form of happenings and environments. Kaprow, A. *The Legacy of Jackson Pollock*, Art News, no. 6, 1958.

6   Ferguson, B. *Exhibition Rhetorics: Material speech and utter sense*. In: Greenberg, R. Ferguson, B. & Nairne, S. eds. *Thinking about Exhibitions*. London: Routledge 1996, pp. 175–191.

7   Ibid. p. 188.

8   Ibid. p. 187.

9   Marchart, O. *Die Institution spricht*. In: Jaschke, B. Martinez-Turek, C. & Sternfeld, N. eds. *Wer Spricht, Autorität und Autorschaft in Ausstellungen*. (eds). Vienna: Verlag Turia + Kant, 2005 pp. 34–58

10   The idea of exhibitions as spaces where audiences can performatively 'shift themselves from being viewers to being participants' is brilliantly introduced in Irit Rogoff's seminal article *How to Dress for an Exhibition*. Hannula, M. ed. *Stopping the Process?* Helsinki: NIFCA 1998, pp. 130–151.

11   Here again the term interpretation should be understood to encompass not only the activities of the education department, but the whole of the institutions activities in relation to its audiences.

WHEN TRUTH DISCOURSE MEETS SPECTACLE

Dorothee Richter

This essay will review some historical perspectives, which influence contemporary cultural practices, posing the question: where does the clash between the visual arts and theatre come from and where is it going?

In recent times, we have experienced an increasing integration of theatre and exhibition practices in terms of display. Evidence of this may be found in the inclusion of scenography and theatrical scenery in exhibitions and installations and video projections in theatre productions, in both cases leading to a general breakdown in what we might see as any strict narration. After some theoretical outlines I will discuss four examples as case studies, firstly the work of Fluxus artists, secondly of Christoph Schlingensief, thirdly of Spartacus Chetwynd and lastly a theatre scene by Renata Burckhardt integrated into the exhibition *Spill the Beans*.

In order to outline some theoretical principles, I will refer to the distinctions Kant drew between different areas in the arts. He not only discussed the arts at length, but situated them in a new, very distinctive light. In Terry Eagleton's view, Kant's theory provided the upcoming bourgeoisie with an ideological background. Not only in his separation of the sensual from the rational, thus installing or giving a name to a friction which underlies modern subjectivity, but also in his definition of the subject in absolute contrast to the object, estranging the subject from its material existence. In this concept the subject is autonomous and remains curiously alone, "the subject is not a phenomenon in the world but a transcendental viewpoint upon it" [1], or as Terry Eagleton puts it: "If freedom is to flourish, if the subject is to extend in colonising sway over things and stamp them with its indelible presence, then systematic knowledge of the world is essential, and this must include knowledge of other subjects." [2]

But this places the subject in a lonely position and interestingly enough it is the sphere of aesthetics that provides these estranged subjects with a form of community. To cite Eagleton again: "What brings us together as subjects is not knowledge but an ineffable reciprocity of feeling, and this is certainly one major reason why *the aesthetic* has figured so centrally in bourgeois thought. For the alarming truth is that in a social order marked by class division and market competition, it may finally be here, and only here, that human beings belong together in some intimate community." [3]

Moreover, the artistic genius as a concept was bound to subjectivity in Kant's view as he derived the genius concept from the abilities of an eternal creator, but transferred it to represent a function of the artistic subject. This creativity may also be traced back to the requirements for an autonomous entrepreneurship. Kant saw the existence of one major break in subjectivity, the sensual (connected with the arts and the body) and the rational (connected with the rational and the mind). A contradiction, which was later problematised by Adorno and

Horkheimer, who pointed out that in this perspective the mind will always contradict and imprison bodily existence.[4]

This very brief theoretical excursion will function as a background showing us how and in which ways the visual arts and theatre, from the enlightenment onwards, are already positioned through their historical conception. Following Kant, both belong to the sensual, but it is obvious that the visual arts are positioned closer to the concept of a mimetic rational truth and theatre is closer to the sensual and the repressed pleasures of the body. To subdue the disturbing pleasures of the body, theatre plays had a strong pedagogical impact in bourgeois society, implying that you have to learn *morals* from theatre plays. In this perspective, two principles (those of the theatre and the visual arts) are at stake when we discuss the clash of theatre practices and visual arts from the 1960s onwards. To put it in even more exaggerated terms: what happens when spectacle meets the truth discourse? Even if today the manifestations of practices in theatre and in the visual arts seem to be almost the same, their context is different, which implies that more differences exist than appear at first sight.

The following simplified matrix outlines these differences approached from a historical enlightenment position like Kant's. I also take the liberty of transferring Peter Bürger's categories in his famous *Theory of the Avant-Garde* (reception, production and usage) to the field of the genres of theatre and the visual arts.[5] The third category is changed by me, for this specific context, and tries to describe the mode of addressing the public, the underlying pedagogy.

	THEATRE	VISUAL ARTS
	Related to the sensual	Related to the rational
PUBLIC (RECEPTION)	Group in a dark space	Individual in an overview situation, able to move around
PRODUCTION	Hierarchical group	Individual genius
UNDERLYING PEDAGOGY	Morals about life, love and war	To behave, to install control inside the subject

In Europe in the 1950s, after the catastrophes of the Second World War, theatre can be observed as a site where informative and timeless values were delivered to the upper and middle classes, or at least this was the current ideology of how a theatre play should be. In this period, as Richard Sennett has noted[6], the public sat more or less immobilised in their chairs and viewed what was staged for them; a situation notably different to pre-French Revolution Europe, when (rich) aristocrats freely moved around the theatre, chatting and commenting on the action on the stage. Also in the museums and galleries of postwar western cities people were encouraged to move around and view the exhibits silently and without indulging in any spontaneous, loud or expressive behaviour.[7] In all cultural venues, the audience behaved in an extremely inhibited manner, for the instance of control was now installed inside the subject; it controlled itself in an environment of total overview and of total visibility (public). Theatre was supposed to be produced in a working process by a large hierarchically organised group, and the visual arts were seen as the product of the ingenious mind and skilful hands of a single individual (production), as sketched in the matrix above.

With the practices adopted during the 1960s the categories of theatre and visual arts collapsed, but remained defined or framed by the institutions, the museums and galleries for visual arts on the one hand and the theatres on the other.

The notion of performativity, which might be used in our context to discuss different image and theatre-based practices, can be traced back to a broad concept of the performative. In 2002, the team of the Munich Kunstverein described this in regard to their approach to curating:

"The concept of performance is derived from the philosophy of language of the 1950s which defined it as the conceptual antipode to competence. Performance here characterizes the concrete use of language and signifies the realisation of expressions in a specific situation by an individual speaker – the applied and embodied language. Competence, on the other hand, is the ideal notion of a speaker who forms an unlimited number of expressions from a limited number of linguistic elements. This implicit metalevel of competence has been negated within the concept of performance by Noam Chomsky and J. L. Austin. Austin's speech act theory in *How to Do Things with Words* implies that language not only has a referential function but also a performative one.[8] The performative, according to his definition, also realises what it characterises – a so-called speech act. "What is meant here is the connection between action and language, such as the connection between the words 'I congratulate you' with the action of shaking hands, or statements like 'I swear', 'I bet', in which the action as such is already implied. The relevant evaluative judgement of performative expressions is, accordingly, not their level of truth, but rather the relative success or failure of their intended meaning. 'Performative' is thus understood as the constitution of a meaning through an act or a certain practice."[9]

The text provided by the team of Kunstverein Munich transfers speech act theory to the visual arts and specifically to curating, comparable to Dorothea von Hantelmann's transfer of speech act theory to the arts in her publication *How to Do Things with Art*.[10] Both approaches can be thought of as paraphrasing Judith Butler's notion of social practices which must be uttered/performed again and again to become effective. In this understanding 'the performative' of any utterance, whether artistic-, curatorial- or theatre-based, is related to its effects.

Fluxus

In the case of Fluxus the collapse of the genres of poetry, visual arts and theatre was mediated through music, insofar as Fluxus events were notated as musical scores. Through this estrangement, everything could be written down in terms of notation and reproduced from this notation or score at every venue by everybody. A good example of the rejection of a pictorially oriented conception of art is La Monte Young's Fluxus event *Composition 5,* in which "the action is limited to allowing one or more butterflies to fly around in the performance room and to see to it that all the butterflies are able to escape." [11] Musical scores thus provided a metalanguage that allowed a levelling of all possibilities of action with written and visual objects and subjects.

For George Maciunas ('chairman' of Fluxus) it was ultimately important to distinguish Fluxus from Happening. He traced Happening back to theatre and to the Baroque ballet at the court of Versailles, whereas Fluxus was positioned against elitist 'high art' and in favour of collective lifestyles; to be understood as a fluid transition between, or unification of, art and life. So Fluxus actions themselves refused artificiality or separation from everyday life. Even the objects that later on became known as Fluxus editions began their lives as embodiments of action scores, ephemera which could be activated and performed anytime by anybody, the only restriction being to label them when publicly performed as Fluxus. The truth discourse of the visual arts is visible in the concept that Fluxus should avoid pretence and be neither dramatic nor skilful. In the words of Emmett Williams: "Fluxus art amusement [should] be simple, entertaining and unsophisticated, concern itself with banalities, require neither special skills nor numerous rehearsals, be neither tradable nor institutionalizable." [12]

Especially the last requirement turned out to be an impossible task; Fluxus became tradable and institutionalised at the cost of denying part of its goals and production processes. For example the multiple authorship in many Fluxus productions, particularly in the editions and films, is nowadays forgotten – the reason being that Fluxus became again part of the visual arts field and was therefore again reduced to the attribution of very specific authorship. The following matrix summarises some main issues of the production and reception of traditional theatre in relation to the neo-avant-garde Fluxus.

	THEATRE	VISUAL ARTS	FLUXUS
	Related to the sensual	Related to the rational	Related to chance operations
PUBLIC (RECEPTION)	Group in a dark space	Individual in an overview situation	In a community — audience could be part of a score or could also engage in re-interpreting a score
PRODUCTION	Hierarchical	Individual genius	In a group group, authorship unclear — production is motivated through musical scores
UNDERLYING PEDAGOGY	Morals about life, love and war	To behave, to install the control inside the subject	re-evaluation of every-day live, political awar-ness, anti-bourgeois

In our context it is important to state that the different productions and authorships were closely interlinked: the events were put on stage and sometimes the event score was written afterwards. The event score consisted of very basic instructions that could be performed in many different ways. Many of the Fluxus editions comprehend conglomerations of these instructions or they proposed certain actions with their usage. So the object character that today marks presentations of Fluxus 'works' is very questionable. For example when Nam June Paik performed an interpretation of La Monte Young's Fluxus event score *Draw a Straight Line*, the remains of the performance were later treated by both art history and the art market as an autonomous art object.

Art/Life:
Christoph Schlingensief

At the centre of the late Christoph Schlingensief's artistic practice were the processes of reshaping the conceptions of 'art' and 'life' and the question of how to represent the personal. He pulled on source material from his personal history and chaotic life events, devoting, with total dedication, his injured personality to his array of chosen media:

"The practice of Christoph Schlingensief (1960–2010) represents a foray through diverse types of artistic engagement – from film-making to activism, from acting to directing, from painting to journalism. The multiplicity of materials that this implies has not only blurred the boundaries between traditional artistic categories but has also entailed a deconstruction and reconstruction of visual worlds; absorbing everything into itself, denying linearity and classical narration, the work makes excessive demands on the viewer's sensory abilities. In the effort to summarise Schlingensief's activities, one feels tempted to apply the term 'universal'." [13]

The above citation comes from the press release for Schlingensief's exhibition *Kaprow City,* shown at the Migros Museum, Zurich, between November 2007 and February 2008. The curator of the exhi-

bition Raphael Gygax notes that
the show, in its first appearance,
was a walk-through stage set
peopled by actors at the Volksbühne in Berlin (a theatre), later
transformed into an installation
for the museum. In these images 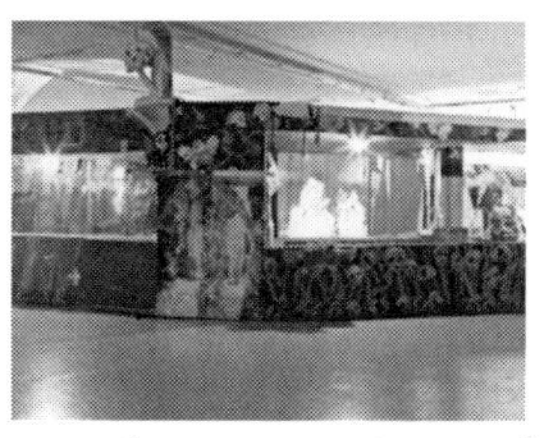
you can have a premonition of the round stage setting, which was stat-
ic in the museum. The original moving stage was reversed into a film
installation, the main film titled *Fremdverstümmelung* which was produced originally for the opera *FREAX* (by Moritz Eggert). The installation at the Migros Museum also consisted of two films done by Schlingensief's father and a 'waschvideo'. In the first room different videos
from surveillance cameras of the theatre version were also shown.

With the transformation from theatre to the exhibition space
the material changed from an atmospheric stage design (background)
into a sculptural art object (foreground). While theatre is produced
traditionally within a hierarchical group consisting of directors, stage
designers, actors, technicians, illuminators, special effects and sound
technicians, musicians, film-makers etc., in the context of the fine arts
all this work is subsumed under the sole author name, in this case
Schlingensicf. Infected by the visual arts environment, the material
gains automatic artwork values, losing the usable, tangible characteristics of stage design. The desire for bodily pleasure, which is more
present in the context of theatre, is therefore hushed to allow for the
more distanced sense of the visual. For the public the conditions of access have also changed, the material world could be entered in the theatre, but only partly so in the exhibition space. So the installation is
influenced by the preconditions of the visual arts paradigms. The artist subject that is on display is positioned as being injured by his family
history, which removes the encounter even further from any social or
political conditions. The installation introduces the desire for a bodily transgression of the muted visitor subject, but it fails to allow this,
blocking any theatrical access to the object. The media critique, which
one could see in the blurred videos, was hardly distinguishable from
its affirmation. Even though the attempt at transformation was an interesting one, the resultant fixed attitude was clearly due to the transfer from theatre context to exhibition space. This fixation was also reflected in the return of the (male) author subject as genius.

	Schlingensief's work in the realm of THEATRE		Schlingensief's work in the realm of VISUAL ARTS
	Related to the sensual	→	Related to the irrational
PUBLIC (RECEPTION)	Group in a dark space	→	Individual in a confusing situation, able to move around
PRODUCTION	Hierarchical group		Individual genius, hurt by family history
UNDERLYING PEDAGOGY	Morals about life, love and war		To behave, to install control and self-discipline inside the subject

Spartacus Chetwynd

Schlingensief's installation was only one part of the Migros Museum's ongoing investigation of the overlapping of theatre and visual arts. A further exhibition at the museum focussed on the work of the British artist Spartacus Chetwynd [14], whose performances employ an interesting approach to recycling material amidst scenery elements that fittingly look as if they have been made from rubbish. In an article for Frieze magazine, Tom Morton describes her work as follows:

"Over the past few years Chetwynd has, with the aid of a flexible troupe of some 20 friends and family members, staged a number of performances that draw on everything from *Conan the Barbarian* (1982) to *The Incredible Hulk,* from the performances of Yves Klein to Hokusai's erotic print… Al-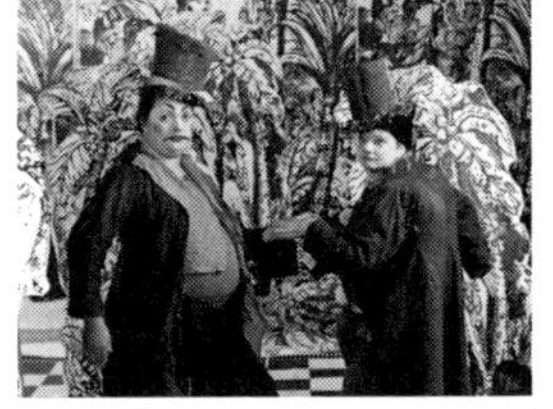though carefully produced, these spectacles seem always to teeter on the brink of joyful anarchy: The performers sip beer, extemporize lines and distractedly check their text messages, as though what's important here is not persuading the audience to suspend their disbelief but instead to introduce a measure of the carnivalesque into everyday life … I can't help but think her works are just as influenced by the let's-put-the-show-on-right-here-kids attitude found in the BBC children's television series *Why Don't You? (1973–1995)*". [15]

Chetwynd's characters act as subjects who can make a claim on culture material and reread it, according to their necessities, against the grain. For example, for her work *The Fall of Man* (2006) she presented aspects of the book of Genesis, Milton's *Paradise Lost* and Karl Marx' and Friedrich Engels' *The German Ideology* as a puppet play. The marionettes, made out of potatoes, were animated on makeshift cardboard stages by her performers, dressed as clowns. In this absurd context the texts, normally laden with history and meaning, were handled with indifference, as if interchangeable with any or all other texts. The inclusion of everyday behaviour from the actors, such as playing around with their mobile phones, creates a tension where the distinction between actors and audience is in danger of breaking down at any time. Yet on the other hand, their care-free attitude and lack of perceptible skill appear to call out to the audience to become one of them, as if their weird sexual performances could be copied in a minute. In many of her performances, Chetwynd seats the audience at the same level as the actors with the division of audience and actors often set up purely through the presence of an installation element, a table for example.

	THEATRE	VISUAL ARTS	Chetwynd
	Related to the sensual	Related to the rational	Related to children's play and the absurd
PUBLIC (RECEPTION)	Group in a dark space	Individual in an over-view situation	In a community — audience is affected by the performance and in a way their presence is acknowledged
PRODUCTION	Hierarchical group	Individual genius	In a group, authorship unclear but in the end subsumed under one artist's name. Production is motivated through do-it-yourself attitude, playfulness
UNDERLYING PEDAGOGY	Morals about life, love and war	To behave, to install the control inside the subject	Re-evaluation of cultural history and media-access, possible fun despite the absurdity of so-called reality

Calling on Dorothea von Hantelmann *How to Do Things with Art* [16] we could argue that not only the spoken word (as Austin has developed at length) but also the play of signs in visual arts refer to actions and make things happen. The transfer of the stage set into the exhibition space brings with it the same problems we have encountered with Fluxus and Schlingensief. The material is transformed from an equipment of an action into a fixed situation that becomes immediately an art object. Also the anarchic element of the life act is subdued through this transformation, the encounter of an event, where possibilities can never be completely controlled, is lost.

Renata Burckhardt:
A Theatrical Scene in an Exhibition

The last example cited here is the scene with the title: *Inclusion/exclusion – acteurs in the art system.* This took place in the exhibition project *Spill the Beans,* curated by Andrea Roca, Zoe Meyer and Renata Burckhardt in February 2010, at the alternative art space Perla Moda in Zurich. As the organisers explained in the press material, the exhibition "focussed on the existing structures, economies and politics of the contemporary art world, showing various works by artists who reflect on, emphasize and criticize these structures and mechanisms and subvert the control of recognition processes in the art world or offensively exploit them for their own purposes." [17] Amidst more object-based artworks, a setting in the exhibition space was designed by the scenographer Melanie Mock and featured a central, raised orange platform which resembled the kind of promotional display stages found at trade and art fairs. The curators used the platform to introduce a number of interventions exploring the dynamics of contemporary art business. The writer Renata Burckhardt wrote a scene for the exhibition, in which actors portraying various art-world types made an appearance, playing out a dialogue amongst the audience in a situation which was not immediately recognisable as a staged scene. The two protagonists started with a typical situation in the art field: a relatively unknown artist (female and not young) shows work to a young hip male curator, who reacts patronisingly. Gradually the two locate themselves on the raised platform in the space, literally 'staging' the power relations they represent. During the ongoing scene, the female protagonist made it clear that her partner was a very influential gallerist and slowly took charge of the situation. This narration was interrupted by reflexions of the actual space (it is cold here) and the actual situation of the actors, partly delivered with megaphones. Even if the message was possibly rather a simple one, namely that money exerts a definite influence on art institutions and their exhibitions programme; the protagonists were expert in expressing their power relationship by subtle changes of attitudes and behaviour patterns. Precisely this inflection was something everybody present in the room had encountered before. Also the references in the scene to the specific space where it happened (the door won't shut) further involved the audience in what was happening. The message of the theatrical intervention transmitted a sudden recognition of one's own position in the art world. The conditions of access became visible.

	THEATRE	VISUAL ARTS	Scene in an exhibition by RENATA BURKCHARDT
	Related to the sensual	Related to the rational	Related to the sensual
PUBLIC (RECEPTION)	Group in a dark space	Individual in an overview situation	In a community — audience is affected by the performance
PRODUCTION	Hierarchical group	Individual genius	Hierarchical in a group but also based on a long term pre-production
UNDERLYING PEDAGOGY	Morals about life, love, war	To behave, to install the control inside the subject	Self awareness

In this example the problem of the static art work is also recognisable, in our spectacular media world it would seem to be not enough to just view it. Yet, to put the audience in the situation of overwhelming emotions, as is often the case in mass media, is also not an option. To enlighten always means to make somebody aware of his or her position and to suggest a possible action, a move towards self-empowerment. All categories of reception, production and pedagogy/usage, that is of the underlying statements, could be resolved and aim at a message that goes beyond the given.

In conclusion it is possible to identify that we encounter nowadays a clash of theatre and visual arts, which melts down the categories in the Kantian sense. But this issue is not only driven by an ideological urge, it is also part of a certain helplessness of the position of so-called 'high art' which is nowadays encountering less support in society and from the political side. The aspect of an overall education is not of much interest for politicians, unless the masses are involved in the process (therefore the notion of art education is in this respect problematic). Meanwhile, in terms of ideological needs, protagonists of the visual arts field appear to be trying to change the exhibition format into something more spectacular. The movement from the Kantian fixed genres to this more recent overlap of cultural genres leads to a situation in which single authorship is more and more neglected in favour of a post-Fordist notion of new free combinations of replaceable and interchangeable pieces. In such times, the question of how the visitor subjects are addressed is a difficult one, and the answer can vary enormously in seemingly similar projects. What remains clear is that the aspect I have termed the 'underlying pedagogy' should never be taken for granted, but rather be carefully discussed in all cases.

1   Terry Eagleton, *The Ideology of the Aesthetics* (Oxford: Blackwell, 1990), p. 72.

2   ibid., p. 73.

3   ibid., p. 75.

4   Theodor Adorno, Max Horkheimer, *Dialektik der Aufklärung, Philosophische Fragmente,* (Amsterdam: Querido, 1947).

5   See Peter Bürger, *Die Theorie der Avantgarde* (Frankfurt am Main: Suhrkamp, 1974).

6   See Richard Sennett, *Verfall und Ende des öffentlichen Lebens. Die Tyrannei der Intimität.* (Frankfurt am Main: Fischer, 2004).

7   See Tony Bennett, *The Birth of the Museum: History, Theory, Politics,* (London: Routledge, 1995).

8   John L. Austin, *How to Do Things with Words,* (Oxford: Clarendon Press, 1962).

9   Sören Grammel, Maria Lind, Katharina Schlieben, 2002. *Curating Per-Form: Reflections on the Concept of the Performative,* http://www.kunstverein-muenchen.de/Folder: ueberlegungen_considerations/essays Filename: en_performative.pdf – 23.05.2002. Accessed 20.03.2011.

10 Dorothea von Hantelmann, *How to Do Things with Art: The Meaning of Art's Performativity,* (Zurich–Berlin: JRP Ringier, 2002).

11 Jürgen Schilling, *Aktionskunst. Identität von Kunst und Leben? Eine Dokumentation,* (Luzern–Frankfurt am Main, C. J. Bucher Verlag, 1978), p. 81.

12 Emmett Williams, *St George und der Fluxus-Drachen,* in Klaus Schrenk ed., *Aufbrüche, Manifeste, Manifestationen. Positionen in der bildenden Kunst zu Beginn der 60er Jahre in Berlin/Düsseldorf und München,* (Cologne: DuMont, 1984), p. 33.

13 Press Release by Migros Museum accompanying the exhibition by Christoph Schlingensief. 2007–2008.

14 Raphael Gygax & Heike Munder (eds.), *Spartacus Chetwynd,* (Zurich–Berlin: JRP Ringier, 2007). Exhibition catalogue.

15 Tom Morton, 2007. *Spartacus Chetwynd,* Frieze, No. 107, May. http://www.frieze.com/issue/article/spartacus_chetwynd/. Accessed 13.5.2012.

16 Hantelmann, cit.

17 Andrea Roca, Zoe Meyer, Renata Burckhardt, Master Project for the Postgraduate Programme in Curating, *Spill the Beans,* http://www.curating.org/index.php/master_projects/spill-the-beans. Accessed 13.05.2012.

HOW TO PERFORM THE CITY?

Sally De Kunst

The Belluard Bollwerk International is a 'small big' arts festival that takes place every year at the beginning of the summer in Fribourg (CH). It has a history of having its own vision of actual artistic trends and showing work of local and international emerging artists in a convivial context.

This is a very personal manual. There is no such thing as one guideline for the Belluard Bollwerk International. At its best, an arts festival in a small town in Switzerland doesn't have just one profile. Rather it exists as a series of mini profiles: it focuses on every project, every artist, and preserves their artistic autonomy in relation to the given context. It is the actual art that defines the diversity of a festival and that also reveals the heterogeneous profile of its habitat.
Festival Belluard Bollwerk International, www.belluard.ch

It is hard to define the disciplines we are creating or presenting. It is said that we are somewhere 'in between'. Which is at the same time complex, challenging and exciting. Our main priority is to find a good balance between artistic autonomy on the one hand, and the link between the artist and the world that surrounds him on the other; between art and society; between an arts festival and its social function in a city. This however does not mean that we do socio-cultural work. Rather the festival investigates 'performativity' in different ways: actions or utterances that through their performance change the situation or the power relations within the given encounter or context.

What follows is my personal manual in 10 steps how to organise the Belluard Festival, with four years of experience in Fribourg.

1. Get to Know Your Context

Fribourg is a small town in the confederation of Switzerland: a de-centralised country with 4 official languages, 26 states, and just as many different mentalities and cultures. Although it is geographically in the centre of Europe, Switzerland seems to have (in the performing arts) a big focus on local production, which is often due to cultural politics and funding bodies. 'Internationalism' in the German-speaking part of Switzerland means mostly an exchange with Germany and Austria. In the French-speaking part of Switzerland there is a strong link with France. Fribourg is a small Catholic town (34,000 inhabitants, of which 1/3 are foreigners) with a renowned university (10,000 students) and is situated on the language and cultural border of these two regions. It is a city where superstitious practices are numerous, where the concentration of shopping centres per inhabitant is the highest in Europe, and where you can find seven tattoo shops for 34,000 residents. This complex combination gives it a sort of 'cosmopolitanism':

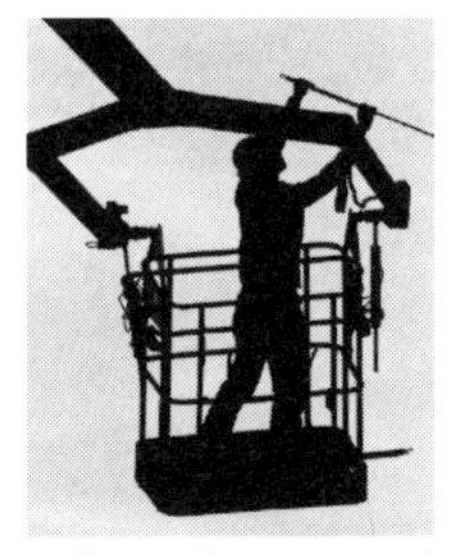

an openness and curiosity. We seem to be situated in a quite remarkable place that turns out to be the perfect context, since running a festival like the Belluard Bollwerk International implies never standing still, advancing constantly, keeping up with the times.

NB: One often gets under the surface of a local context by means of artistic projects. In 2010 the German artist Thomas Bratzke treated a building with acupuncture. The performance-installation *Building Therapy* revealed in its research that Fribourg is the Mecca of alternative therapy and superstition. One example of this is the practice of the 'faiseurs de secrets': people who have a gift of healing others over the telephone.

2. Think Global, Act Local

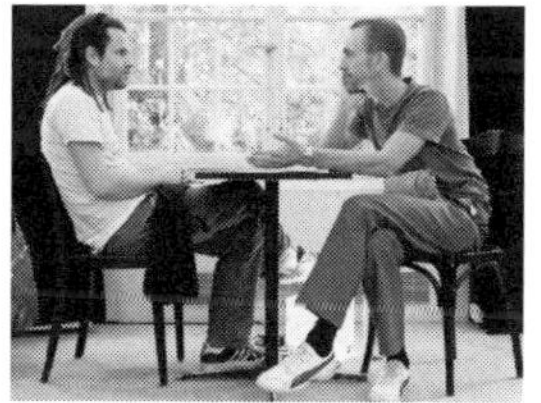

There is a risk involved in what we do at the Belluard Festival, in producing and presenting atypical projects, either in their form or their content. Within the given cultural political situation – which as already mentioned, is much focused on the local – it remains a challenge every year to organise an atypical international festival which is firmly anchored in Fribourg. This, however, doesn't mean that I am pleading for a return to localisation. The result of globalisation is that the romantic idea of cultural origins or local roots has more or less lost all meaning. Authenticity doesn't refer to provenance any more, but rather to the successful arrival of a cultural practice in a new setting, ideally with its own strong-willed flair. It is in this sense that locality becomes interesting to a festival like Belluard Bollwerk International: by producing international artistic works that create an interactive relationship with a local context, scrutinising it at the same time. By encouraging local artists to think outside of the box and trying out new formats. By organising a contest with a leitmotiv that challenges artists and practitioners from other fields, and that offers a supervised residency to get to know the city and local society. By involving local spectators in an active way so that they become performers or participants in an artistic project. By using other locations in the city and reaching an audience of passers-by. By being actively involved in both local and wider ranging artistic activities.

NB: We often realise projects that are licences or creative commons, such as the *Complaints Choir* (2008) or the *Human Library*

(2010). This year the Fribourg theatre director Sylviane Tille staged *The Great Public Sale of Brilliant but Unrealised Ideas*©, an auction of artists' ideas instead of oeuvres. Seventeen ideas by international and local artists, such as Santiago Sierra, Miranda July, San Keller, Jean-Damien Fleury, … were assessed by experts and sold by auctioneer Bernhard Piguet from the Maison des Ventes in Geneva, for money or 'creative capital' (artistic ideas). The evening degenerated brilliantly into anarchy and active participation by the Fribourg audience.

3. Watch, Listen and Talk, Talk, Talk

In concrete terms, the way choices are made to put the festival together every year is very intuitive: I let myself be led by what I see, hear, read, by the discussions I have with artists and by questions of society they are dealing with. A mutual interest is very important. Artists should also have an interest in practical matters and reality. To put together the programme I am often in dialogue with a lot of different people: the artists, but also my team, the members of our association, politicians, foundations, sponsors, colleagues in the national and international art fields, journalists, local authorities, experts in different fields, the owners of certain locations in Fribourg that we want to use, the audience… I consider my practice as a director of an arts festival as a constant flux of dialogues with many people.

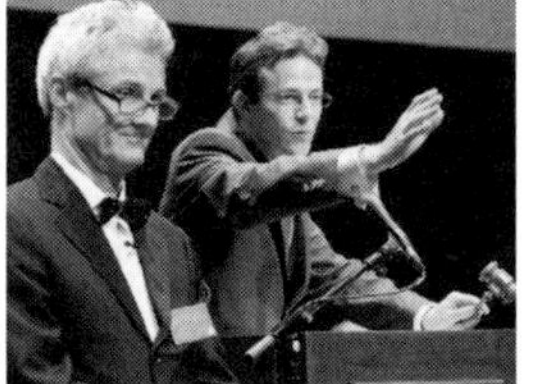

NB: Through an informal discussion with librarian Madeleine Dietrich in Fribourg I found out about the creative commons *Human Library*. I invited Sylviane Tille to organise her version in 2010 in the State & University Library of Fribourg. The catalogue contained 60 human books – people with a speciality or particular knowledge – and 15 dictionaries (simultaneous interpreters). The project was a huge success, with festival and library visitors.

4. Work Directly
with the Client

Although the festival spreads out markedly across the city, we do have one main venue: the Belluard (or 'Bollwerk' in German) is an old fortress from the Middle Ages – reminiscent of Shakespeare's Globe Theatre – half of 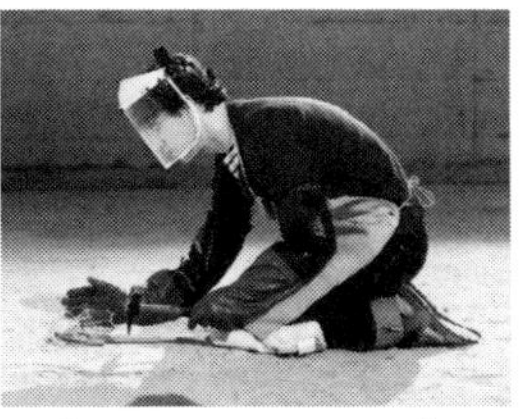 which is open-air, and which has a theatre stage. The site was occupied in 1983 by artists who founded the Belluard Bollwerk International, and since then it has been the heart of the festival every year. It is a real eye-catcher, a magnificent, but also very dominant building, where you cannot just present any performance or art project. So this space plays a part in simply making decisions. In the Belluard we present more 'conventional' projects, not in terms of their ideas, but in their form, like concerts and performances. Sometimes artists use the space in a different way. This year, for example, the musicians/composers Antoine Chessex, Valerio Tricoli and Jérôme Noetinger used the architecture of the fortress to create the sound piece *Espèce d'Espace*. It was the Belluard as had never been *heard* before. However, the space also hosts theatre pieces, such as Forced Entertainment's new creation *Tomorrow's Parties* or *External* by the young British company GETINTHEBACKOFTHEVAN (2011). Another space we often use is the Nouveau Monde theatre at the Ancienne Gare. It is a classical black box that allows us to present performances, lecture performances, films or other smaller stage projects, such as *L'effet de Serge* by Philippe Quesne (2008). The space also lends itself to other forms, for example the 'Oral cinema' piece *[wirvwar]* by Swiss artists Gilles Aubrey & Stéphane Montavon (2010), in which the audience could lie down on pillows and close their eyes while listening to a soundscape based on field recordings from Fribourg and elsewhere. Besides these more 'classical' stages, the Belluard Festival produces a lot of work in relation to the context of the city and its inhabitants. Many projects take place in the public space or in other spots or buildings in Fribourg. We've done projects in the university, in shopping centres, a library, old warehouses, a law court, in city gardens, on the streets, in the open air swimming pool, behind the cathedral … For this site-specific work and for the stage pieces, we operate directly with the client: every artist proposes a concept or project, and together we look for the right setting for the project (never the other way round).

NB: Taking the time for a long walk through the city with an artist, and showing them several places and sites, turns out to be very constructive. Often a space inspires the initial proposal. The British artist Sheila Ghelani modified her performance installation *Covet Me, Care For Me,* in which the visitors can break a blown glass heart, after having decided to present the work at the Werkhof, a beautiful, partially renovated old boat warehouse in Fribourg.

5. Entice Artists
with a Leitmotiv

In order to place more emphasis on artistic input as the starting point, the year-long call for proposals of the Belluard Bollwerk International, a traditional window in the festival programme, changed its rules as from 2008. Every year we choose a 'leitmotiv', often in dialogue with other artistic practitioners: in 2008 *Mis-Guided* with Wrights & Sites, a group of artists/researchers from the UK; in 2009 *Kitchain* – re-inventing our festival centre – with Oliver Schmid, Patrick Aumann and Adrian Kramp, three architects from three different practices in Fribourg; in 2010 *Urban Myth* in collaboration with the Belluard office team; in 2011 *Hope* with Elke Van Campenhout, a dramaturge from Belgium. These people are invited because they are working on a topic that is to us relevant at that point in time. Either because it relates to the urban and social context *(Mis-Guided),* because it concerns the festival as a community and meeting place *(Kitchain),* because it is a subject that is very present as much in Fribourg as globally *(Urban Myth)* or because a lot of artists are dealing with it and it is a current political issue *(Hope).* These keywords are not themes, but rather a pair of glasses to contemplate what is really happening in the field of art. The leitmotiv, by the way, does not dominate the entire communication of the festival. As Fribourg is a city in a constant state of change, in which urban transformations are as much criticised as acclaimed, the first call in 2008 took into consideration this everyday reality. Under the label *Mis-guided in Fribourg* and co-directed by the English collective Wrights & Sites, six interventions in the public space were realised for the festival. These projects did not take visitors to historical or picturesque parts of the city, but rather showed the hidden side of the city: the commercial zones, the changing and expanding districts. In a playful way the six projects questioned urban society, and this without the slightest hint of nostalgia, but rather from a subtle, critical point of view.

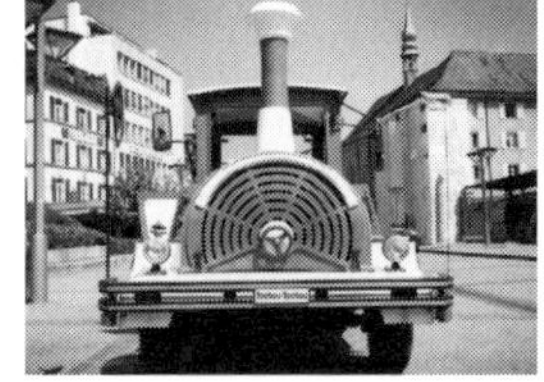

NB: The *Mis-Guided* projects in 2008 not only embraced festival visitors, but also caught the attention of passers-by and tourists. To our pleasant surprise two of the projects, *Tschou-Tschou* by Alexander Hana, an alternative tour with the Fribourg tourist train to the commercial outskirts of Fribourg, and *Hier, aujourd'hui, demain* by Robert Walker, a guided tour with 3-D glasses through the constantly mutating quarter of Pérolles, were after the festival taken over by the Fribourg Tourism Office for its 2009 summer programme.

6. Take
Risks

A jury of 8 people (half local, half international, consisting for example in 2011 of an architect, a graphic designer, a teacher/artist, an artist, a curator, a performing arts programmer, a dramaturge and myself) selects between one 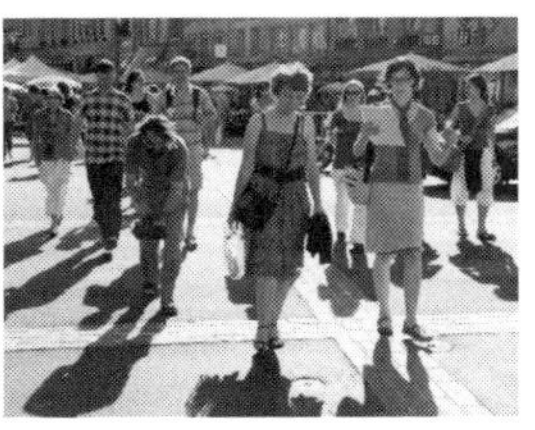 and nine proposals – depending on the nature of the call and the projects – out of the average of 250 to 550 applications we receive every year. The final selection takes two days, and consists of long discussions, and a mapping of the chosen projects. This part of the festival practice is very important, as it influences my choices as a programmer. First of all, we receive lots of proposals from artists and other practitioners that I don't know, and whom I wouldn't meet in my usual networks – although I try to avoid these. Secondly, these artists often have a completely different view of the leitmotiv: it's like a stone that we throw in the water and which sends out ripples in many directions. Thirdly, the final selection on the table is the result of a really tough debate. Some projects that end up in this way in the programme, I would not have selected personally. However, through the group discussion I find myself seeing certain things from a different angle and discovering new perspectives on the festival, which is very refreshing.

NB: In 2010 the jury decided to choose the project of *Anonymous*, an artist who wanted to keep his identity a secret; a scheme that put at risk the festival as an institution. We couldn't sign a contract with an anonymous artist, couldn't wire money to his account, couldn't take out any insurance, ... During the festival *Anonymous* made various unannounced interventions, and the quest to discover his identity became a real treasure hunt in the city of Fribourg. On the philosophical level this project tackled different questions about authorship and art.

7. Stay up
to Date

Even though – after 28 years – we are institutionalised, we like to think that we are still a 'small big festival' that stays in touch with contemporary influences at the level of society and the arts. Every year the festival's programme allows us to welcome a new generation of artists, and with them, new ideas.

Whereas the 2008 festival focused more on the urban situation in general, the 2009 festival was heavily influenced by the economic crisis and the issue of the consumption of art. Empty shop windows were spreading in Fribourg, according to the newspaper *La Liberté* on 28 April 2009, a phenomenon also to be seen in other towns. Within this context, the Belluard Festival 2009 invited three artists and two artist duos to open a shop in the city of Fribourg for a period of ten days. Their projects were a reflection on consumption, economic transactions and the economic position of artists.

2010 was the year of *Urban Myths* (see 5), but also an edition where many north-south issues infiltrated the programme.

When the Belluard Festival launched the call for proposals for 2011 in May 2010 under the title *Hope*, we thought it necessary to develop a contemporary understanding of the word. We believed that hope could be a subtle, divisive force in every situation, relation and ethical set-up we commit to, rather than dreaming of a bloody revolution. One year later, in June 2011, at the time of the festival, the world had changed completely… However, we believe that hope is just that: something that changes all the time, that is intangible and that implies actions, revolutions and movement. For us, 'being hopeful' doesn't mean accepting the simple coherence of any activist position, we rather prefer to stay at the more indefinable level of unresolved poetics and questioning proposed to us by different artists from different backgrounds.

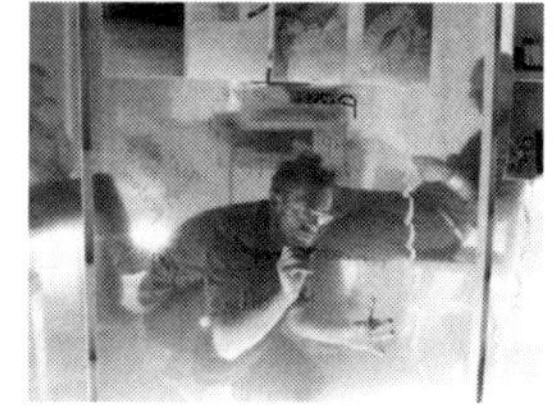

NB: Reality quite often overtakes art. When in 2010 artists Nicholas Galeazzi (CH) & Joel Verwimp (B) proposed to research the link between Colonel Gaddafi & Damien Hirst in their performative copyshop *Coyotl: Imprimerie des mythes,* and this was one of the 'myths' picked up by our graphic designer René Walker for his publicity campaign with anonymous posters, we could never have foreseen the huge media scandal this would cause around the time of our press conference. The copyright of one of the series of posters that said 'Gaddafi invited to Fribourg', was tracked down by – of all possible Swiss media – the *Trib-une de Genève* as belonging to the Belluard Bollwerk Interna-tional, and this at exactly the time that one of the two Swiss hos-tages was about to be set free by the Libyan government. Some Swiss newspapers wrote that the Belluard Festival put the lives of the hostages in danger, and a tough media and political de-bate about our campaign and festival ensued, continuing until the release of the hostages.

8. Create
a Buzz

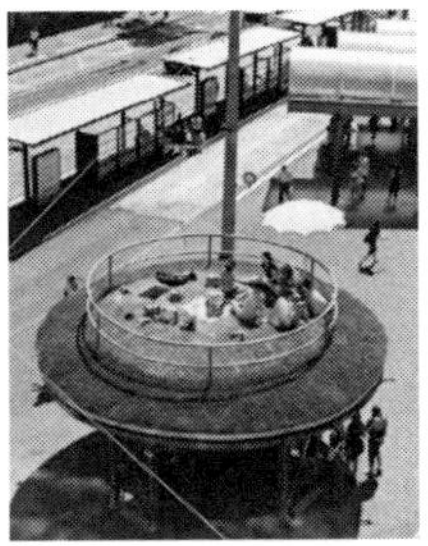

The Festival Belluard Bollwerk International has a history of pro-ducing and presenting art works that have in some cases caused scandals, but which have always created a buzz. Passed on by word of mouth, many projects of the past 28 years continue to lead a life of their own, often distorted, exaggerated or sensationalised. Mostly the rumours spread uninten-tionally. However in 2010, the festival launched the call *Urban Myth* with the deliberate intention of causing a stir. In some of the realised projects the 'myth' was not created through an action. Several projects were not announced before the festival, and their performativity exist-ed rather through the word of mouth and the suggestion of what might still happen, or the recounting of what had happened.

NB: Although the festival has a playful, distinct communication, it is often the projects in the urban space that catch the attention of passers-by, and create unconventional publicity. One of the catchiest examples was *Die Insel* (2008), by the German artist Christian Hasucha, an island covered with grass on scaffold-ing in front of the train station on one of the busiest squares in Fribourg. It could be rented free of charge for three-hour time slots. The tenants were at the same time spectator and perform-er, on a platform that questioned territory in the urban space.

9. Work with a Community of Practice

The projects *Human Library* (see 2) or *The Great Public Sale of Brilliant but Unrealised Ideas©* (see 2) are examples of a *community of practice*, according to the cognitive anthropologists Jean Lave and Etienne Wenger "a group of people that shares an interest, a practice and/or a profession". The group can develop itself by means of sharing and exchanging knowledge and experiences.

The group can, however, also be formed with the goal of obtaining knowledge about a certain field. Contemporary artists appeal to specialists to help to develop their work. This can be an artistic support, but also and more often this is a knowledge exchange with specialists from other fields: an engineer, a scientist, an architect, a shaman, a cook, a politician,… The selected artists are then invited for a group residency in Fribourg together. They get the opportunity to meet each other and the team, to visit the city, and meet specialists that can help them develop and produce their project. Since we don't have a venue or studio, these residencies are a key moment in the year to prepare the festival, and to collaborate with the artists and other people in Fribourg. All these specialists or participants and their colleagues, friends and relatives are consequently part of the *community of artistic practice*. The exchange of knowledge that takes place during a festival (or its production phase) is more a form of sharing a tacit knowledge; a knowledge that is not so much tangible and explicit, but that can be transferred through artistic projects between different domains and people. All members of a community get a sort of stimulus by what they create together: shared knowledge gives new perspectives, new forms, new art, for a changing society.

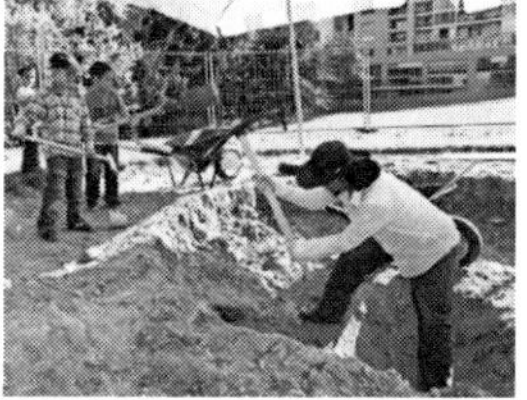

NB: Often the simplest concepts present the biggest challenge, and can consequently result in the biggest community of participation. *The Digging Project* by the Brussels based artists Kosi Hidama & Gosie Vervloessem (2011) for example, was a poetic project – digging a hole for ten days in a public garden in the centre of Fribourg – that was, however, logistically very complicated to realise. The city architect, the city engineers, the Archaeology Service of the State of Fribourg, a geo-biologist and a magnetiser were just a few of the experts that were consulted for the research and production.

10. Be a Good
Host

An important aspect of the festival is hospitality. A cutting edge artistic programme can only prosper in a convivial atmosphere where a broad audience (or 'community') feels welcome. This hospitality can be interpreted 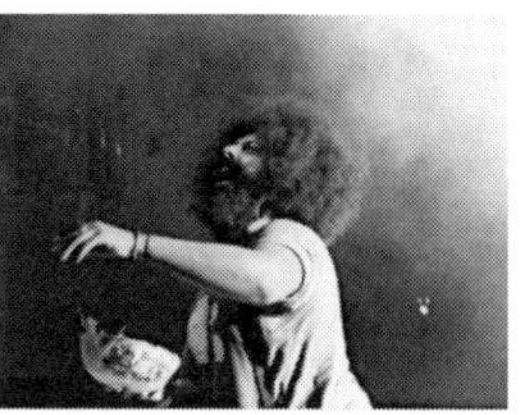 in very concrete terms: by creating a time-space to host people to meet, eat, drink, discuss, … In reference to the idea of the festival as a temporary community, as a place that, over two weeks, offers both a professional context for strong work of international artists and a festive setting for exchange between artists, locals, visitors and professionals, the Belluard Bollwerk International launched a call for proposals for a 'kitchen' for its 2009 edition. For at the heart of every artistic process there is always a kitchen: a cooking place, an eating and meeting place – a place that nourishes creative discussions. And after all, you will always find the most interesting encounters in the kitchen at parties…

To reinforce and encourage this idea of social gathering, Antonio Louro (P) & Benedetta Maxia (I) designed a modular table-based system – *Kitchain* – that invited people, through their actions, to turn the entire Arsenal (an old military warehouse next to the Belluard) into a huge kitchen. The audience could decide between an active or passive role: active because you really could prepare your own meal at one of the cooking corners; passive because you could observe our professional cooks Jean Piguet, Arnaud Nicod and Maïté Collin at work and taste their delicious meals. *Kitchain* also included a bar, and provided space for smaller projects and parties. Its flexibility allowed the festival to create different layouts and to renew the kitchen space concept every year. *Kitchain* has turned out to be a huge success, attracting a larger audience every year since its introduction. (blog: www.kitchain.net)

NB: A festival is at its core a 'party', so it should also be festive. Parties form an essential part. A musical highlight of recent years was the hilarious, brilliant and unpredictable performance of the American musician-comedian-beatboxer Reggie Watts in 2010.

EASTSIDE PROJECTS
MANUAL DRAFT
#2

Gavin Wade

This is a manual for Eastside Projects – it explains what the space is made of, how it was set up, who it is for, how it can be used and what it can offer. Spaces do not often come with instruction manuals. Eastside Projects was designed from experience and speculation on future audiences, inhabitants and workers of the space, to expose its specific context and encourage its use. As would be necessary for operating a machine or learning a subject a manual may be necessary for the full use of Eastside Projects. In this way we seek to open Eastside Projects to new forms of engagement.

Situation

Eastside Projects is an artist-run space, a public gallery for the city of Birmingham and the world. It is organised by a founding collective comprising Simon and Tom Bloor, Céline Condorelli, Ruth Claxton, James Langdon and Gavin 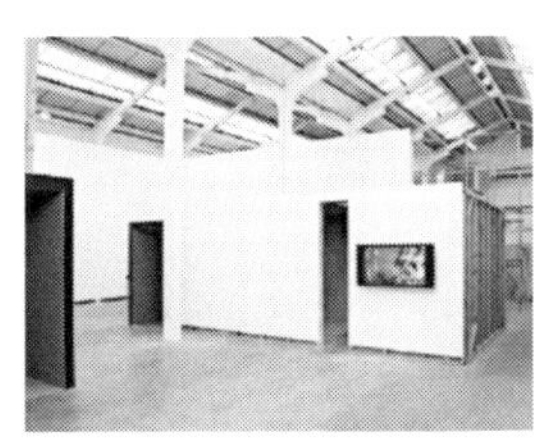 Wade, who first conceived and now runs the space.

Eastside Projects seeks to question the role and function of art within the urban environment by inviting and presenting experimental contemporary art practices, and fully participating in and supporting the cultural activity of the city both inside and out. Eastside Projects is free and open to the public as well as to multiple forms of involvement from artists and other practitioners.

Eastside Projects is to be considered intrinsic to the structure of the city and part of the sphere of public support through government subsidy. This is correct and proper as part of the fight to keep at bay the monopoly of cultural homogeneity. It works to establish the artist-run space as a public good.

Eastside Projects is a not-for-profit organisation, and works in partnership with Birmingham City University; it is revenue-funded by Arts Council England West Midlands.

Eastside Projects is set within an industrial building, originally a cabinet maker's premises, in the centre of Eastside, Birmingham, and in close proximity to other art production and exhibition spaces; Ikon Eastside, the Custard Factory and VIVID. The building was renovated using Arts Council England West Midlands funds and includes a large main gallery space, 225 square meter; a second smaller gallery, 70 square meter (equipped for video projection); and an artists' residency studio. Birmingham City University's Visualisation Research Unit (VRU) offices and studios for image and sound editing are also on site. Building renovations and development of the exhibition space were led by Support Structure: Céline Condorelli and Gavin Wade.

Purpose

If previous gallery structures tend to lull you into passivity then East-side Projects demands, through its design, that you are active. This activity is a prompt for further work beyond the public space of the gallery into and onto the public sphere. This should be the purpose of the gallery.

Display Device

The exhibition space was developed in response to the following questions: How do architecture and design support exhibition-making alongside the curation process? Can architecture and design be used as a form of curation as part of a gallery programme? Can we imagine a context that actively and explicitly produces exhibitions, art and exhibition-making, rather than embody or represent them? Can exhibitions also display means, relationships and underlying ideologies in the representation of space?

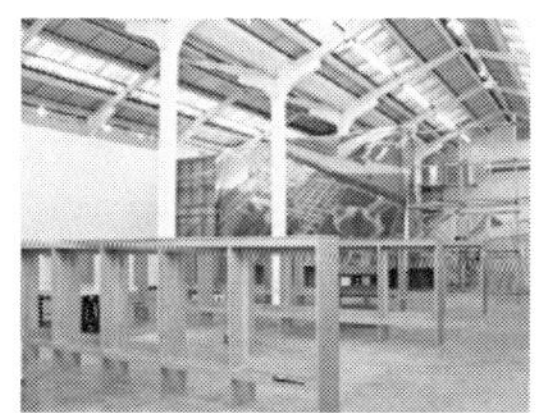

The gallery becomes a project-making machine, the artist-run space a space of production: of sensibility, of exhibitions and of a specific understanding of objects, context and experience. In this way the exhibition space enters a discourse of performativity, with a constructed context that engages in its subject rather than merely offering it for consumption. Eastside Projects is a display device designed specifically with and in support of a programme, in order to work alongside it as a form of curating, with the languages of design and building supporting its process.

Such an art space is being imagined in order to produce critical questions on the production of art, its perception, consumption and possible engagements through the filtered display of the art space.

Artworks as Existing Conditions

Eastside Projects considers design, organisational structures and architecture to be an integral part of its programme; each aspect of the gallery is in the process of constant evolution. Existing conditions are constructed through and with the exhibition programme. Artists are invited to set the existing conditions for the gallery. Work may remain. Work may be responded to.

Occupying the existing building with a very thin and fragile layer – a lining – with a temporary, ad-hoc aesthetic, the first exhibition

This is the Gallery and the Gallery is Many Things forms the first response to the site, and sets the initial alteration to existing conditions. This is clearly added on to the building, like a scaffolding, and as such allows further possibilities for change. In order to accumulate experience and put the building through a learning process, some traces should remain from what has happened previously. The gallery is a collection. The gallery is an artwork.

Long Term
Works

The Eastside Projects office is the artwork *Pleasure Island* by Heather and Ivan Morison. The structure is built from harvested red wood trees from a wood in Wales belonging to the artists. Originally commissioned for the 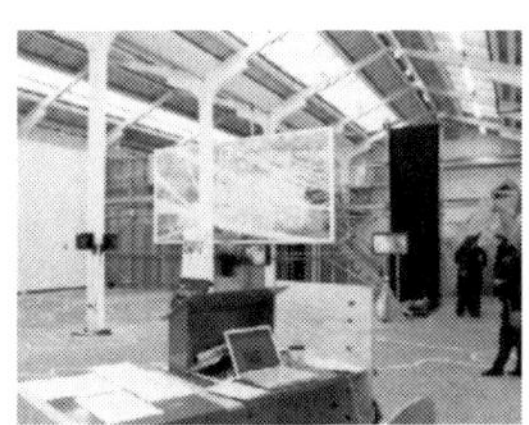 Wales Pavilion at the 52nd Venice Biennal in 2007, the building has been adapted for Eastside Projects as a long term commitment to exploring the nature of artworks within the space. New features within the structure include a kitchen, desks, shelving and a larger entrance. The artists will present a series of puppet shows within *Pleasure Island* as part of the gallery programme. The first show at the launch of Eastside Projects on 26 September 2008 was titled *I Love You Pleasure Island* and performed by Owen Davies and Suzy Kemp.

Other long term works have been installed by artists Matthew Harrison, Peter Fend, ISAN, Mark Titchner, Lawrence Weiner, Barbara Holub, Scott Myles and Susan Collins.

References as
Existing Conditions

At least three exhibition precedents have provided references and an underlying ethos for the first exhibition and continuing evolution of the gallery as an ongoing artwork.

1. El Lissitzky's *Abstract Cabinet* (1926/1930), at the International Kunstausstellung Dresden and Hannover Museum represents a clear and radical emergence of the artist-curator generating a constructed environment for artworks by Piet Mondrian, Naum Gabo and Lissitzky himself. It functioned as an artwork in itself, intertwined with the selection and integration of other artists' works. The *Abstract Cabinet* can be used as a model for an art space, a display device designed specifically to support different

directions in a programme. We might think not of El Lissitzky's aesthetics but of his approach to spatial design as a form of curating, the building and graphics supporting and producing the curation process.

2. Peter Nadin Gallery (1978–1979), New York, by Peter Nadin, Christopher d'Arcangelo and Nick Lawson, which had a continuous exhibition titled *The Work Shown in this Space Is a Response to the Existing Conditions and/or Work Previously Shown within the Space.* Artists included Daniel Buren, Peter Fend, Dan Graham, Louise Lawler, Sean Scully and Lawrence Weiner. The artists directly responded to each other's work, developing a cumulative environment. Two of the artists (Fend and Weiner) contributed semi-permanent works to the first exhibition at Eastside Projects. Nadin et al's 1978 project began with the text "We have joined together to execute functional constructions and to alter or refurbish existing structures as a means of surviving in a capitalist economy." The text forms the starting point for Eastside Projects' gallery policy and strategy. Just as Nadin et al's exhibition started with the 'empty' gallery space, *This is the Gallery and the Gallery is Many Things* followed suit in an unravelling of function, design and execution by the practitioners forming the gallery and the artists.

3. *This is the Show and the Show is Many Things,* 1994, Museum van Hedendaagse Kunst, Ghent, curated by Bart de Baere. The exhibition included Honoré d'O, Fabrice Hybert, Louise Bourgeois, Suchan Kinoshita, Jason 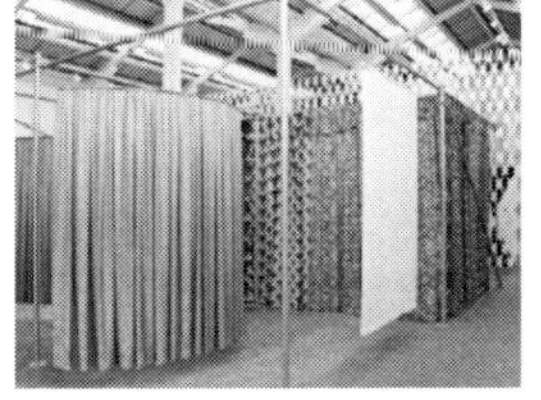 Rhoades and Luc Tuymans, who collectively planned the exhibition as a joint enterprise, defining relationships between each other and redefining functions of the museum space. The title of the first Eastside Projects show, *This is the Gallery and the Gallery is Many Things,* is adapted from this exhibition and also functions as a policy and slogan.

First edition: Celine Condorelli, James Langdon
& Gavin Wade (ed.), *Eastside Projects Manual,*
Berlin, New York: Sternberg Press 2009.

BELLY
OF THE WHALE

Sibylle Omlin

The intrinsic context of the relation between performance, time and space was specified in the project *Belly of the Whale* (2010–2011) [1], which was developed in a display of various institutions. We thought up a special event format specifically for this project: the relay of events and spaces.

Seventeen artists participated in five exhibition sites, with its own specific circumstances: a white cube, an alternative space, an experimental exhibition space in the nature of a display window, a park and the public space.

Because performance now as ever depends on an ephemeral, albeit repeatable action, it needs new forms of extension in the narrative cultural space. One possibility would be this concatenation of exhibitions, when seen in the context of research on performative practice and performative installations. The transformation from one to the other, from performance to installation, from one spatial apparatus to another, is the heart of the research in this project.

The chain of exhibitions within the relay not only changed places but also changed subject matter, formats and artists, who used their own means and media to examine the performance. Each of the artists invited to participate in the relay had two appearances or performances in the project.

For example, the artist Katja Schenker – whose performances cleverly combined physical strength, material and physical forces in a live situation at the Kunstverein Konstanz involving a paper landscape that filled the room, expanded out from a compressed paper cube – made furrows and folds in the paper during a one-hour action, which was then shown in the exhibition space for a month under the title *moll* (minor). [2] The main act of the performance – the crumbling and pressing of the paper – though was not visible to the public. [3]

Other artists like Dorothea Rust or Berclaz de Sierre, in turn, were on the road with a store of material. Dorothea Rust for instance installed this material – which included shoes, bags, climbing ropes, carpets, hooks, apples and pages of paper – in dance performances and installations at the Kunstraum K3 in Zurich and in a transformation of the same materials in the park of Château Mercier in Sierre, Switzerland.

1   www.installaction.com

2   *Arbeiten an der Erdoberfläche,* Nuremberg, Verlag für moderne Kunst Nürnberg 2011

3   Today, there is a video documentation of the performance as part of the whole work.

Janusz Baldyga, PL

The performer Janusz Baldyga, from Warsaw (born 1954 in Lublin), started out in artistic action theatre, which played an important socio-cultural function in Poland during the 1970s. Co-founder and member of the Pracownia group of artists (1976–81), co-founder of the Pracownia Gallery in Warsaw together with Jerzy Onuch and Łukasz Szajna (1976–79), member of the Akademia Ruchu (Movement Academy) since 1979. Today he works as a performer and sculptor. His objects often stem from performances – as when he covered tables with a cloth and constantly wound them with string, or balanced on a wooden board which he broke step by step, giving rise to a circular object. For the project *Belly of the Whale* he presented two performances, in Constance and in Sierre. In the Double Flag Performance, on the tennis court in Sierre, he shifted a 2 × 3-metre wooden board from the horizontal into the vertical using various iron brackets and his own physical strength. This created an installation which remained standing for the rest of the symposium.

Christophe Fellay, CH

Percussionist and composer (born 1966). Christophe Fellay is primarily active in sound installation and soundscape. He developed and installed a large soundscape in San Francisco, for example, while he was there on a scholarship. He increasingly interprets his percussion instruments as spatial sculpture, which generates a surround sound through its positioning within the architecture, and he often extends his instruments with samplers and loudspeakers.

Christophe Fellay's project for *Belly of the Whale* was presented in the Marks Blond art space in Bern, and proceeded from the idea of connecting visitors to the project space with the city and its sounds. The noises on Spychergasse were collected by a microphone mounted on the display window of the venue and amplified into the space, turning it into a soundscape that enabled the city to be perceived like a real or imagined living body. The outside, on the other hand, formed an extended space for the perception of the sounds of the alleyway and the traffic. Christophe Fellay also performed his conceptual music with various drums, percussion instruments and live electronics in Bern and Sierre.

Simon Kindle, FL/
Sophie Hofer/ Katrin Keller, CH

Born in 1983 in Vaduz. Since studying visual art at the Lucerne University of Applied Sciences and Arts he has primarily worked in installation, scenography and performance. The action *Vaduz, my pleasure – es ist uns ein Vergnügen (+[pozitif, -iv])* consisted in positioning a performance object (which contained the artist himself) in front of the Kunstraum Vaduz, a speech by Sophie Hofer, an artist colleague from Biel, and the possibility of interacting with the audience, which could set the artist in motion in the performance object. This turned the object into a sculpture, and the speech became the inauguration of a work of art in the public space.. The small town of Vaduz, already over-endowed with such works, thus acquired another one, if only temporarily.

Simon Kindle invited his colleague Katrin Keller to Sierre. The two performers – clothed in black and shod in curious buskins – observed the symposium for two days without uttering a single word. The artists' reflection of the symposium in this silent role confirms their thoughts as performance. The artists were also interested in whether deliberate, publicly visible observation, as a silent action by two people, would influence the atmosphere/essence of a symposium. As perhaps it did.

Pe Lang, CH

Sound performer (born 1974). Pe Lang works with sound installations, performance and composition. He often focuses on minimal kinetic systems: very simple electronic devices that can be combined with various materials to create unusual sound sources. His work is dominated by a highly reduced, minimalist use of material (watch glasses, batteries, electric wire, etc.), which is intended to produce sounds through simple linkages and circuits.

Numerous compositions and sound performances for Transmediale Berlin, Elektra Montreal, Sonic Arts Amsterdam, Dissonanze Roma, ISEA Singapore, Bitforms Gallery New York and elsewhere. Pe Lang has received numerous prizes and commissions (Bundesamt für Kultur, Swiss Art Awart, artists-in-lab).

For the project *Belly of the Whale* he conceived a live sound performance at K3 in Zurich, and at the Château Mercier in Sierre he set up an electrically controlled vibration in a plastic membrane to make small spheres rotate and produce a puzzling noise for the visitors to the public park.

Davor Ljubičić, DE

Davor Ljubičić grew up in Bosnia (born 1958), stu-died at the Academy of Visual Arts in Sarajevo (1980–84) and has lived in Germany since 1992, when he fled from Banja Luka during the Balkan Conflict. His is an expressive, spatial artistic practice – primarily in graphite or pencil – which often takes place in a performance setting. In his current installations he also works with found materials, simple electronics, mirrors and sound elements, which he frequently integrates into his painting or arranges spatially.

At the art space K3 in Zurich Ljubičić installed an existing object together with a table, two found milk churns and a sound installation: *O.T. (TWINS)*, video object, 2008/09. The sound was created by scraping his fingernails along the milk churns. The milk churns in turn have their own story. He obtained them from friends who split up their belongings while getting divorced and worked them up in his studio. For Sierre he staged the drawing performance

O.T.C. ora et labora (2010/11) in the entrance to the tower. Large-format graphite drawings hung in the space, and a video recording – again with irritating scraping sounds – projected into the site showed the artist drawing with a piece of graphite attached to a heavy metal cross.

Valerian Maly/ Klara Schilliger, CH

The Bern-based artists Klara Schilliger, born in 1953 in Sursee, and Valerian Maly, born in 1959 in Tübingen, have been working together since 1984 in the areas of performance art and installation. For certain specific works (usually with the direct involvement of the audience) they use the term 'installAction'. Their intermedia installations and performances are often site-specific interventions that are preceded by project-related research. Maly/Schilliger have presented numerous exhibitions and performances in both established art institutions and alternative spaces and festivals in Europe, the US and Asia. In 2008 they were awarded the Art Prize of the City of Bern.

As part of the exhibition *A travers le champs* in Goms in Oberwallis (2008), Klara Schilliger and Valerian Maly carried out a two-part action. *In Gold geritzte Ranken* was an installAction developed in 2008/2009 in the late Gothic parish church of Münster and dedicated to its high altar. The work consisted on the one hand in the initiation and publication (at Easter 2009, in time for the 500th anniversary of the consecration of the altar) of an art guide, on the other in a spatial installation, referring to the coming publication, of variable objects in the church itself. Maly and Schilliger's work thus oscillates between action and object and is aptly described by the neologism installAction: the two artists use structures and systems to install something that continues to exist over a longer period of time; and they take action to bring something about temporarily, but also to leave something behind.

For the stop-over of *Belly of the Whale* in the alternative space Marks Blond in Bern Maly and Schilliger developed a new installation and performance around the Jonah story. With charcoal produced from vine grafts from the vineyards around Mercier Castle according to an old recipe of the Renaissance painter Cennino Cennini (c. 1370 to c. 1440 in Florence), they wrote the biblical text of Jonah and the Whale, word for word, in Hebrew, Arabic and German, onto the walls of the art space in an action lasting two weeks. The action was accompanied by readings from the interlinear translation of the Bible in Hebrew, Arabic and German.

Victorine Müller, CH

The body and the allusive effect of light play a central role in Victorine Müller's performances and installations. With her works she finds contemporarily relevant portrayals of the human figure, which she positions in or between large transparent envelopes or spatial items. She has a tendency towards mythical human creatures, sensuality, dream and spirituality. In the past years she has also shown her sculptures and drawings away from her performances in museum spaces, most recently at Weiertal, Winterthur (2013), at Saint-Merri Church Paris (2012), Maison Rouge, Paris (2012), Kunsthalle Wil (2011), Konkordienkirche Mannheim (2010), in Kunstmuseum Solothurn (2008), Kunsthalle Wien, Projektraum Karlsplatz (2008) and Centre PasquArt Biel (2007). In exhibition spaces her large-format transparent objects are presented under theatrical lighting, which alters their physicality.

For the Kunstraum Vaduz Victorine Müller developed a new installation of light objects and opaque papier-mâché figures entitled *Pressentiment* (2010). In Sierre she installed her *Erdling* (2009), a transparent, whale-shaped sculpture, with lighting effects on the palace terrace.

Boris Nieslony, DE

Born in Grimma in 1945, Boris Nieslony spent his childhood and youth in homes. He became an artist through an action: from 2 October 1966 he lived for nine months inside a chalk circle on Georgplatz in Hanover. Nieslony studied painting in Berlin from 1969 to 1974, but he then switched to performance in Hamburg. After his studies he carried out large-scale performances at Künstlerhaus Hamburg and Künstlerhaus Stuttgart (*Das Konzil,* 1980, which involved 70 artists for 30 days), while also building up a performance network. In 1985 the performance group Black Market International was formed, originally consisting of seven artists. In 1986 Boris Nieslony founded the Art Services Association (ASA) for performers and theorists.

Nieslony understands his work as being equally oriented towards form and content. An essential theme is the art of encounter. In this sense – not only in contrast to the classical art market – meetings and collaborations with other artists are a part of his work. He has founded or co-founded many initiatives, groups and projects, some of which last a long time. They include a series of performance conferences, which have combined theory and practice since 1995, and the performance archive *Die Schwarze Lade.* For the project *Belly of the Whale* Nieslony was a guest and observer of the symposium, and he carried out a performance in the billiards room of Mercier Castle: for an hour he layed on his side on the billiards table and placed sunflower seeds into his ear from a pile of them on the green baize.

Denis Romanovski, SE

For Denis Romanovski, who was born in 1970 in Minsk and now lives in Stockholm, performance is primarily a social act. Formerly active as a top athlete (cross-country skiing), Romanovski raises issues about event and media culture, for example transmitting his direct physical experiences as a participant in the Vasaloppet ski marathon via live connection to an art audience in Stockholm. He is particularly interested in the phenomenon of karaoke, which not only represents an artistic platform of live performance, but is also fascinating in its installation aspect.

For the project *Belly of the Whale* he set up an empty aquarium marked *NO FISH HERE* (2010) in the park pool and ... fished in the pool.

Dorothea Rust, CH

The interesting contribution to the project by Dorothea Rust, who first trained as a dancer, later as an artist, was her spatial physical actions, based on the medium of dance but also integrating materials, gestures and objects. She travels bearing a fund of material and objects – rugs, rucksacks, fishing boots, watering cans, rope, slips of paper with words, apples, but also movements and sung tones – with which she develops site-specific performance installations and situations. At the K3 art space in Zurich she adjusted a public space with her ropes, objects and apples. *Newtons Äpfel* (2010/11) made her paraphernalia hover in defiance of gravity. At the finissage she threw around 6 000 envelopes – all of which were authentic postal items and addressed to her – out of the window into the courtyard. She brought the apples and a few objects to Sierre, and distributed them around the park. In a blindfold performance she then had the audience direct her in words to the places where the objects were installed.

Katja Schenker, CH

The performance artist Katja Schenker has recently attracted attention primarily through site-specific installations and in performances emphasising material. Her work with fabric, tubing, parachute silk, asphalt, concrete, bricks and other materials take their starting points from a simple physical action. But the works remain behind as objects after the performance or action. In the courtyard of the administration building of the Swiss Federal Office of Topography in Bern she asphalted a square by hand and planted it with shrubs. For a sewage plant she invented a mixture of earth that is porous but can solidify and form a wall. Holes dug by hand, self-produced conglomerate rock, doubled floors: with her materials and her own physical strength Katja Schenker creates large-format, architecture-like surfaces in interior and exterior spaces. Topographies, actually. For the project *Belly of the Whale* at the Kunstverein Konstanz she developed a new performance with paper, which had seven times the surface area of the floor of the large skylight gallery (134 square metres): *moll*. Before the exhibition, she and numerous helpers (but no machines) folded it down to the volume of 1.6 × 1.8 × 0.7 metres in a sports hall. At the opening of the exhibition an inconspicuous white bale stood in the centre of the hall, tightly held together with strings. Katja Schenker pulled at the strings, unfolded the bale and tugged the crumpled paper into all the corners of the space, creating a bizarre paper landscape that resembled a glacier in the bright light of the gallery.

Some of the paper went on to Sierre, into the library of Mercier Castle.

Stuart Sherman, USA

The presentation of a famous performance object by Stuart Sherman (1945–2001) could be seen at the K3 in Zurich in cooperation with the theatre expert Klaus Hersche. The performer Stuart Sherman was an innovative performance artist and author who also wrote plays for the theatre and screenplays for film and video. He called his performances, which he began to create in the 1970s, 'spectacles'; they were precisely planned, amazingly rhythmic demonstrations of particular everyday objects, which Sherman presented on a simple folding table – often set up in parks and on street corners – to the accompaniment of absurd linguistic gestures and scraps of text. But they could also be theatrical texts, which he performed with the utensils on the table: *Faust, Hamlet, Oedipus* as a one-man show. He filmed his spectacles on video; the tapes are now kept in the Museum of Modern Art/Electronic Arts intermix, and Sherman's archive is held by the Fales Library of New York University. His performance table, with various utensils and a suitcase, could be seen at K3. Klaus Hersche (previously director of the Belluard Festival in Fribourg, CH) reconstructed the work with the performance table on the basis of film material and his own memories of the artist Stuart Sherman. The table stayed with Klaus Hersche in 2000 after Sherman had given a performance at Belluard Bollwerk and then gone travelling. He left it with Klaus Hersche because he didn't know when he would have permanent accommodation again. Stuart Sherman died of AIDS in 2001.

Berclaz de Sierre, CH

Born on 15 April 1986 in Paris, lives in Siders and is a conceptual artist primarily concerned with the identity of the name. His own biography plays a central role here: on finishing his studies in Geneva in 1998 a namesake – also an artist – forbade him the use of his own name. Berclaz de Sierre has used this pseudonym as his label since then. Namesakes continue to be crucial to his work. For example, he seeks out the namesakes of important but deceased artists such as Leonardo da Vinci, Sandro Botticelli, Arnold Böcklin, Paul Klee, Albert Anker or Jean Tinguely. He contacts these people by telephone or through the Internet, visits them where they live and asks for an interview, video recording and photographic portrait. The stories he experiences while doing this have their own significance. Recently he has also become interested in the names of products. From mail order catalogues he orders items of clothing and shoes, furniture or home furnishings bearing the name of famous artists and stars, and combines them into spaces, exhibitions and installations. For the project *the Belly of the Whale* he created a Gilbert & George room with furniture, rugs and bags. In Konstanz he arrived with mattresses *Konstanz* and bed linen *Bodensee*, and in Sierre he presented items of clothing and underwear with the label *Gilbert & George* on Mercier Castle's hall stairway.

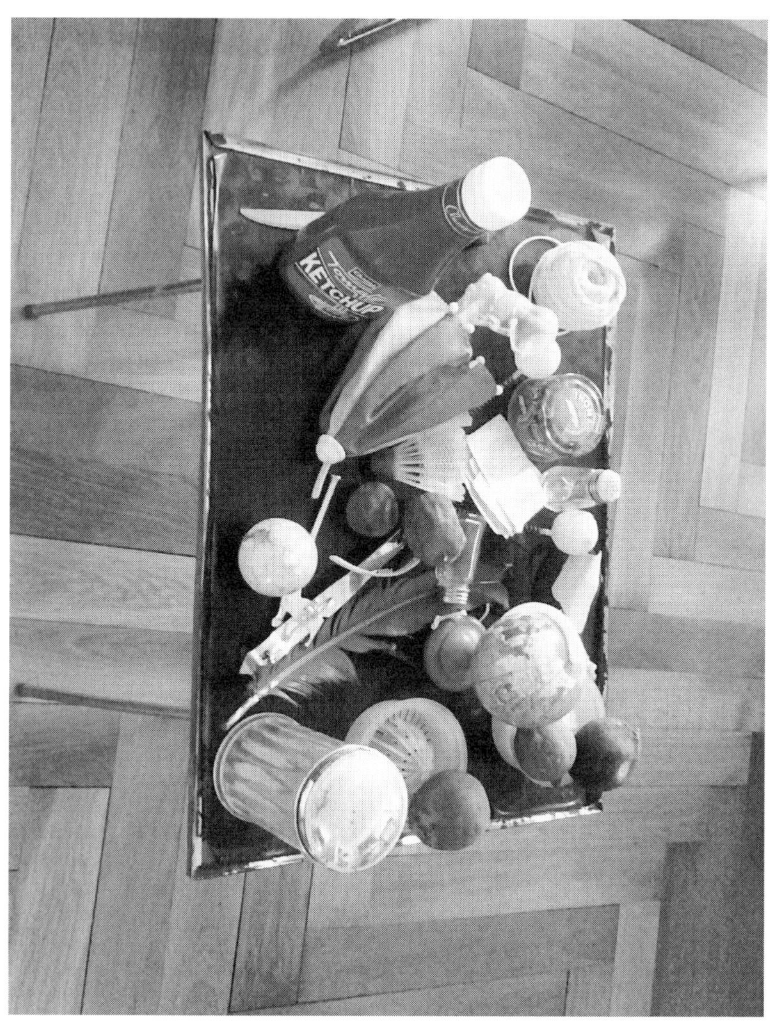

Stuart Sherman

10.10.2010, Zurich
Talk about the American performance artist Stuart Sherman
(1945–2001) with Klaus Hersche, presentation of *Stuart's Table*.
©Sibylle Omlin

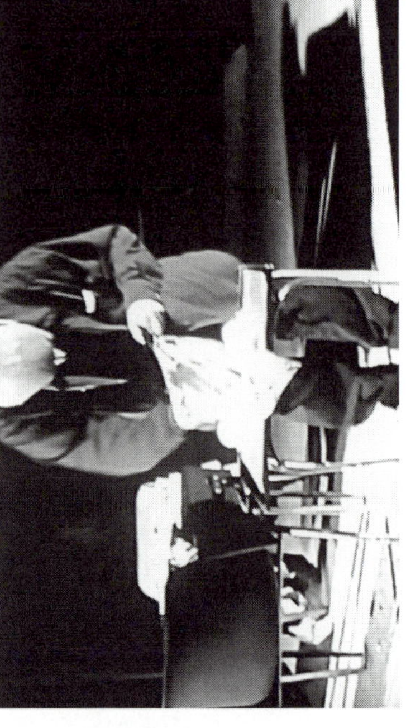 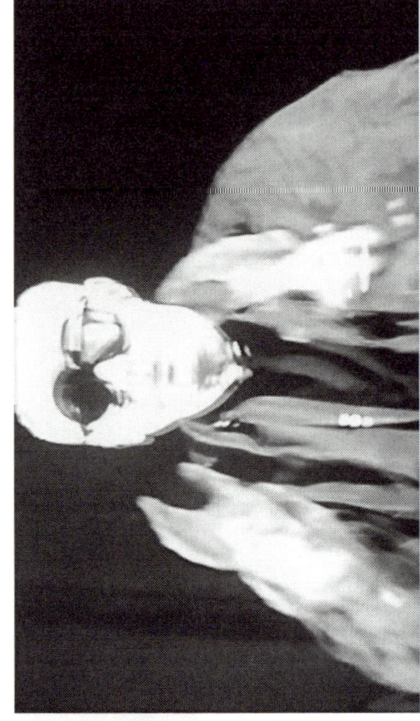

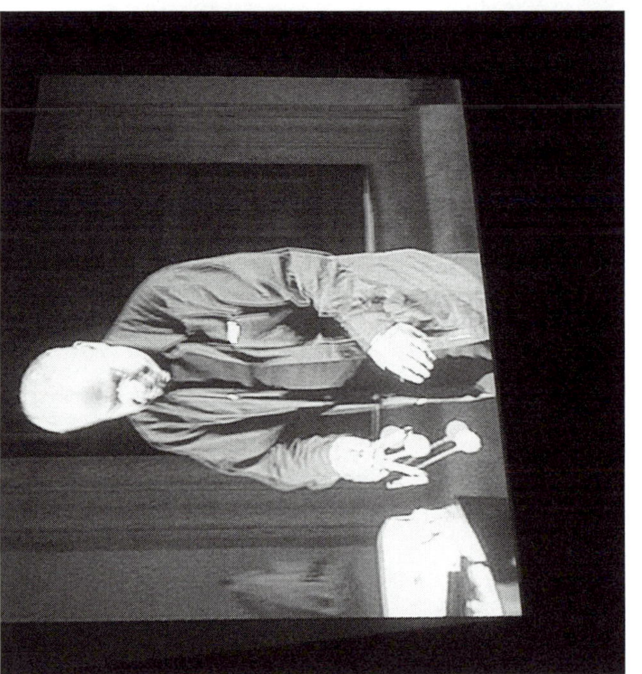

Stuart Sherman

10.10.2010, Zürich
Gespräch über den amerikanischen Performer Stuart Sherman
(1945–2001) mit Klaus Hersche, Präsentation von *Stuart's Table*.
© Sibylle Omlin, Ingrid Kaeser

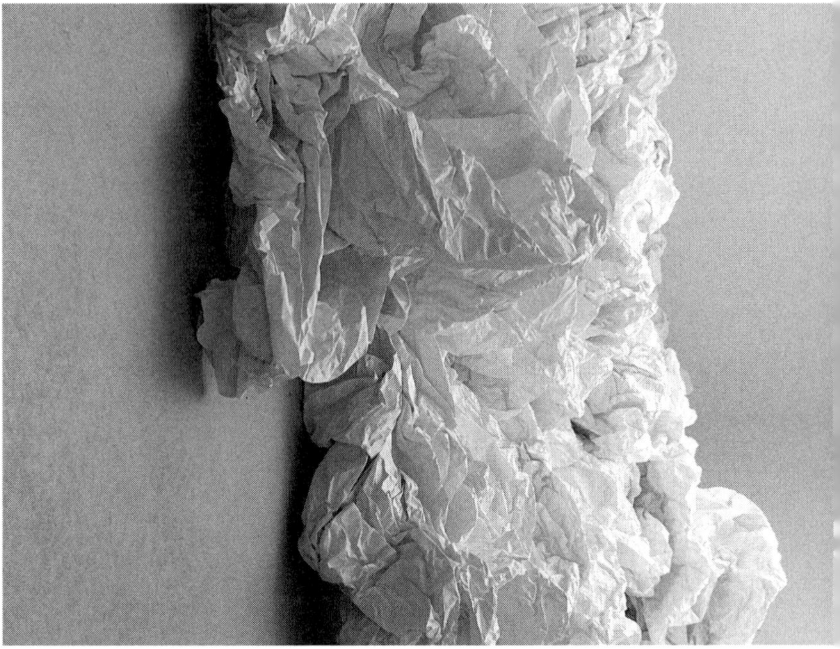

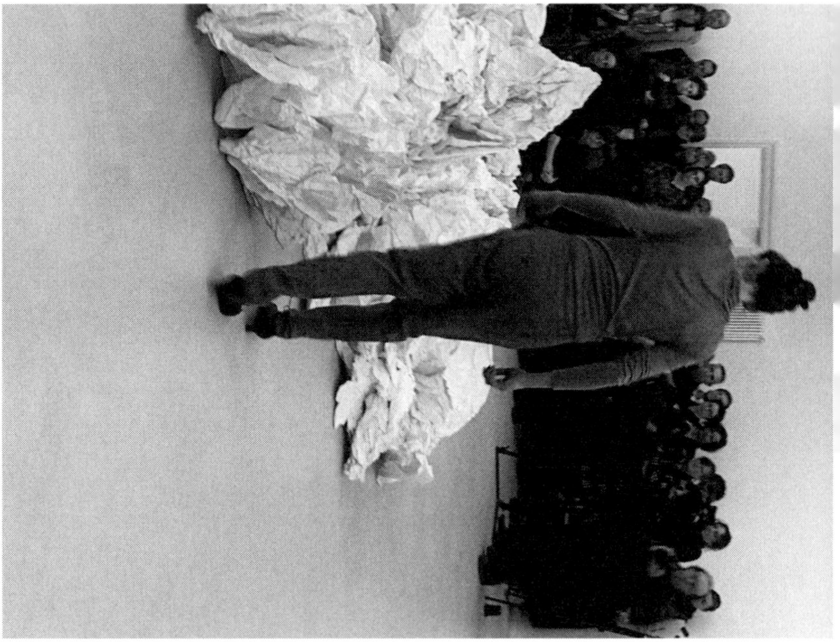

11.2.2011, Constance
Opening by the performative installation *moll* with Katja Schenker
at the main hall of Kunstverein Konstanz.
©Sibylle Omlin

Katja Schenker

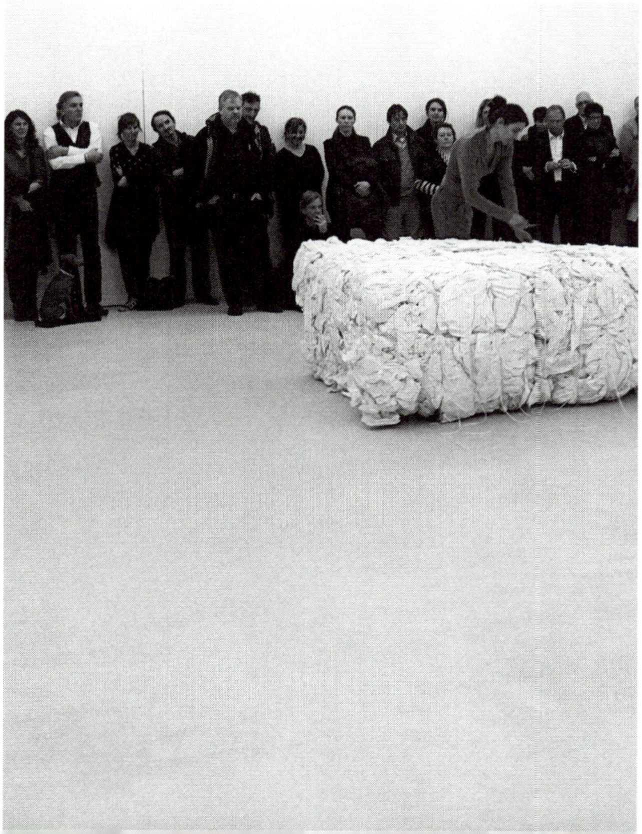

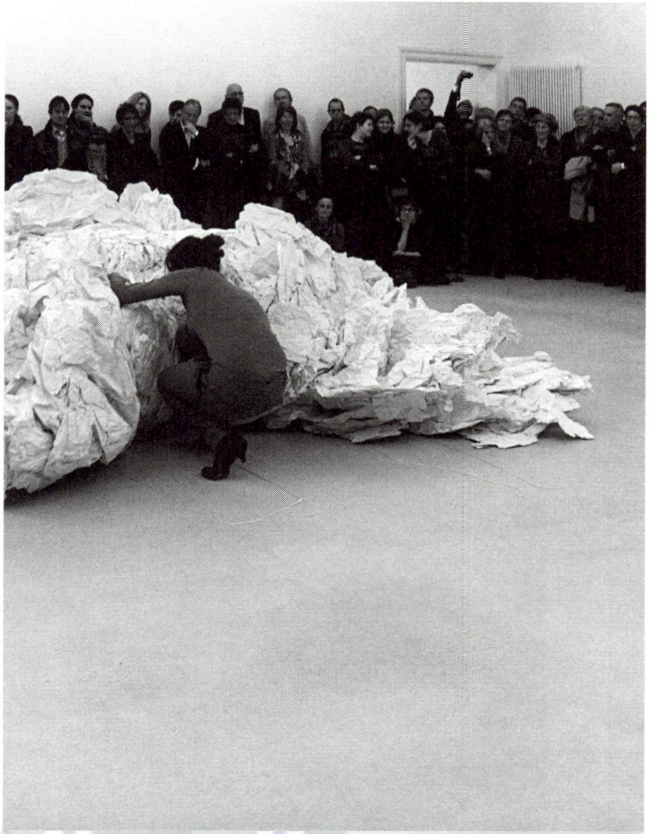

11.2.2011, Konstanz
Vernissage der performantiven Installation *moll* von Katja Schenker
im Oberlichtsaal des Kunstvereins Konstanz.
©Sibylle Omlin

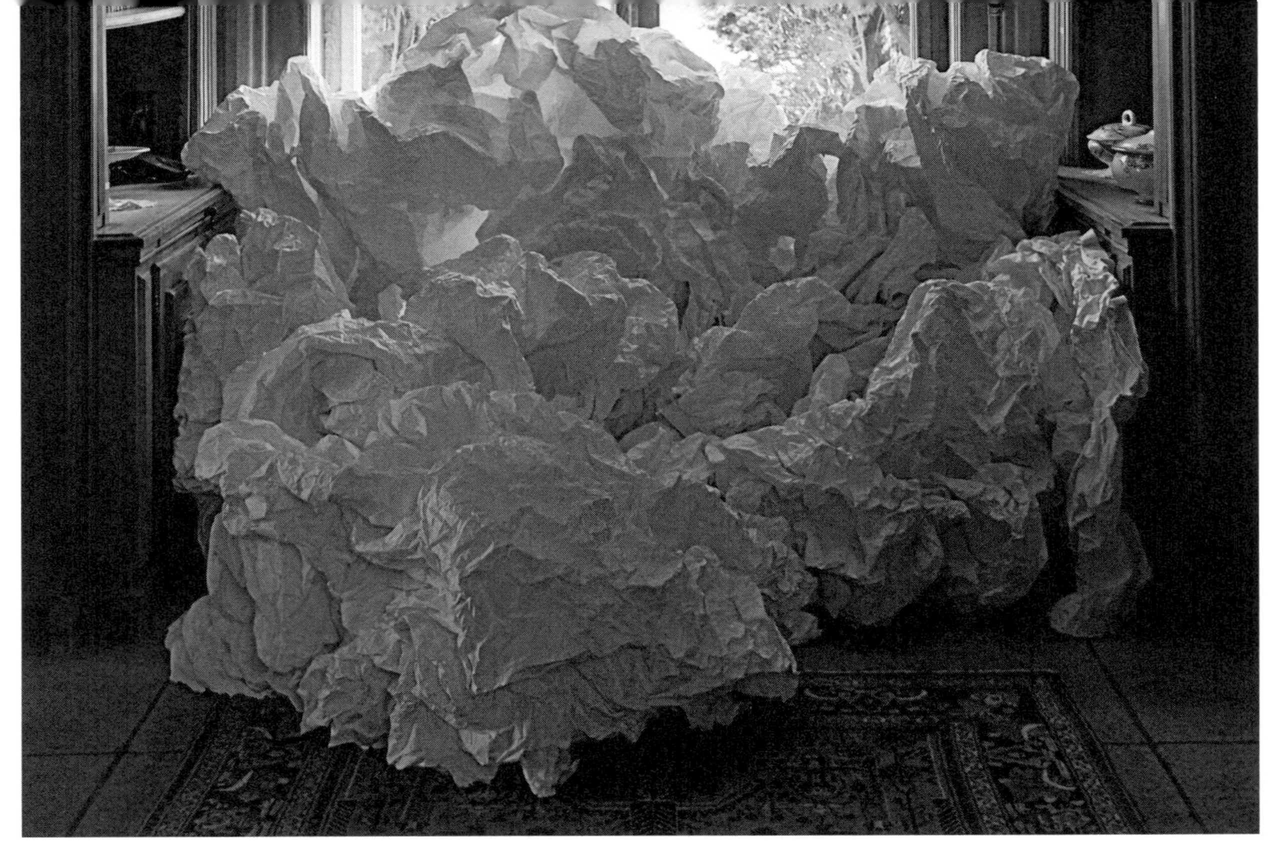

Katja Schenker

8.–10.5.2011, Sierre
Installation *moll* by Katja Schenker at the library
of Mercier Castle. ©Sibylle Omlin

Katja Schenker

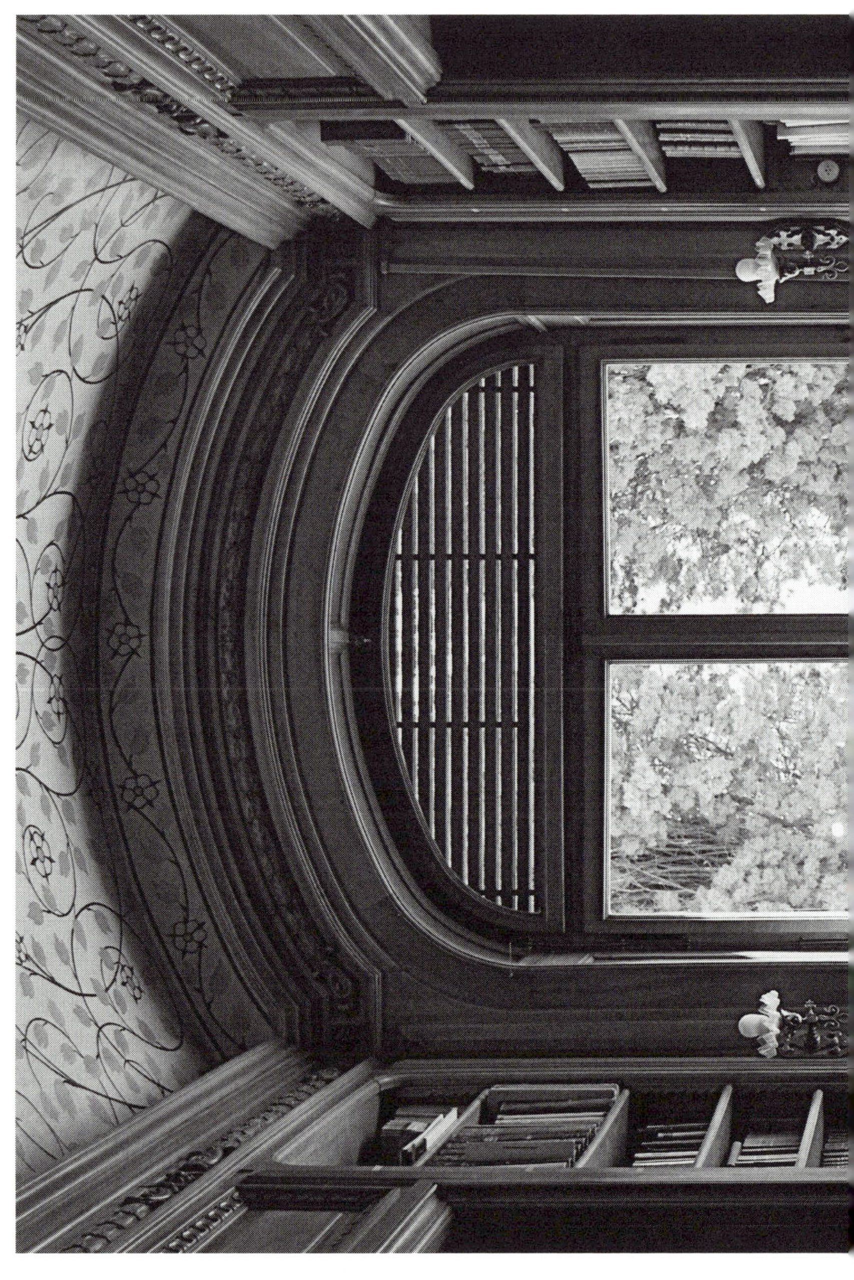

8.–10.5.2011, Sierre
Installation *moll* von Katja Schenker in der Bibliothek
von Schloss Mercier. ©Sibylle Omlin

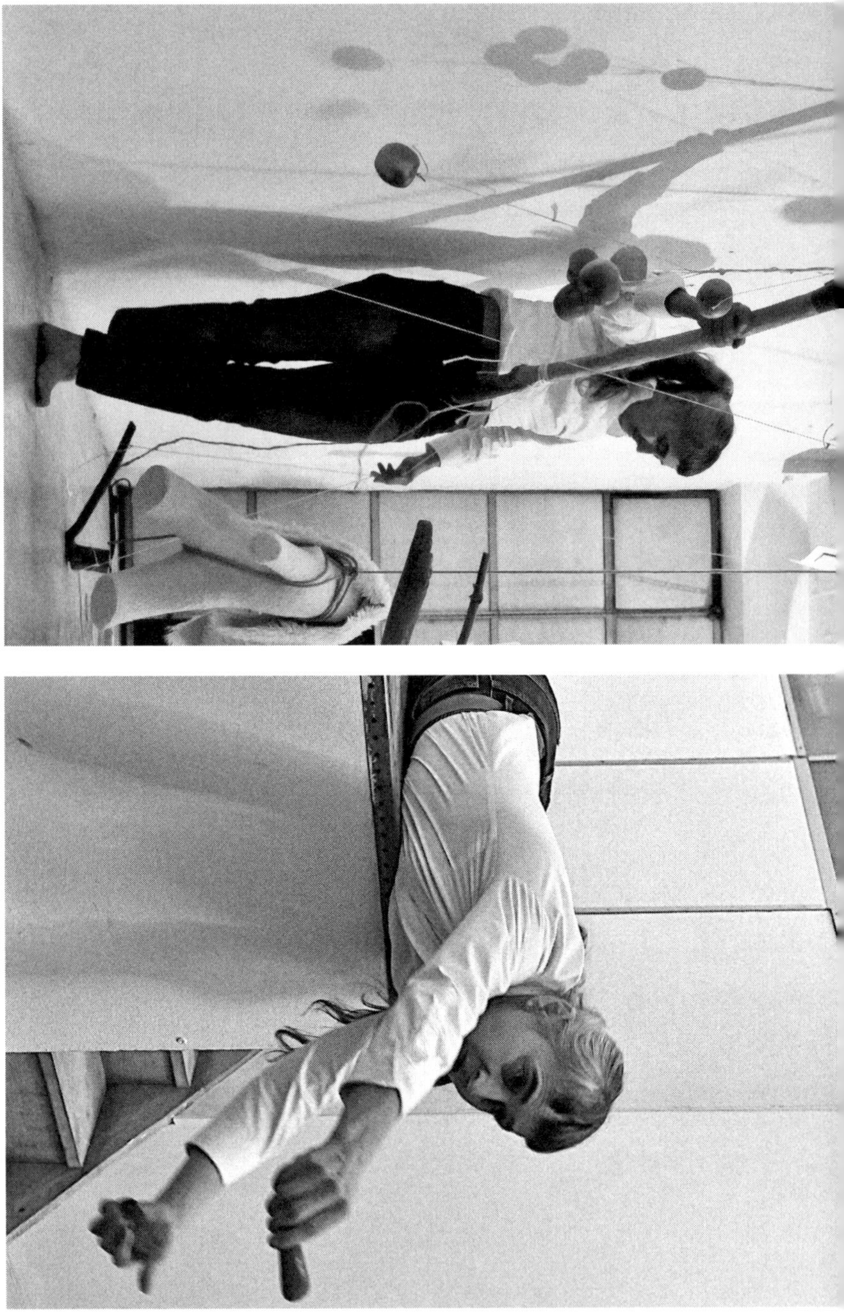

1.10.–17.10.2010, Zurich
Dorothea Rust, *Newtons apple*. Performative installation at Kunstraum K3
with closing day action on 17.10. © Christian Glaus

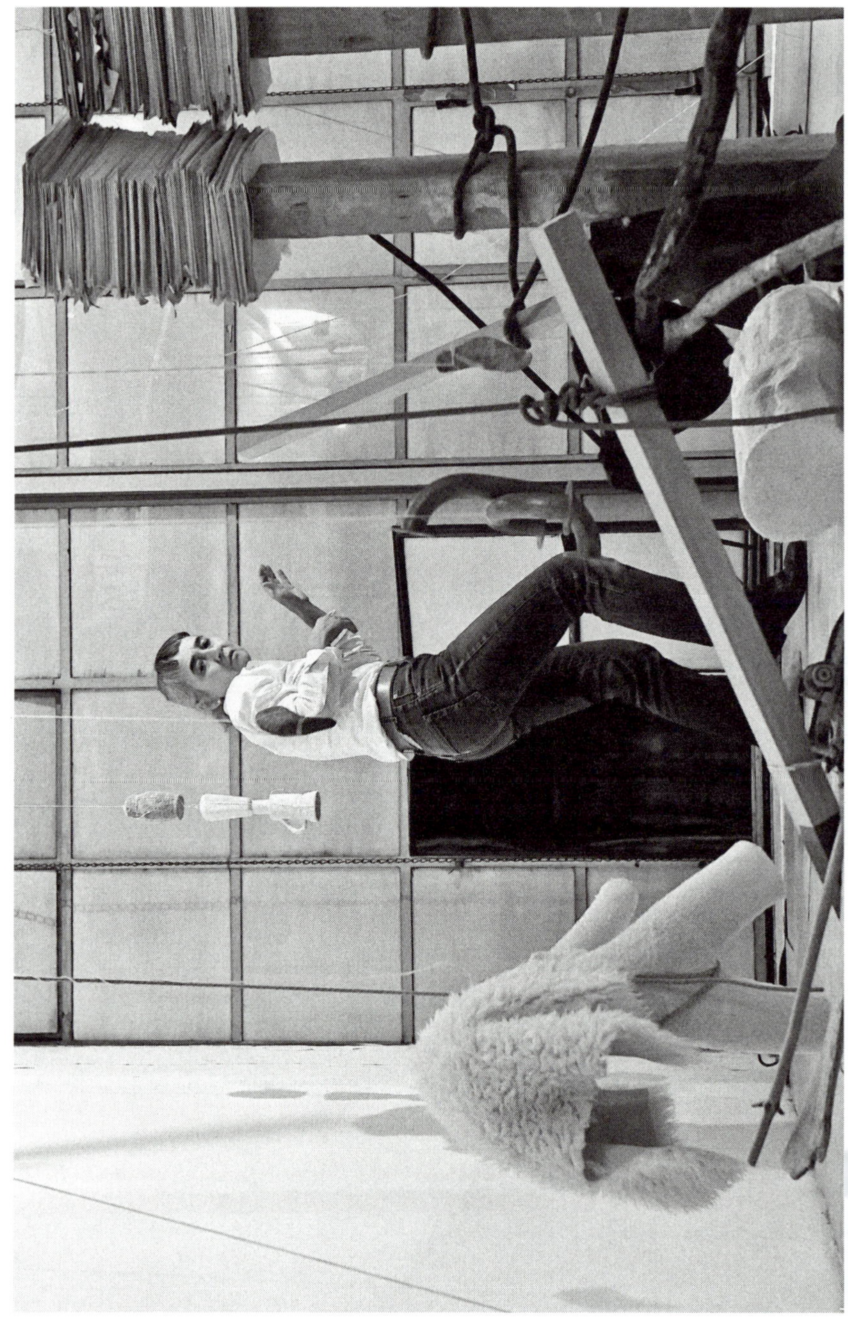

Dorothea Rust

1.10.–17.10.2010, Zürich
Dorothea Rust, *Newtons Äpfel*. Performative Installation im Kunstraum K3
mit Schlussperformance am 17.10. © Christian Glaus

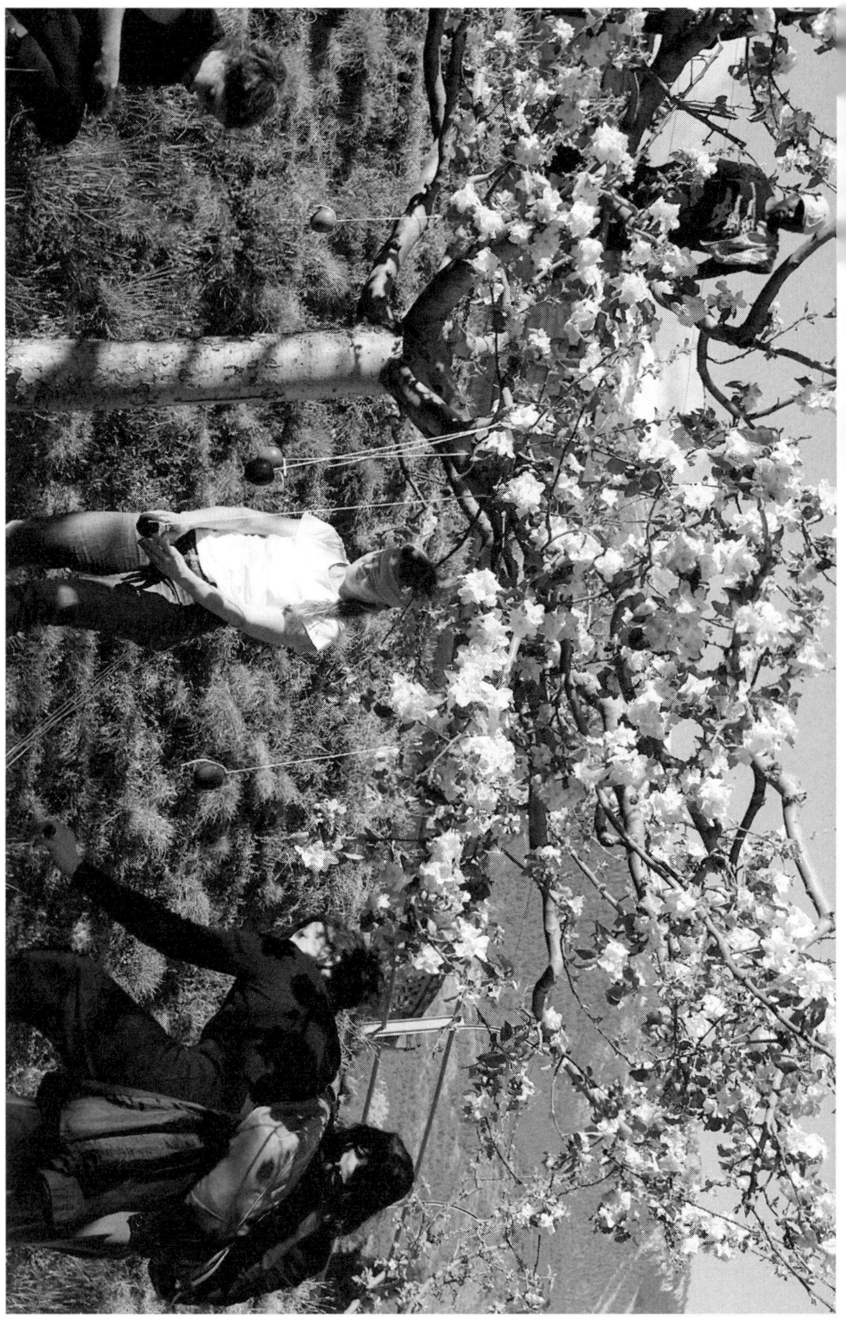

8.4.2011, Sierre
Dorothea Rust *Newtons apple*. The The blindfolded artist
is guided by her public through the park of Mercier Castle.
©Davor Ljubičić

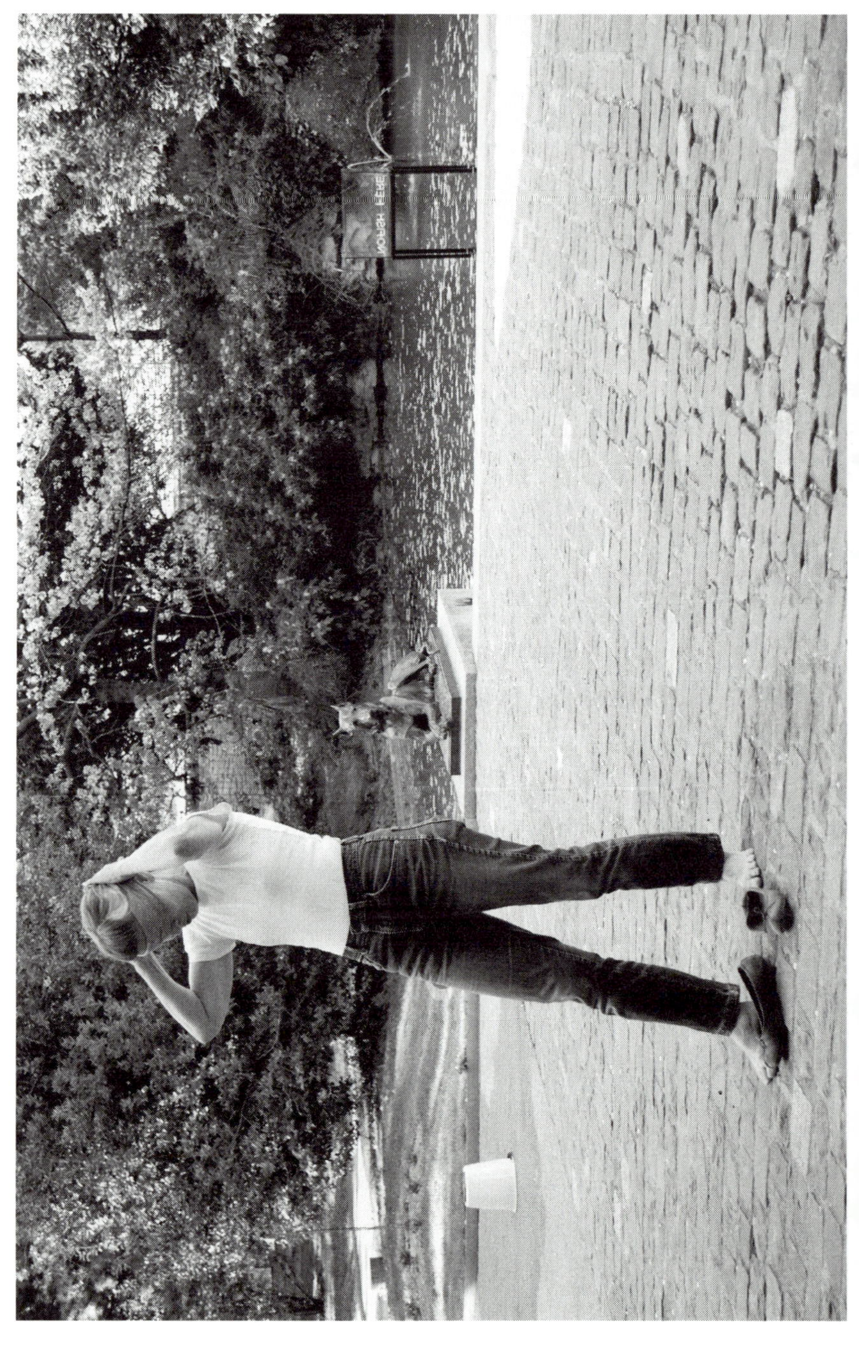

8.4.2011, Sierre
Dorothea Rust, *Newtons Äpfel*. Die Künstlerin lässt sich vom Publikum mit verbundenen Augen durch den Park von Schloss Mercier dirigieren. ©Davor Ljubičić

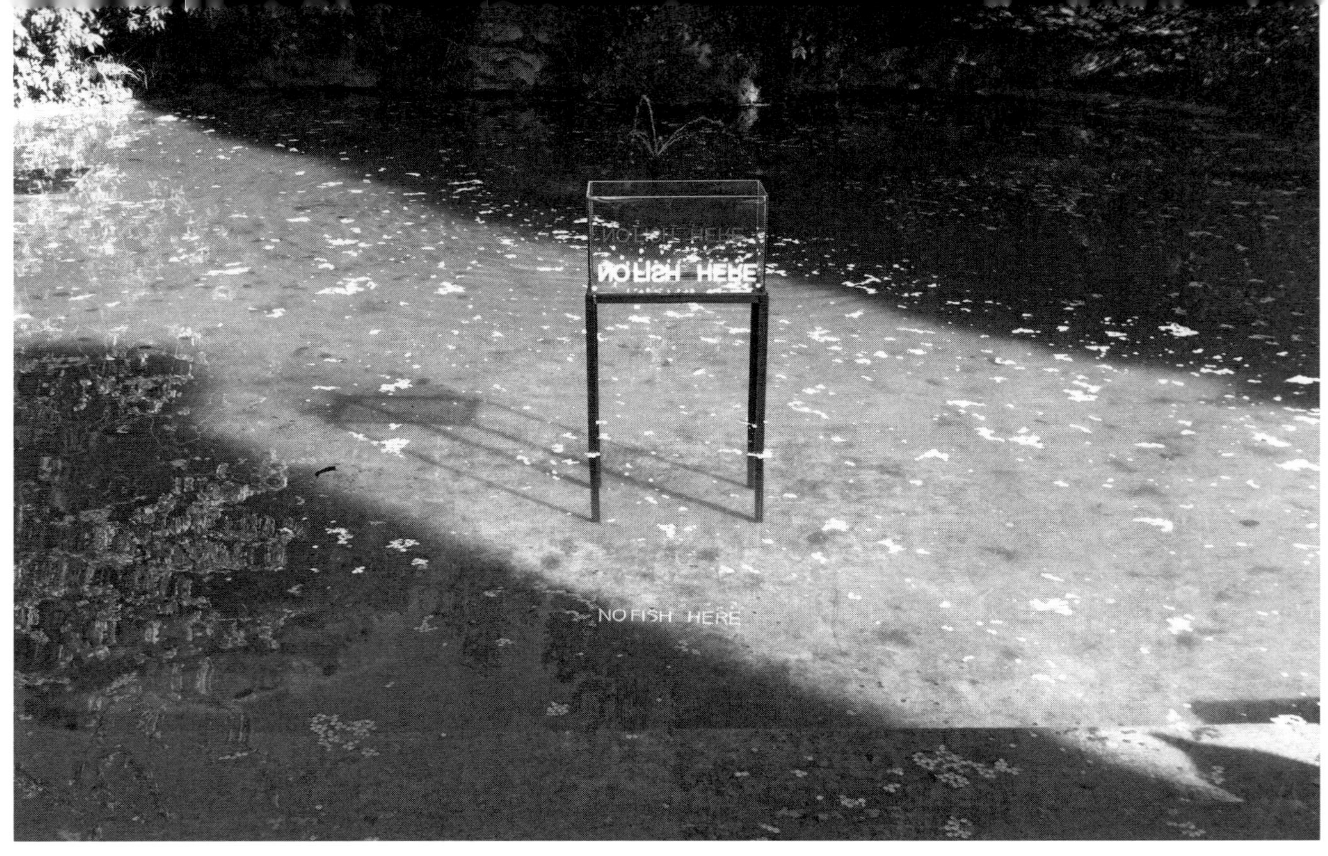

Denis Romanovski

9./10.4.2011, Sierre
Denis Romanovski, *No Fish here*, installation/performane with aquarium
in the pond of Mercier Castle. ©Davor Ljubičić

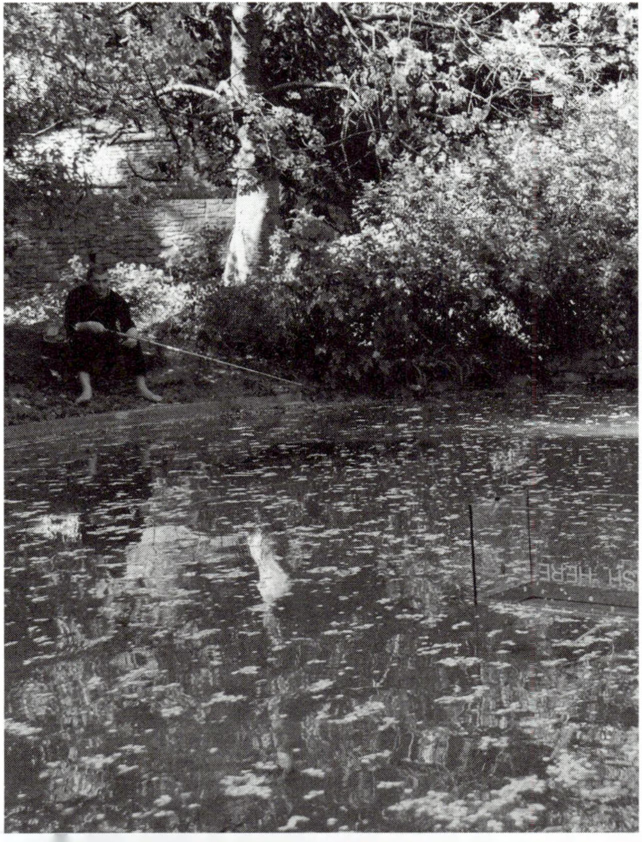

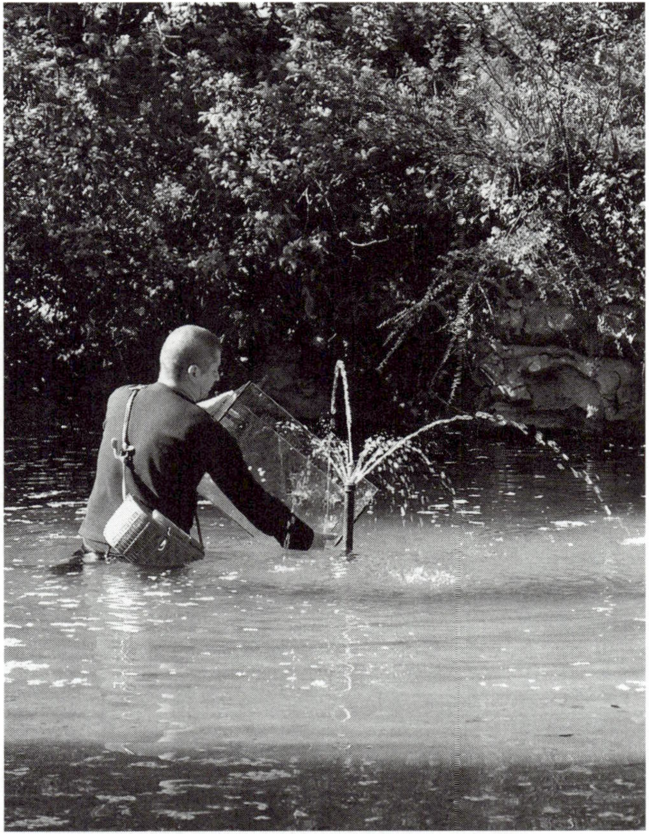

Denis Romanovski

9./10.4.2011, Sierre
Denis Romanovski, *No Fish here*, performative Installation mit einem
Aquarium im Schlossteich auf Schloss Mercier. ©Davor Ljubičić

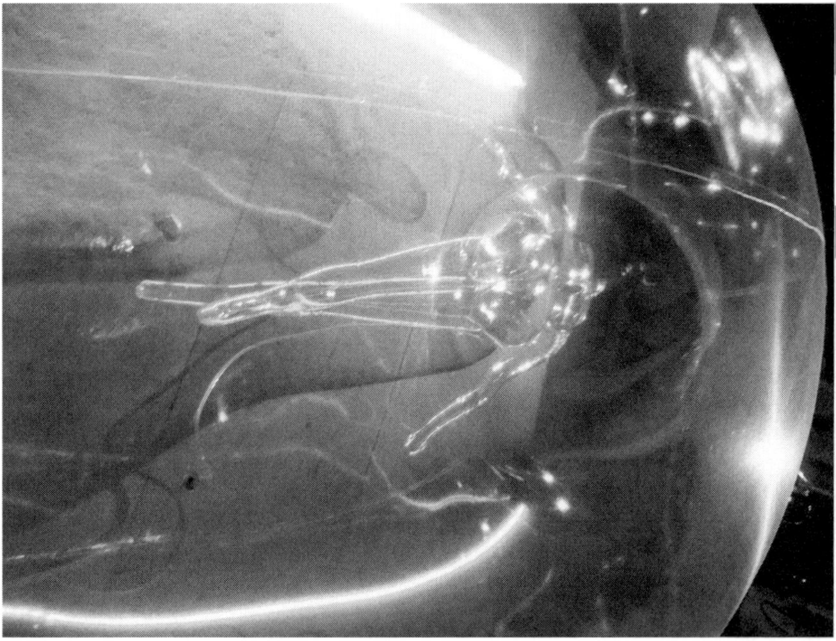

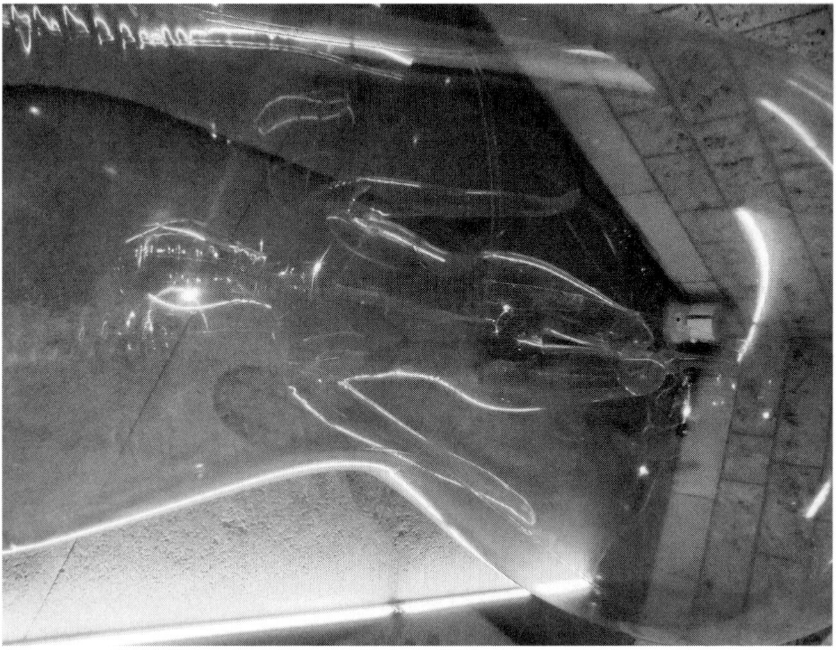

8.4.–11.4.2011, Sierre
Victorine Müller, *Erdling,* installation, Mercier Castle, Sierre/Terrasse.
© Victorine Müller

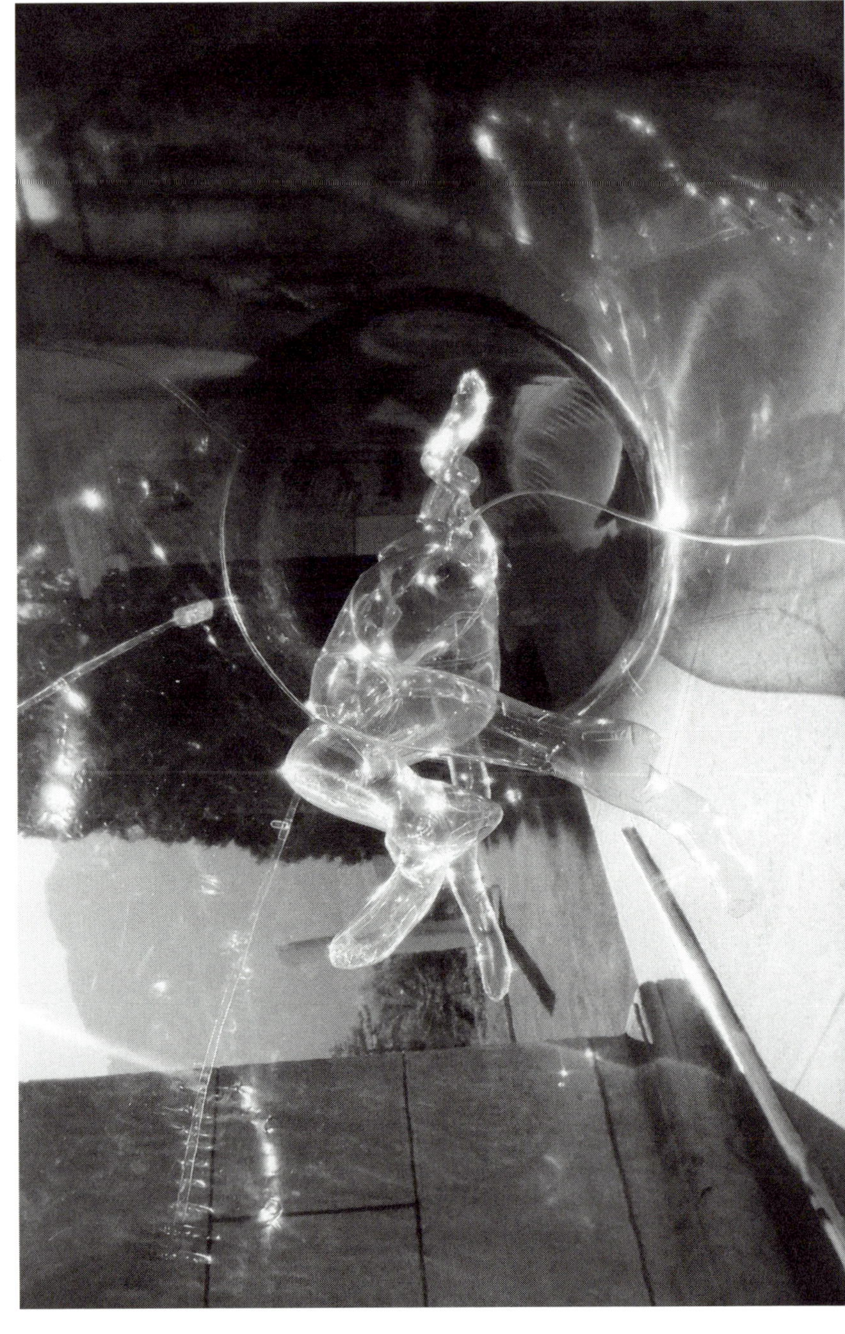

8.4.–11.4.2011, Sierre
Victorine Müller, *Erdling*, Installation, Schloss Mercier, Sierre/Terrasse.
© Victorine Müller

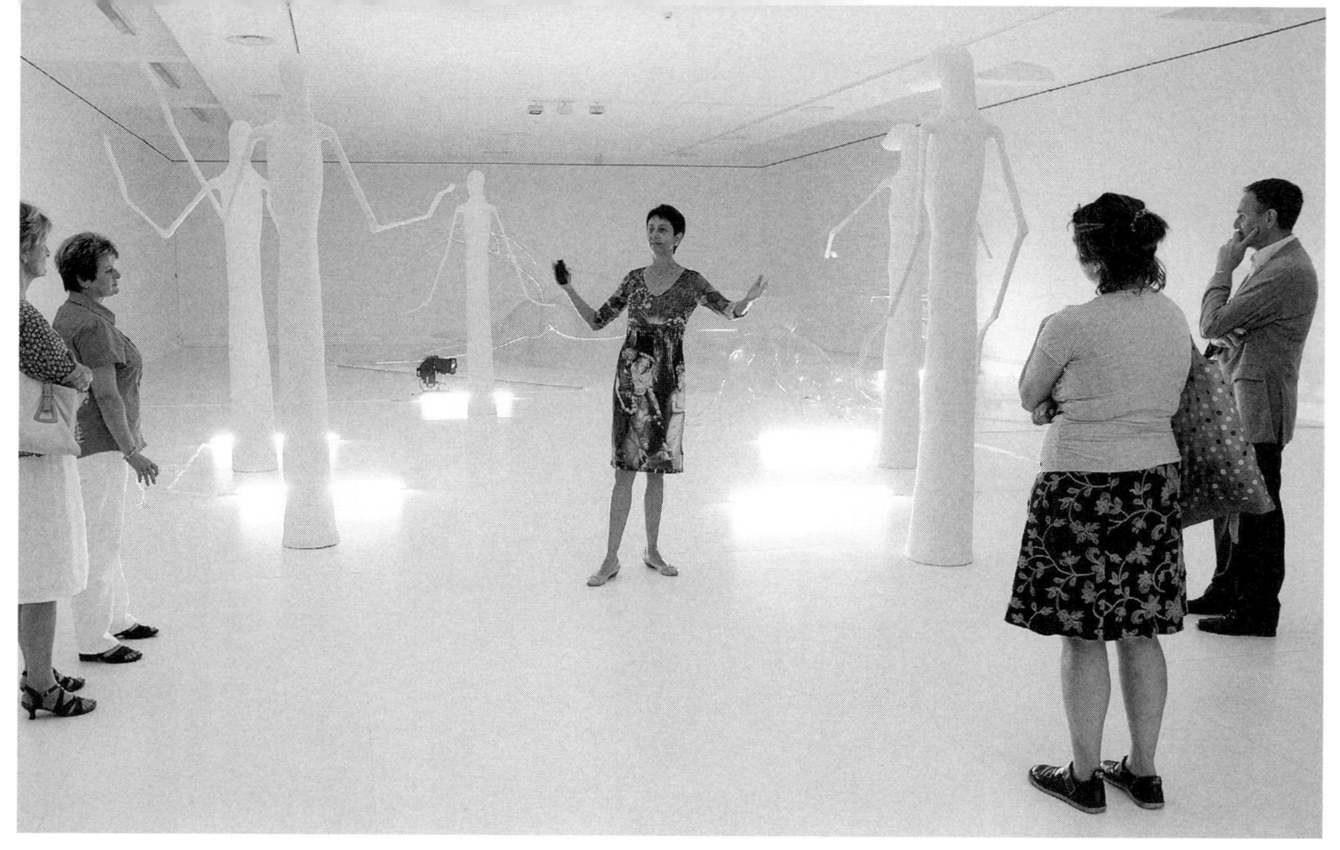

Victorine Müller

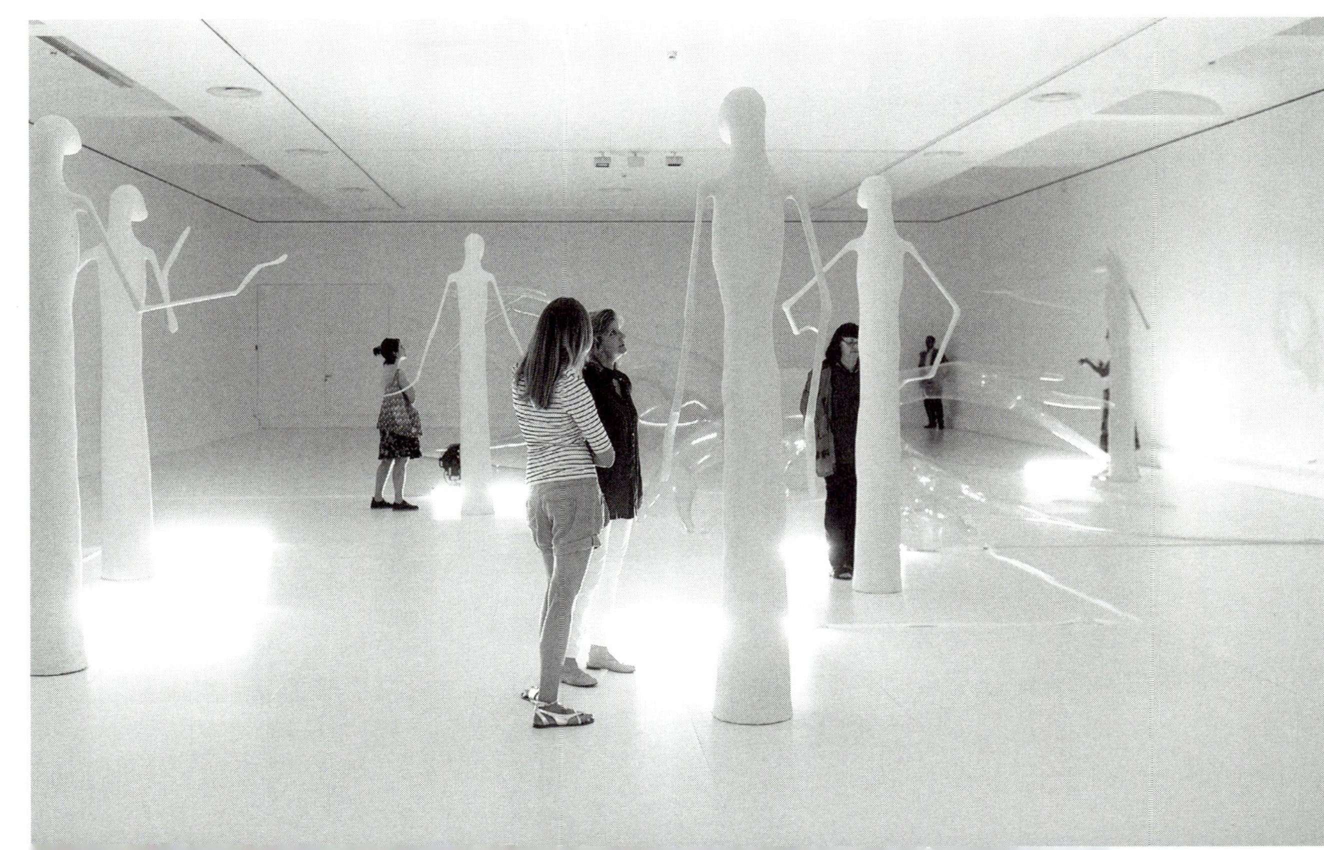

Victorine Müller

28.5.–18.7.2010, Vaduz
Victorine Müllers Installation *Pressentiment* im Kunstraum Engländerbau.
Schlussperformance am 18.7. ©Michael Zanghellini

Klara Schilliger / Valerian Maly

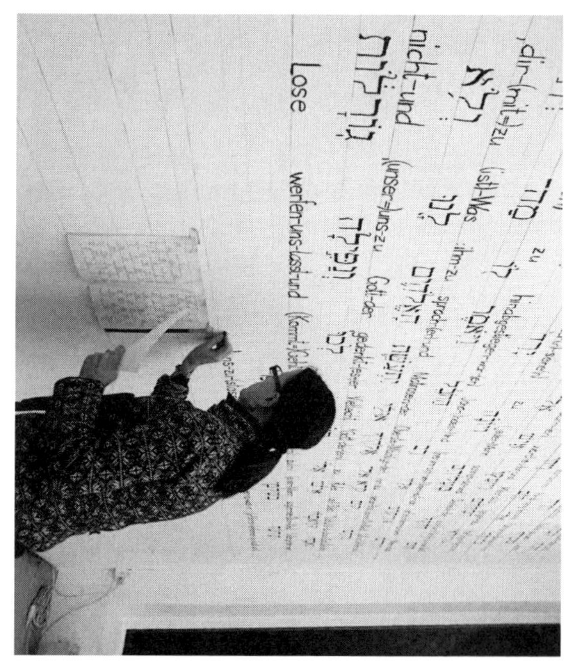

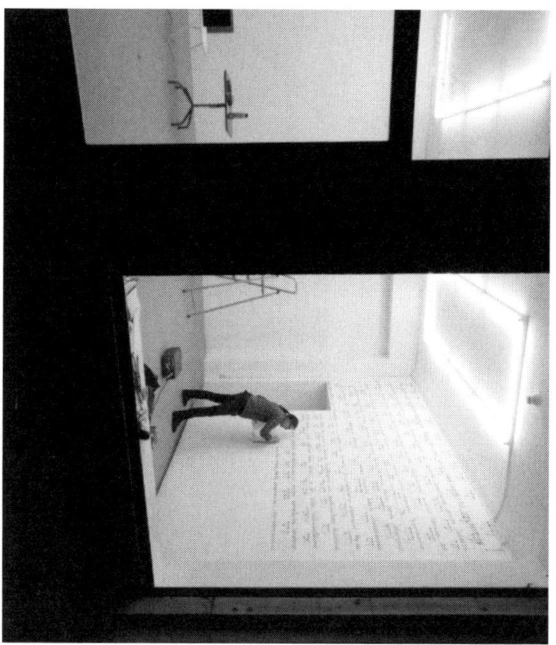

11.11.–28.11.2010, Bern
Buch Jonah – Install-Action by Klara Schilliger and Valerian Maly.
Set uf of the exhibition, writing work of the bible text of Jonah and opening
performance on 11.11.2010 at Marks Blond Bern. © Valerian Maly

Klara Schi¨liger / Valerian Maly

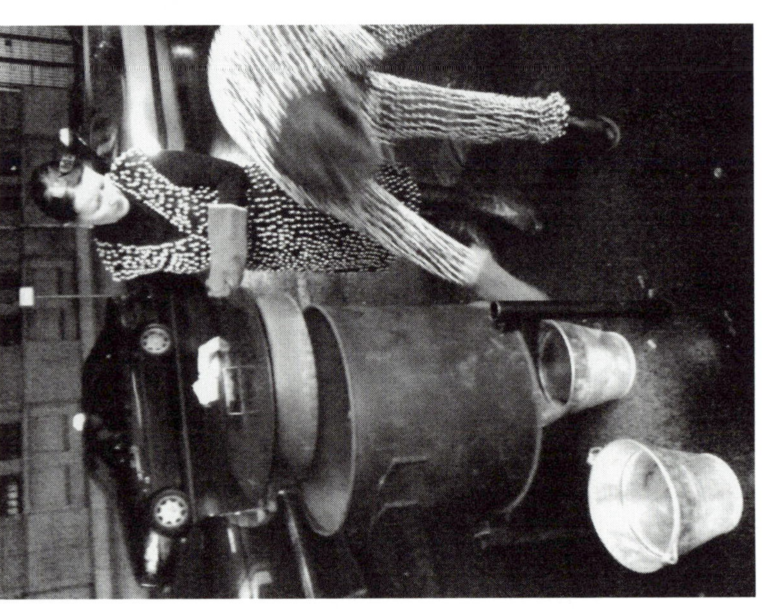

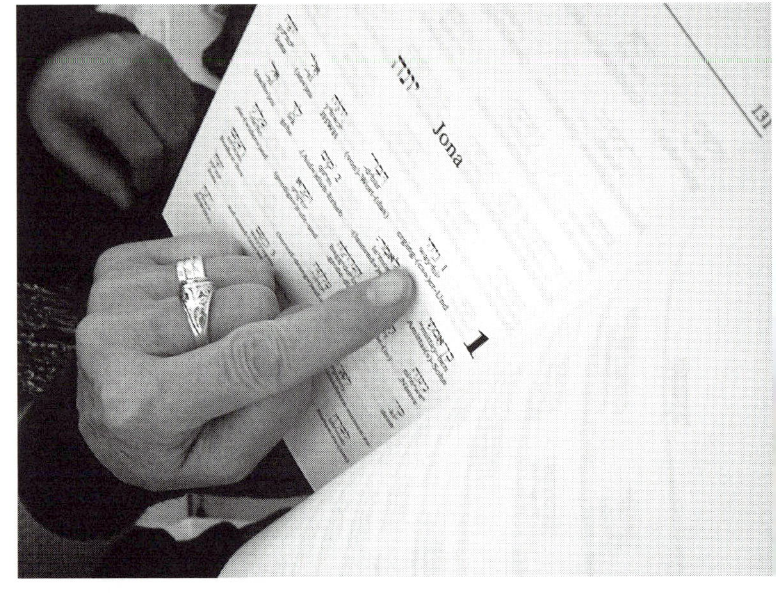

11.11.–28.11.2010, Bern
Buch Jonah – Install-Action von Klara Schilliger und Valerian Maly.
Aufbau, Schreiben des Bibeltextes aus dem Buch Jonah und Eröffnungsaktion
am 11.11.2010 bei Marks Blond Bern. ©Sibylle Omlin

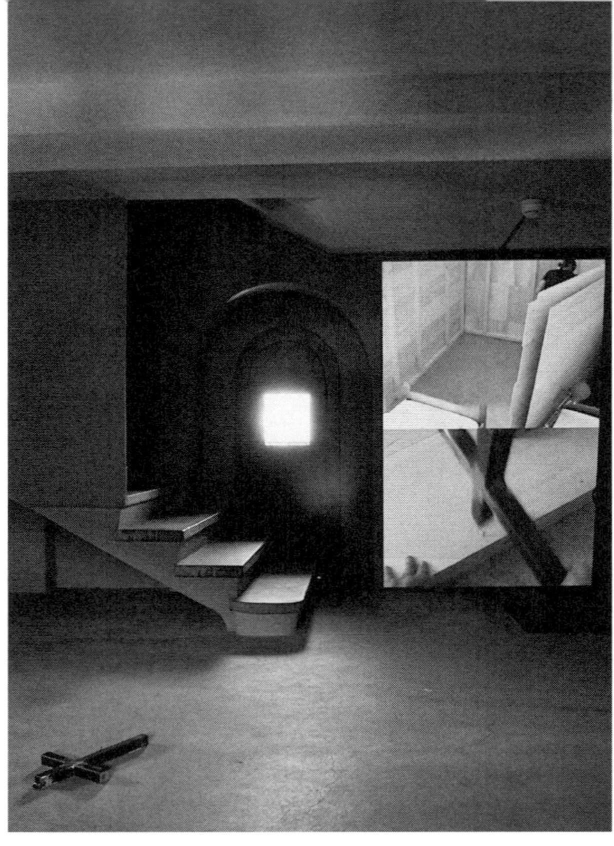

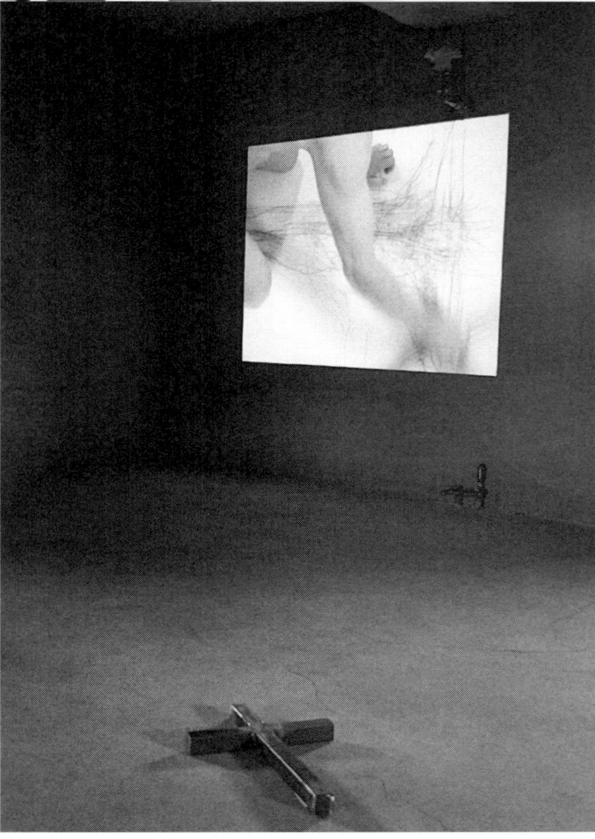

Davor Ljubičić

8.–10.4.2011, Sierre
Davor Ljubičić, media installation *ora et labora*
with drawings, metal cross, video. ©Davor Ljubičić

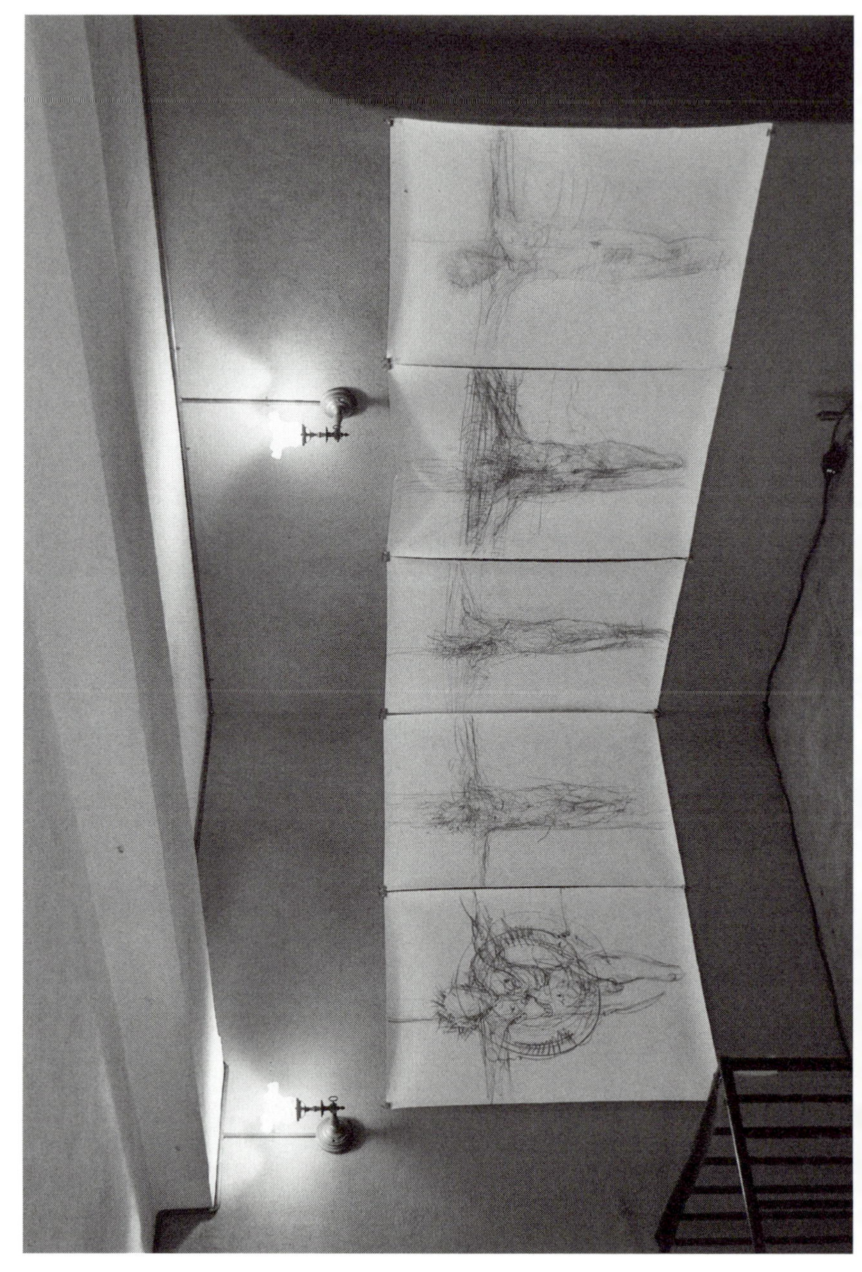

Davor Ljubičić

8.–10.4.2011, Sierre
Davor Ljubičić, mediale Installation *ora et labora*
mit Zeichungen, Metallkreuz, Video. © Davor Ljubičić

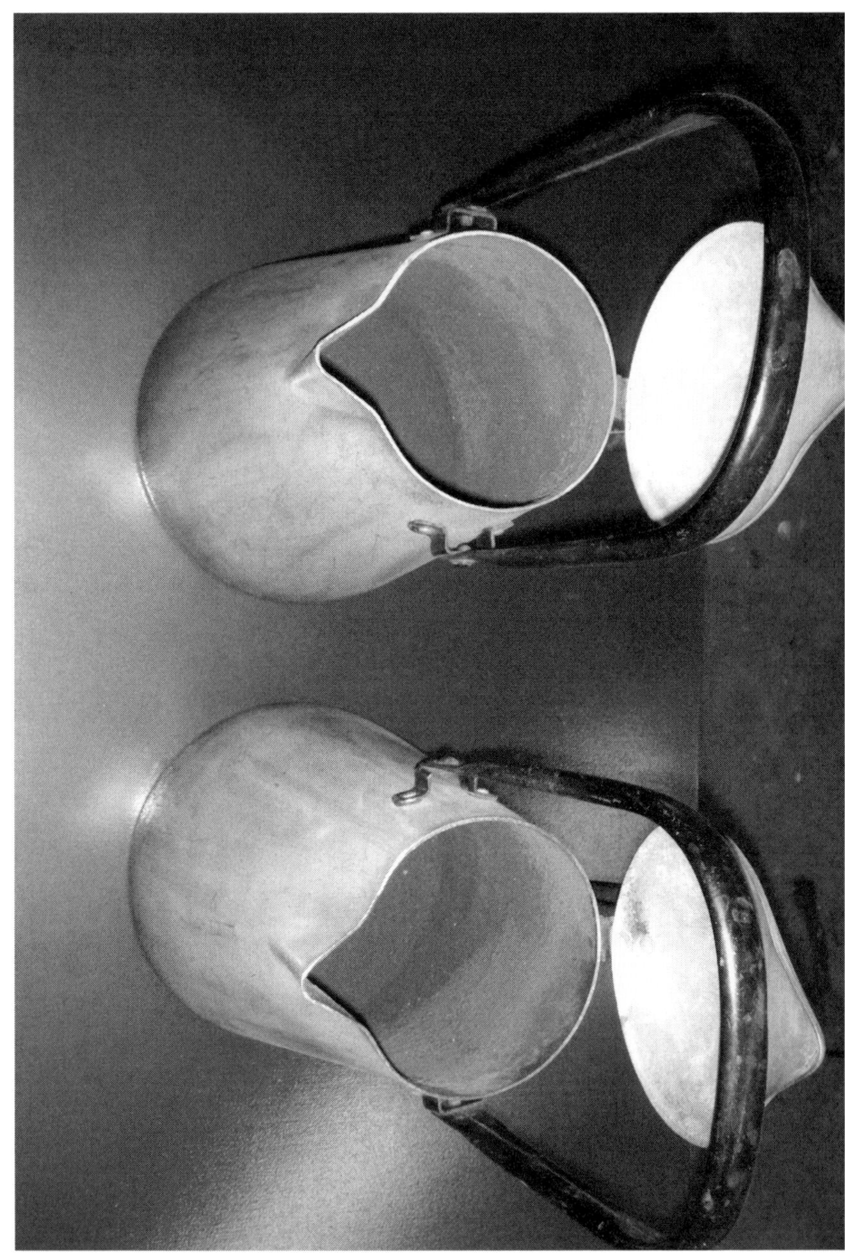

1.–17.10.2010, Zurich
Davor Ljubičić, installation *O.T. (TWINS)*
with objects, table, sound (scratching the milk can)
at Kunstraum K3. ©Ingrid Kaeser

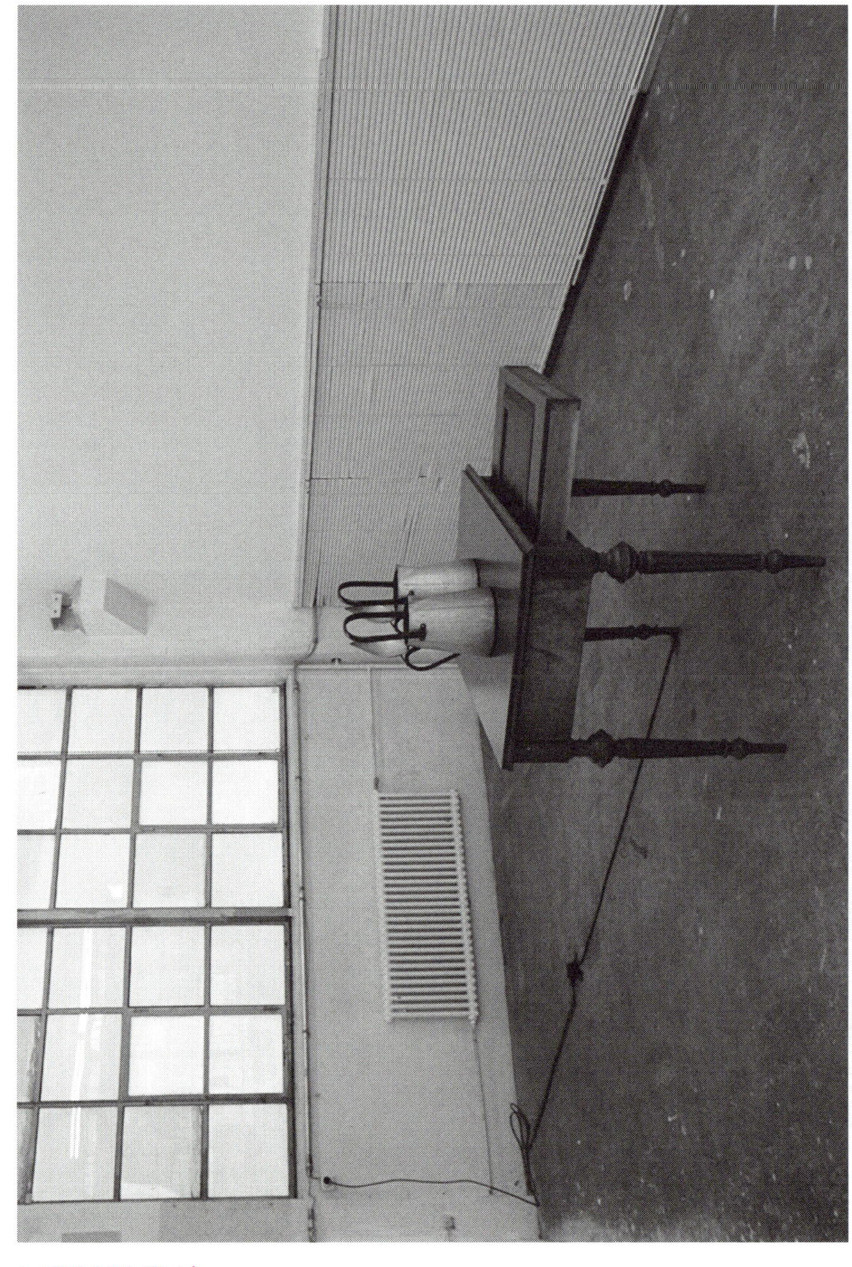

Davor Ljubičić

1.–17.10.2010, Zürich
Davor Ljubičić, mediale Installation *O.T. (TWINS)* mit 2 Milchkannen,
Tisch und Sound (Kratzgeräusche von Fingernägeln auf der Milchkanne)
im Kunstraum K3. ©Ingrid Kaeser

SMOKY
POKERSHIP

VERLAG *für* MODERNE KUNST

IMPRESSUM
Herausgeberschaft und Konzept
Sibylle Omlin

Gestaltung
Bonbon – Valeria Bonin, Diego Bontognali
und Pierrick Brégeon, Zürich

Texte
Sally De Kunst, Barnaby Drabble, Katya
García-Antón, Federica Martini, Sibylle
Omlin, Dorothee Richter, Gavin Wade

Übersetzung
Michael Turnbull (Deutsch › Englisch),
Nikolaus G. Schneider (Englisch › Deutsch)

Lektorat
Ines Gebetsroither, Silvia Jaklitsch, Sibylle
Omlin, Katharina Sacken (Deutsch),
Michaela Alex, Helmut Gutbrunner, Steve
Tomlin, Michael Turnbull (Englisch)

Herstellung
DZA Druckerei zu Altenburg GmbH
©2013, Sibylle Omlin, Verlag für moderne
Kunst Nürnberg, die Künstlerinnen und
Künstler sowie die Autorinnen und Autoren

Bildnachweise (Kunstschaffende)
Evelyn Bermann (Simon Kindle/Sophie Hofer),
Christian Glaus (Dorothea Rust), Ingrid
Kaeser (Davor Ljubičić), Davor Ljubičić
(Janusz Baldyga, Katrin Keller, Pe Lang, Davor
Ljubičić, Denis Romanovski, Dorothea Rust),
Valerian Maly (Klara Schilliger/Valerian
Maly), Sibylle Omlin (Janusz Baldyga, Boris
Nieslony, Christophe Fellay, Victorine Müller,
Katja Schenker, Stuart Sherman), Stefan Postius
(Janusz Baldyga, Berclaz de Sierre), Michael
Zanghellini (Victorine Müller).

Bildnachweise (Texte)
Thomas Hirschhorn (S. 16), Christoph
Schlingensief (S. 17, 59), Santiago Sierra (S. 25),
Dexter Sinister (S. 28), Charles Filch (S . 31),
Spartacus Chetwynd (S. 61), Belluard Bollwerk
International Fribourg (S. 68, 69, 71, 74, 75),
Sylviane Tille (S. 70), Wrigth & Sites (S. 72),
Christian Hasucha (S. 76), Kosi Hidama
& Gosie Vervloessem (S. 77), Reggie Watts
(S. 78), Eastside Projects Birmingham (S. 80,
81), Heather & Ivan Morisn (S. 82), Eastside
Projects Birmingham (S. 83)

ISBN 978-3-86984-413-8
Printed in Germany. All rights reserved.
Erschienen im
Verlag für moderne Kunst Nürnberg GmbH
Königstrasse 73, D–90402 Nürnberg
www.vfmk.de

Bibliografische Information der Deutschen
Nationalbibliothek. Die Deutsche Nationalbibliothek verzeichnet diese Publikation in der
Deutschen Nationalbibliografie; detaillierte
bibliografische Daten sind im Internet über
http://dnb.ddb.de abrufbar.

Distribution in Großbritannien
Cornerhouse Publications
70 Oxford Street,
Manchester M1 5 NH, UK
Phone +44-161-200 15 03
Fax +44-161-200 15 04

Distribution weltweit
D.A.P. Distributed Art Publishers, Inc.
155 Sixth Avenue, 2nd Floor,
New York, NY 10013, USA
Phone +1-212-627 19 99
Fax +1-212-627 94 84

DANK AN
Künstlerinnen und Künstler sowie Autorinnen
und Autoren, Federica Martini, Barnaby Drabble
(Koorganisatoren Symposium April 2011)

Partner/finanzielle Unterstützung
Kunstraum Engländerbau Vaduz; K3 Zürich
(Sandi Paucic); Marks Blond Bern (Daniel
Suter); Kunstverein Konstanz e.V. Konstanz
(Michael Günther); Fondation Château Mercier
Sierre (René-Pierre Antille); Pro Helvetia;
Ernst Goehner Stiftung; Ecole cantonale d'art
du Valais, Sierre; HES-SO, fonds stratégique;
Loterie Romande; Jubiläumsstiftung Raiffeisen;
Migros Kulturprozent; Ernst und Olga Gubler-
Hablützel Stiftung; Kanton Bern/Swisslos Kul-
tur (Valerian Maly/Klara Schilliger); Stadt
Bern, Bürgergemeinde Bern (Marks Blond Pro-
ject, Bern); Kanton Wallis (Berclaz de Sierre,
Christophe Fellay); Kulturstiftung Liechtenstein
(Victorine Müller); Liechtensteinische Landes-
bank Vaduz (Simon Kindle und Sophie Hofer);
Stiftung Fürstlicher Kommerzienrat, Guido
Feger, Vaduz (Simon Kindle und Katrin Keller);
Kanton Solothurn (Victorine Müller); Kanton
Zürich Fachstelle Kultur (K3); Regierungspräsi-
dium Freiburg (Kunstverein Konstanz); Kultur-
förderung Kanton St.Gallen (Katja Schenker),
Stiftung Ostschweizer Kunstschaffen (Kat-
ja Schenker), Freunde und Förderer des Kultur-
zentrums am Münster e.V.; Sappi Schweiz AG,
Kunstgiesserei, Stadt Gossau (Katja Schenker)

Projektmitarbeit
Ingrid Kaeser (Assistance)
Jérôme Lanon (web)

prohelvetia

RAIFFEISEN
Raiffeisen Jubiläumsstiftung

ERNST GÖHNER STIFTUNG

SMOKY POKERSHIP

Raum, Kunst,
Ausstellung,
Transformation,
Performance

Sibylle Omlin
(Hg.)

Einleitung

Dieser Band versammelt Beiträge von internationalen Theoretikerinnen und Theoretikern, Kuratorinnen und Kuratoren sowie Kunstschaffenden, welche die Beziehung zwischen Performance und Installation im aktuellen Ausstellungsdiskurs untersuchen. Zentrales Anliegen ist es, Möglichkeiten zu entwickeln, das Installations- und Ausstellungsdispositiv neu zu denken und den performativen Annäherungen von Kuratoren und Kunstschaffenden an die Ausstellung neue Impulse zu geben sowie institutionelle Formate aufzubrechen. Wichtig ist auch die Frage, wie sich dabei die Werke und die Ausstellungssettings selbst verändern – formal, zeitlich, in Bezug zum Publikum.

Der Begriff der Performance-Installation oder ‹installaction› impliziert ein Live-Element, das von einem räumlichen, installativen Setting ausgeht; die Performance unternimmt in diesem spezifischen Kontext eine Transformation im Raum. Die Handlung des Performenden bleibt sichtbar für die Dauer der Ausstellung oder kann sogar weitere Eingriffe beinhalten, wie in meinem Beitrag beschrieben. Was als Relikt oder Objekt von solchen performativen Handlungen zurückbleibt und welche Qualität ihnen als Objekte der Ausstellung innewohnt, wird im Aufsatz von Federica Martini reflektiert.

Der Bezug zu Geschichte und Theorie von zeitgenössischen Ausstellungsprojekten im Bereich von Performancekunst, Installation und Relational Art markiert die Überlegungen in allen Beiträgen dieses Buches. Wesentlich ist dabei die Frage, wie Performance die kuratorische Praxis und das Format einer Ausstellung programmiert und festschreibt. Wie werden durch Transformationen zwischen Installation und Performance neue Besucherbeziehungen in der Ausstellung hergestellt? Diese beiden Fragen stehen im Zentrum der Beiträge von Katya García-Antón und Dorothee Richter. Katya García-Antón reflektiert die Möglichkeiten von Relational Art in Ausstellungsformaten bis hin zur vollkommenen Verweigerung gegenüber dem Publikum, während Dorothee Richters Artikel sich dem Nachdenken über den Unterschied zwischen dramatischen Bühnenformaten und dem performativen Ausstellungsformat, das mehr und mehr auch als zeitbasiertes Format gelesen werden will, verschreibt. Barnaby Drabble wiederum fasst die Beziehung zwischen ausgestelltem Werk und Betrachter als einen Dialog von Stimmen.

Alle in den Beiträgen reflektierten Beispiele und theoretischen Referenzen drehen sich um eine partizipative und prozessorientierte Ausstellungspraxis und münden in eine zentrale Überlegung: inwieweit das Ausstellen oder das Organisieren von Festivals selbst Teil einer performativen Angelegenheit geworden sind. Gavin Wade und Sally De Kunst reflektieren in ihren Artikeln ihre kuratorische Arbeit in einem zeitgenössischen Kunstraum in Birmingham (UK) und beim Performance-Festival Belluard Bollwerk in Freiburg (CH), wobei die

Praktiken des Palimpsests und des konzeptuellen, situationsbezogenen Arbeitens im Fokus stehen.

Die Beiträge wurden anlässlich eines von der Ecole cantonale d'art du Valais ECAV unter dem Titel *Perform the exhibition. Kuratorische Praxis zwischen Performance und Installation* organisierten Kolloquiums diskutiert, das vom 8. bis 10. April 2011 im Château Mercier in Sierre stattfand. Dieses wiederum bildete den Abschluss eines längeren Ausstellungsprojekts, *Bauch des Wals* (2010/11), das von Sibylle Omlin initiiert und kuratiert wurde (www.installaction.com). Das Ausstellungsprojekt regte Arbeiten – Performances, Installationen, Performance-Installationen – von 17 eingeladenen Kunstschaffenden an (Janusz Baldyga, PL; Christophe Fellay, CH; Simon Kindle, FL; Katrin Keller/Sophie Hofer, CH; Pe Lang, CH; Davor Ljubičić, DE; Valerian Maly/Klara Schilliger, CH; Patricia und Marie-France Martin, CH/BE/FR; Victorine Müller, CH; Boris Nieslony, DE; Denis Romanovski, SE; Dorothea Rust, CH; Katja Schenker, CH; Berclaz de Sierre, CH) und versuchte, die im Buch behandelten Fragen durch kuratorische Forschung und künstlerische Praxis an fünf verschiedenen Kunstorten/räumlichen Settings zu erhellen. Der Bildteil zum performativen Ausstellungsprojekt *Bauch des Wals* erzählt seine eigene Geschichte zu diesem Anliegen.

Die Herausgeberin

TRANSFORM THE EXHIBITION SPACE

Performative Praxis zwischen Performance und Installation

Sibylle Omlin

Die Performancekunst in Europa ist in den letzten zwanzig Jahren in Bewegung geraten. Aufwendige räumliche Settings, ‹long duration performance›, der Gang in die Landschaft und die verstärkte Verankerung in Ausstellungssituationen und Kunstinstitutionen durch performative und partizipative Projekte sind nur einige Merkmale der neuen Phänomene im Umfeld der Performance.

Die räumliche Praxis der Performancekunst ist in den letzten zwei Jahrzehnten zunehmend ins Interesse der zeitgenössischen Kunst gerückt, vor allem ihre performative und installative Verschränkung. Diverse kuratorische Formate wurden in diesem Kontext sowohl in Kunsträumen las auch auf Festivals, im Museum und im öffentlichen Raum erprobt. Seit den musealen Untersuchungen der Performancekunst durch Institutionen wie das Museum of Modern Art New York[1], das MOCA in Los Angeles[2], das Museum für Gegenwartskunst Frankfurt[3], die Villa Arson in Nizza oder in der Schweiz das Migros Museum[4], um nur einige Beispiele zu nennen, ist die Loslösung der Performance aus dem Moment des Live-Ereignisses heraus und ihre Fixierung auf den Raum und auf das Objekt ein Thema.

Als handelnde und physisch agierende Form ist die Performancekunst zwar nach wie vor der Bildfindung der visuellen Kunst und der Aufführung im Theater eng verbunden, aber ebenso der Musik, dem Tanz, dem *spoken word* sowie der prozessorientierten Kunst.[5] Neue performancespezifische Formen wie Interaktionen im öffentlichen Raum, performative Installationen in Offspaces, ‹long duration performance›, partizipative Settings u. a. m. verlangten nach neuen Formaten im Ausstellungsbereich.

Die theoretische Reflexion über die Transformation der Performance in die räumliche Installation und umgekehrt steht jedoch nach wie vor nur in Ansätzen zur Verfügung. Am konkretesten sind die Reflexionen zum Bereich der Performance als Transformation oder Partizipation im sozialen Raum gediehen (‹relational art›). Deshalb setzt dieser Aufsatz die theoretische und praktisch-künstlerische Erforschung der Transformation von räumlichen Dispositiven der Performance-Installation ins Zentrum. Dabei nehme ich die Performance als Ausgangslage für ein Ausstellungskonzept, das zwischen Ereignis/Aufführung und Installation im Ausstellungskontext schwankt und verschiedene zeitliche und räumliche Momente beinhaltet. Der Aufsatz dreht sich somit weniger um die Symbiose von Aktion, Ereignis und Installation im Ausstellungsraum als vielmehr um die Frage der Transformation und der zeitlichen Dauer von performativen Ausstellungsformaten und den daran beteiligten künstlerischen Objekten, Handlungen, Materialien. Dieses Interesse bildete auch die Ausgangslage für ein mehrteiliges Ausstellungsprojekt an fünf Kunstorten (Kunstraum Vaduz, Kunstverein Konstanz, K3 Project Space Zürich, Marks Blond Project Bern, Château Mercier Sierre), an dem zwischen 2010 und 2011 siebzehn Kunstschaffende beteiligt waren.[6]

Solche Fragen lauteten beispielsweise: Wie kann aus der Performance, aus dem Ereignis oder der Handlung der Performance, aus dem Material der Performance etwas entstehen, das dauerhafter ist als nur ein Performance-Foto? Wie transformiert sich eine Performance in eine Installation, wie hinterlässt sie räumliche Bezüge?

Ich ging dabei von folgenden Thesen/Beobachtungen aus:

1. Der Einbezug von Objekten oder Materialien in die Performance ist bereits dazu angelegt, dass das Objekt auch losgelöst von der Performance ein Eigenleben führen kann.

2. Die Installation als Form des an einen Raum gebundenenn thematischen oder politischen Ereignisses bietet sich als räumliche Erweiterung der Performance an. Dabei hat vor allem die Transformation oder Metamorphose der Performance einen entscheidenden Anteil.

3. Das Ausmass der Performativität in einer Installation im Hinblick auf ihre Erscheinung und Intensität kann nicht vollständig vorhersehbar und kontrollierbar sein (vgl. vor allem den Installationsbegriff von Thomas Hirschhorn). Das macht die Installation zu einem künstlerischen Medium, das die Performance in eine räumliche Präsenz und Dauer transformiert.

4. Die Transformation von ephemeren Materialien wie Sprache oder Wetterphänomene in den Raum, in eine räumliche Installation kann mit einem skulptural-installativen Moment verbunden sein.

In diesem Kontext ist auch der Begriff der ‹installaction› von Interesse, der von den Schweizer Performern Valerian Maly und Klara Schilliger geprägt wurde. Maly/Schilliger verorten ihre Arbeit vor allem im Zwischenbereich von Performance und Installation, da ihre Performances und Installationen oft – aber nicht ausschliesslich – ortsbezogene Interventionen sind, denen projektbezogene Recherchen vorausgehen. Die Künstler befassen sich heute mit dem Ausstellen von Performance-Materialien und -Relikten im Kontext des Ausstellungsraums.[7] Auch Roman Signers Transformationsbegriff kann hier herangezogen werden. Er nennt seine Interventionen und Handlungen, die die Transformation eines Materials, eines Ortes durch technische Hilfsmittel (oft Explosionen) oder Naturkräfte implizieren, schlicht ‹Skulptur›.[8]

Von der Sprechakttheorie zur Ästhetik der Installation

Die zentrale Theorie, die sich hinter der Performance-Handlung verbirgt, ist jene des Sprechakts (‹speech act›), der jedem Performance-Element im Vollzug jenen performativen Charakter zubilligt, der das Wesen des authentischen Vollzugs von Performance vor Publikum ausmacht.[9] Judith Butler hat in der Interpretation dieser Theorie auch später noch betont, dass sich der performative Charakter einer Sprech-

handlung, einer Handlung überhaupt, nur im sich ständig erneuernden Vollzug dieser Handlung festmachen lässt. Heute wird auch darüber nachgedacht, ob die Performance nicht ebenso immer schon auf ihre Nachträglichkeit hin angelegt ist, also auf ein Dokument oder ein fixierendes Bildmedium hin geplant und aufgeführt wird.[10] Auch die Narration des Ereignisses, der Diskurs darüber, bildet einen wesentlichen Bestandteil der künstlerischen Performance.

In den letzten zwanzig Jahren der Geschichte der zeitgenössischen Performancekunst ist deshalb eine Verlagerung des Interesses weg vom Körper des Performenden hin zum relationalen Raum und Kontext der Performance zu beobachten. Das Anliegen des Raums, welcher für die Performance vorgesehen ist – Bühne, öffentlicher Raum, Landschaft, Neue Medien – fordert in der Entwicklung der Performance neue Formen heraus, beispielsweise jene des Environments oder der lang anhaltenden, eingreifenden Aktion, der politisch engagierten Projekte oder der Handlungen der Kunst im gesellschaftlichen Raum.[11] Die Performance steht in diesem Kontext für die Belebung, Bewohnung und Inbesitznahme dieses Raums durch den Körper des Künstlers, der Künstlerin.

Für die Entwicklung der zeitgenössischen Performancekunst in den letzten zwanzig Jahren ist jedoch nicht nur der Begriff des verkörperten Ereignisses im Raum von Bedeutung, sondern mehr und mehr auch jener der Installation und der relationalen Handlung/Narration.[12] Wenden wir uns deshalb dem Konzept von Installation etwas intensiver zu.

Die Installation steht für die Konstruktion eines durch den Künstler definierten Raums im Raum der Kunst. Wie die Performancekunst nahm das Auftauchen der Installation seinen zeitlichen Anfang in der politischen Umbruchzeit um 1968, in der bisher geltende Konventionen und Institutionen in Frage gestellt wurden.

Die Installation wie die Performance geben sich mit dem angestammten Raum für die Kunst – dem Museum, dem Ausstellungsraum – längst nicht mehr zufrieden. Beide Kunstformen tendieren zur Expansion in den öffentlichen Raum, zur Expansion in einen gesellschaftlichen Interventionsraum. Performance und Installation haben so den Kontext der Kunst erweitert und hinterfragt. Auch die Position des Betrachters/des Zuschauers ist davon betroffen. Der Betrachter im Museum, der die Wände entlanggeht, um Bilder oder Fotos zu betrachten, ist zum Flaneur geworden, der sich frei im Raum der Installation oder Performance bewegt und sich seine Blickwinkel und Standpunkte sucht. Die Kunstschaffenden im Bereich Performance und Installation erwarten vom Betrachter eine Beweglichkeit im Raum, die Standorte an verschiedenen Stellen im Raum nötig machen. Die Beziehung zwischen Werk und Betrachter in den installativen und performativen Kunstformen wird als Teil des beweglichen Raums mitgedacht.

Die Transformation der Installation

Der 1961 erstmals von Dan Flavin für eine Arbeit mit Leuchtstoffröhren verwendete Begriff der Installation bezeichnete bereits damals diesen lebensweltlichen Raum, der für künstlerische Fragen relevant wurde. Leuchtstoffröhren aus dem Alltag, elektrisches Licht, elektrische Leitungen und Installationselemente aus der Haustechnik wurden von Flavin in künstlerische Arbeiten einbezogen. Der alltägliche Kontext verleiht dem Begriff ‹Installation› eine entsprechende Bedeutung. Flavin benutzte ihn, weil ihm jener des ‹environment› zu soziologisch klang.[13] Elektrisches Licht für einfache Raumwahrnehmungen zu gebrauchen war in seinen Augen eine radikal einfache künstlerische Handlung. Diese Einfachheit und Radikalität wurde in der Folge sowohl für die Installation als auch für die Performancekunst bedeutsam. Das Inszenatorische, das sich mit solch ästhetischen Fragen verbindet, ist denn auch zentral in beiden Kunstformen. Ebenfalls in den 1960er Jahren wurde der Begriff der Installation durch die Arbeiten und Interventionen von Gordon Matta Clark – seine *anarchitectures* bezeichnen direkte Eingriffe an aufgelassenen Gebäuden und industriellen Anlagen – bereits wieder einer Form von Dekonstruktion unterzogen, wenngleich die dekonstruierende Geste etwas Transformiertes hinterliess. Die Transformation ist somit den beiden Kontexten – Performance und Installation – inhärent.

«Was unter dem Begriff der Installation entsteht, sind weniger Werke denn Modelle ihrer Möglichkeiten.» Mit dieser Feststellung legitimiert Juliane Rebentisch in ihrer *Ästhetik der Installation* einen für die Installationskunst grundlegenden Unbestimmtheitsfaktor, ein kontinuierliches Überschreiten von Gattungsgrenzen. Nach Rebentisch stellt die Installation prinzipiell den jeweiligen Kontext ästhetischer Erwartungen in Frage.[14]

Die Art der Konkretisierung, die im Falle einer Installation am Werk ist, wird durch die Prozessualität des Rezeptionsvorgangs und seiner auf den Körper des agierenden Rezipienten bezogenen Einmaligkeit charakterisiert. Dies bedeutet eine primäre Subjektivierung der ästhetischen Reflexion. In diesem Zusammenhang weist installative Kunst durchaus Ähnlichkeiten mit weiteren zeitgebundenen und performativen Kunstformen auf, die unter den Stichworten Aktion, Happening, Performance und Body Art versammelt werden. Wie Paul Schimmel 1998 in seiner Studie gezeigt hat, implizieren diese Kunstformen ein verändertes Verständnis des rezipierenden Publikums.[15] Der Betrachter ist nicht mehr der passive Empfänger eines durch künstlerische Medien repräsentierten Inhalts.[16] Im Gegenteil, die Reaktionen des Zuschauers sind ebenso integraler Bestandteil von performativen Kunstformen wie auch die Aktion des Künstler-Protagonisten und die verwendeten Requisiten.

Diese Reaktionen sind auf Körperpräsenz bezogene Handlungen, die das Event vorantreiben und dadurch diskursive, zeitlich erfahrbare und real erlebbare Situationen erschaffen. Solche Kunstwerke beanspruchen nicht die kontemplative Versenkung und Anschauung des Publikums, sondern involvieren «die ganz leibliche Polysensualität und die für das Werk jeweils konstitutiven Handlungsbezüge des Rezipienten»[17].

Vergleicht man die Involviertheit des Betrachters bei zeitgebundenen, performativen Kunstformen mit dem Betrachterbezug innerhalb der installativen Kunst, so ist feststellbar, dass in der raumgreifenden, installativen Kunst die Körperlichkeit und Bewegung des Betrachters ebenfalls als handelnde Werkkonstituente involviert ist und die Basis für seine Erfahrungsgestaltung in der Wahrnehmung einer Installation bildet. Da jedoch die ästhetische Technik, eine Erfahrung zu provozieren, nicht auf die Aktion des Künstlers/Performers (Performance) oder auf seine Anweisungen (Happening) zurückgeht, sondern auf die räumliche Gestaltung selbst, wird sie als ‹situativ› bezeichnet.

Die Untersuchungen über Orts- und Situationsspezifik in der Kunst wiederum nehmen als Anhaltspunkt nicht die räumliche Fixierung des installativen Werkes an, sondern dessen performatives Potenzial.[18] Denkt man an den Wahrnehmungsprozess, der beim ästhetischen Erschliessen einer Installation stattfindet, wird man feststellen, dass Installationen zeitabhängige Kunstformen sind.[19] Bei der Betrachtung der Installation wird der Zeit des Spazierens und Flanierens im Raum eine präzise Funktion in der generell für ästhetische Erfahrung notwendigen Gebundenheit der Wahrnehmung zugeschrieben. Diese einfache Tatsache bestimmt zugleich die Beschaffenheit und die installative Organisation des jeweiligen Ausstellungskontextes, der zugleich der Betrachterraum ist.

Raumgestaltung in der Installation wird von der Idee diktiert, dem Betrachter seine Bewegung und seine Sichtperspektiven selbst so weit wie möglich vorzuschreiben. Genau dadurch aber lässt sich diese Bewegung als narrativ oder gar kinematisch beschreiben. Das Erschliessen des installativen Raums wird von einem raumzeitlichen Vorher-Nachher bestimmt, das zugleich die Bewegung des Betrachters und seine vermeintlich freie Wanderung durch den Raum diktiert. Denkt man unter diesen Voraussetzungen an die Art und Weise, wie ein installativer Raum wahrgenommen wird, kann von einer Rhythmisierung oder Dramaturgie wahrgenommener Wirklichkeitsausschnitte als Sukzession von Eindrücken gesprochen werden.

Ein wichtiges Beispiel im Bereich der Installation, welche performative und narrative Elemente in den installativen Raum integriert, sind die Arbeiten des Schweizers Thomas Hirschhorn. Der Künstler verfremdet Präsentationsweisen im Bereich der Installation. Aus Holz, Karton, Polyurethanschaum, Plastik- und Aluminiumfolie, Packpapier und Klebeband baut er chaotisch anmutende, unüberschaubare Gefüge, in denen man sich als Betrachter leicht verliert. Damit verbunden

sind Recherchen zu einer bestimmten Art von historischem Ereignis oder philosophischem Gedankengut, die sich in einer performativen Auseinandersetzung mit dem Publikum niederschlagen.

Unzufrieden mit den aufgezwungenen Definitionen und Beschränkungen einer kapitalistischen, multinationalen Globalisierungsrhetorik, macht Thomas Hirschhorn sich das kommunikative Potenzial des Denkens zunutze. Sein Werk, in dem der materielle Wert hintangestellt ist, umfasst verschiedene installative Modelle, die vornehmlich aus billigen Verpackungsmaterialien der Konsumindustrie gefertigt sind. Er überführt so die Begierden des Kapitalismus in einen Zustand dauerhafter kreativer Anarchie. Hirschhorns zeitlich begrenzte Denkmale für Benedict de Spinoza (1999 und 2009, Amsterdam), Gilles Deleuze (2000, Avignon), Georges Bataille *(dO-CUMENTA11,* 2002, Kassel), die sich mit dem Ort in Form eines kommunalen Engagements auseinandersetzen, folgen einer Logik der Kurzlebigkeit, der Anhäufung und der potenziellen Offenheit.

Für sein *Bataille Monument* kartografierte Hirschhorn die Stadt Kassel mehr als ein Jahr lang unter persönlichen und sozialen Gesichtspunkten und fügte das Monument für die Dauer der *dOCUMENTA11* aktiv in das Leben einer marginalisierten lokalen Gemeinde in der Friedrich-Wöhler-Siedlung ein.[20] Unter Verzicht auf traditionelle Kategorien der Wissensproduktion holt das Werk die zum Ritual formalisierte Sammel- und Ausstellungsfunktion des Museums in den öffentlichen Raum zurück. Der philosophische Rekurs auf Georges Bataille ist gezielt. Thomas Hirschhorn schreibt dazu: «Georges Bataille untersuchte und entwickelte das Prinzip des Verlustes, des Sich-Ausgebens, der Gabe und der Masslosigkeit. Ich verehre ihn wegen seines Buches *La part maudite* und seines Textes *La notion de dépense.* Die Wahl Georges Batailles bringt mit sich, dass sich ein breites und komplexes Kraftfeld öffnet, zwischen Ökonomie, Politik, Literatur, Kunst, Erotik, Archäologie.»[21]

Das *Bataille Monument* bestand aus acht Elementen, die miteinander verbunden waren:
— einer Skulptur aus Holz, Karton, Klebeband, Plastik
— einer Bibliothek ‹Georges Bataille› mit Büchern, die einen Bezug zum Werk Georges Batailles haben; sie sind geordnet nach Wort, Bild, Kunst, Sport, Sex (Mitarbeit: Uwe Fleckner)
— einer Bataille-Ausstellung mit Werk-Topografie, Plan, Büchern von und über Georges Bataille (Mitarbeit: Christophe Fiat)
— verschiedenen Workshops, die über die gesamte Ausstellungsdauer (9.6.–16.9.2002) liefen (Mitarbeit: Manuel Joseph, Jean-Charles Massera, Marcus Steinweg u. a.)
— einem Imbiss mit Getränken und Esswaren
— einem TV-Studio, von dem täglich eine kurze Sendung vom *Bataille Monument* im *Offenen Kanal Kassel* ausgestrahlt wurde
— einem Fahrdienst mit Fahrzeugen und Fahrern, der die *Documen-*

ta11-Besucher zum *Bataille Monument* (und zurück) brachte und die Bewohner des Quartiers zur *dOCUMENTA11*
— einer Website mit Webkameras vom *Bataille Monument* aus (24 Stunden, sieben Tage).[22]

Das Monument wollte durch seinen Standort, seine Materialien und seine Ausstellungsdauer nicht nur den Denkmalbegriff in Frage stellen, sondern einen speziellen Raum bzw. eine spezielle Zeit für Diskussion und Ideen schaffen. Hirschhorns Monumente betonen den Blick von unten, den Blick für das Bewegliche, Soziale und Nichtrepräsentative. Das *Bataille* 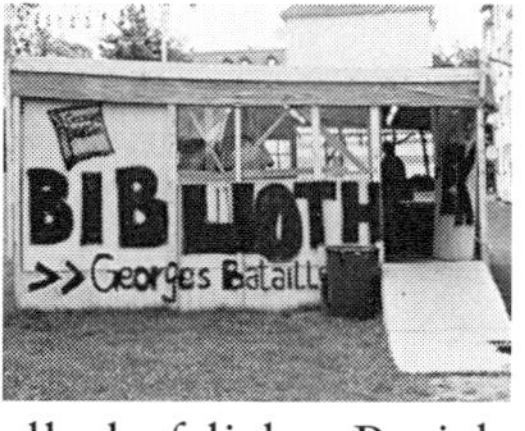
Monument war somit auch ein gesellschaftliches Projekt, das Verbindungen zu einem nichtexklusiven Publikum ermöglichte und Bezüge schuf, die sonst in diesem Quartier nicht möglich gewesen wären. Die Installation war auch in diesem Projekt Vorwand oder Anlass, performative Handlungen mit einer Besucher/innengruppe durchzuführen, Ereignisse medial zu transformieren und Inhalte zu vermitteln.

Performance als bildhaftes Ereignis und Aufführung

Parallel zur Entwicklung des Installations-Dispositivs haben die Formung der Performance zum Bild, ihre Wiederholbarkeit als bildhafte Handlung und die Exposition von Performance-Relikten diesem Medium auch den Weg ins Museum, in die klassische Ausstellungssituation geöffnet.[23] Ausstellungen zur installativen Performancekunst, Tanzperformances im White Cube und monografische Ausstellungen zu einzelnen Performancekünstlerinnen und -künstlern lassen in dieser Kunstform eine Transformation erkennen. Das Publikum wird zwar nach wie vor zum direkten Betrachter und Komplizen einer Live-Handlung, die Performer wählen aber zunehmend auch räumliche Displays, um ihre Handlung im Raum der Ausstellung konkret zu verankern.

Die Kulturtheorie hat zudem Ende der 1990er Jahre die Diskussion um die Begriffe der Aufführung, der Performanz und der Performativität der Künste von Deutschland aus um die Theaterwissenschaftler Erika Fischer-Lichte und Hans-Thies Lehmann neu lanciert.[24] Ausgehend von den Überlegungen des ‹linguistic turn› in den 1950er Jahren in den USA (John R. Austins *How to Do Things with Words)* wurde in den 1990er Jahren angesichts des ‹iconic turn› die Diskussion auf «How to do things with images/art» ausgeweitet. Der Gebrauch der Bilder und der bildhaften Handlungen schien für Theater- und Tanzperformances attraktiv zu sein, der Griff der sozial agierenden Kunst

in den öffentlichen Raum und in den Raum der klassischen Kulturinstitutionen war Programm. Die Performance in der bildenden Kunst, die sich verschwörerisch und nur von Eingeweihten betrachtet als Ritual in der Abge-

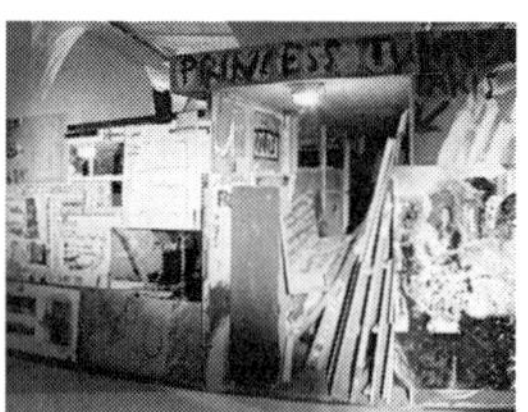

schiedenheit von Insider-Festivals vollzog, wurde durch internationale Grossanlässe auf institutionellen Bühnen neu inszeniert. Christoph Schlingensief – zu Beginn noch vorwiegend als Theatermann bekannt – fegte mit mit seinen Installationen und Performances durch die Biennalen und Museen. Jonathan Meese inszeniert umgekehrt als Künstler Grossperformances wie *Jonathan Meese ist Mutter Parzival* an der Berliner Staatsoper.

Der ‹performative turn› griff sogar auf Konzepte des Wissens und Erkennens über. Wissen als Schauspiel, also der Wechsel vom Modell des Wissens zu dem der Aufführung in seiner (Selbst-)Beschreibung, wurde für die Interpretation von Performativität in Theater- und Kunstforschung Ende des 20. Jahrhunderts eine paradigmatische Leitfigur.[25] Analog zu den theoretischen Überlegungen zum Raum in den 1970er Jahren durch Henri Lefebvre *(La production de l'espace)* und Michel de Certeau *(L'Invention du quotidien – Art de faire)* erfuhr die Performance eine Transformation in den Raum, der auch den gesellschaftlichen Raum miteinbezog.

Die Verbindung
von Performance und Installation

Trotz der anhaltenden Verschmelzung von Bühnen- und Ausstellungsformaten bestand weiterhin ein Interesse, im Kontext der bildenden Kunst die ihr inhärenten Transformationsprozesse im Umfeld der Performance zu beleuchten. Eine für diese Entwicklung wichtige Ausstellung war *Mise en Scène. Theater und Kunst* im Grazer Kunstverein im Jahr 1998, die der Verbindung von Aufführung und Bühnenelementen gewidmet war. Das Thema wurde 2002 von Andreas Baur und Stephan Berg aufgegriffen, die für ihre jeweiligen Institutionen in der Stadt Esslingen und in Hannover (Kunstverein Hannover) 2002/03 die Ausstellung *On stage* veranstalteten.

Im Jahr 2003 entstand ein von Angelika Nollert (heute Leiterin des Neuen Museums für Kunst und Design Nürnberg) geleitetes Projekt, das den Begriff der ‹performativen Installation› in verschiedenen Ausstellungen in unterschiedlichen Kunsträumen in Deutschland und Österreich untersuchte – in der Galerie im Taxispalais in Innsbruck (2003), im Museum Ludwig in Köln (2003/04), im Museum für Gegen-

wartskunst Siegen (2003/04), in der Secession in Wien (2004) und in der Galerie für Zeitgenössische Kunst Leipzig (2004).[26] Jede Ausstellung war für sich autonom und griff einen möglichen Aspekt des Themas auf. Der Begriff der ‹performativen Installation› wurde für diese Ausstellungsserie kreiert und als künstlerisches, gegenständliches Werk mit Ereignischarakter verstanden.[27]

In der Ausstellungsserie *Performative Installation* wurden sehr unterschiedliche Konzepte von performativer Installation erforscht von konstruierten Situationen von Wirklichkeit im Ausstellungsraum, partizipativen Medieninstallationen, bei denen die Bevölkerung zum Mitwirken aufgefordert wurde, bis hin zur Ausstellung *Body Display,* die den Ausstellungsraum der Wiener Secession als Bühne auffasste und den darauf agierenden Körper in seiner Eigenschaft als Projektionsfläche für öffentliche Identitäten zeigte. Die Arbeiten präsentierten somit performative, installative, referenzielle und kommunikative Vorgänge. Die Ausstellung als ‹Display› stand dabei für eine räumliche Form der Präsentation, die die Rezipient/innen unmittelbar und aktiv in das Geschehen miteinzubeziehen versuchte.

Die inhaltliche Verknüpfung von Performativität als Handlungselement wurde als Resultat eines Ereignisses geleistet. Das Endprodukt der Installation wurde mit dem Adjektiv performativ in seinen Eigenschaften charakterisiert: «Es geht bei der performativen Installation nicht um die Auflösung des Werks im Ereignis, sondern um das Ereignis als konstituierende Kraft der Installation, um die Symbiose von Ereignis und Werk.»[28]

Anliegen des Ausstellungsprojekts war die Lancierung eines Begriffs und nur ansatzweise seine Präzisierung. Der Begriff der Installation war in diesem Ausstellungsprojekt von 2003/04 zu einem Universalbegriff geworden. Er subsumierte viele künstlerische Ausdrucksformen, die sich einer näheren Definition entzogen. Im Fokus des Interesses stand das ästhetische Phänomen, dass das Theatrale der Ausstellung anders organisiert werden muss als das Theatrale in einem Bühnenraum mit seinen für das Publikum vorgegebenen Zeitformaten der Präsenz. Von seinem Ursprung abgeleitet bedeutet das Wort erst einmal das Einsetzen von Raum und Objekten als Vorgang und als Ergebnis. Installation setzt etwas zueinander in Beziehung und will den Betrachter in diesen Beziehungsraum mitnehmen. Sie kann alles inkorporieren und zusammenfügen. Vor allem ist Installation auch ein wertender Begriff, der über seine raumgreifenden Eigenschaften und seine Erlebnisqualität eine Fähigkeit besitzt, sich einen originären, singulären und individuellen Kontext zu schaffen, der jenem der Performance ähnlich ist. Der Begriff der Installation scheint somit in der Lage zu sein, einen Eigenkontext der Kunst zu schaffen, der sich in besonderer Weise mit dem Aussenkontext des Kunstsystems zu beschäftigen vermag.

Fazit

Die Performancekunst ist somit ein Feld für situative und ortsbezogene Aktivitäten, die räumliche Situationen heute reflektiert und aktiv miteinbezieht. Dass der Kontext – also der Spielort, der Raum und das Publikum – die Performance unmittelbar mitgestaltet, ist eine der grossen Herausforderungen an dieses Medium. Mit ‹unmittelbar› ist gemeint: schneller, reaktiver, unerbittlicher, als es für andere Kunstformen, wie die Malerei, die komponierte Musik oder das Theater, gilt. Daran zeigt sich auch, dass das weite Feld der Performance eine Differenzierung notwendig macht. Historische, mediale und kontextuelle Bezüge werden immer wichtiger, um sich in der Masse von Angeboten und Auslegungen klar zu positionieren. «Ob es sich um eine spontane Initiative von Künstlerinnen in temporären Räumen oder um eine Performance von etablierten Institutionen wie Theatern oder Theaterfestivals handelt, beeinflusst, wie diese wahrgenommen werden, und wirkt auch auf die Arbeiten zurück», betont die Performancekünstlerin Dorothea Rust, die selbst auch als Performance-Organisatorin aktiv ist.[29]

Performancekunst bleibt nach wie vor eine künstlerische Strategie, mit der die Performer Überraschungen, dichte Momente, Verwunderung und Verwirrung bis hin zu Unverständnis auslösen. Das betrifft nicht zuletzt auch die Ästhetik der performativen Installation.

1   *Marina Abramovič: The Artist Is Present,* Museum of Modern Art, New York, 14. März–31. Mai 2010. Die Künstlerin zeigte da ihre längste für den Kontext des Museums entwickelte *long duration performance.*

2   Siehe die Ausstellungen von Paul Schimmel seit 1998, für das MOCA, Los Angeles, z.B. Paul Schimmel (Hg.), *Out of actions. Aktionismus, Body Art und Performance 1949–1979.* Ostfildern Ruit: Hatje Cantz 1998.

3   Udo Kittelmann, damals noch Chefkurator am Museum für Gegenwartskunst in Frankfurt, untersuchte das Verhältnis von Lebenswelt und Performance im musealen Kontext, wie beispielsweise die Ausstellung *Das lebendige Museum* im Museum für Gegenwartskunst Frankfurt im Jahr 2003 zeigte (ohne Katalog).

4   *While Bodies Get Mirrored. An Exhibition about Movement, Formalism and Space,* 6. März–30. Mai 2010; *Christoph Schlingensief, Querverstümmelung,* 3. November–3. Februar 2008.

5   Vgl. Sibylle Omlin (Hg.), *Performativ! Performance-Künste in der Schweiz.* Zürich: Pro Helvetia 2004.

6   *Bauch des Wals. Performative Arbeiten und Installationen von 13 Kunstschaffenden,* 28. Mai 2010–10. April 2011, www.installaction.com. Siehe S. 87ff.

7   Nach wie vor in Gebrauch ist auch der Begriff der 'living sculpture' (geprägt durch die britischen Kunstschaffenden Gilbert & George) oder jener der performativen Skulptur, der von Victorine Müller verwendet wird und zeitlich begrenzte, körperhafte Setzungen im Raum bezeichnet.

8   Peter Zimmermann (Hg.), *Roman Signer: Werkübersicht 1971–2002.* Zürich, Unikate 2003, 3 Bde. Paul Good, *Zeit-Skulptur– Time Sculpture. Roman Signers Werk philosophisch betrachtet – Roman Signer's Work in Philosophical Perspective.* Zürich: Unikate; Köln: Walther König 2002.

9   John. L. Austin, *How to Do Things with Words,* Oxford: Clarendon Press 1962.

10   Vgl. Philip Auslander, *Liveness: Performance in a mediatized culture.* London/New York: Routledge 1999, vor allem das Kapitel ‹Against ontology› S. 38–45.

11   Vgl. Omlin 2004.

12   Der relationale Aspekt der Performativität wird vor allem im Beitrag von Katya García-Antón herausgearbeitet, siehe S. 21ff.

13   Johannes Stahl, Installation. In: Hubertus Butin (Hg.): *Dumonts Begriffslexikon zur zeitgenössischen Kunst.* Köln: DuMont 2002, S. 122–126, hier: S. 124.

14   Juliane Rebentisch, *Ästhetik der Installation.* Frankfurt am Main: Suhrkamp 2003, S. 103.

15   Schimmel 1998.

16   Lea Vergine, *Body Art and Performance. The Body as Language.* Mailand: Skira 1974/2000.

17   Gerhard Graulich, *Die leibliche Selbsterfahrung des Rezipienten – ein Thema transmodernen Kunstwollens.* Phil. Diss. Essen 1989, S. 17.

18   Für eine kritische Darstellung des englischsprachigen Forschungsstandes vgl. Peter Osborne, ‹Review on recent Literature on Installation›. In: Caroline Arscott (Hg.), *On Installation,* Oxford Art Journal, vol. 24 (no. 2). Oxford 2002, S. 145–154.

19   Vgl. Rebentisch 2003, S. 146–162.

20   Der Künstler arbeitete zur Errichtung des Monuments mit Jugendlichen des Boxcamps Philippinenhof zusammen; jeder Jugendliche wurde für seine geleistete Arbeit bezahlt.

21   www.bataillemonument.de [Seite nicht mehr aktiv].

22   www.bataillemonument.de [Seite nicht mehr aktiv]. www.hirschhorn.documenta.de.

23   Der Performer Boris Nieslony ist der Ansicht, dass die Performancekunst in den 1970er Jahren eigentlich im Galerieraum entstanden ist, also immer mit dem Raumdispositiv agiert hat. Die Entwicklung der Performance in einer Festivalkultur sei vor allem ein europäisches Phänomen. Gespräch mit dem Kunstschaffenden am 8. April 2011.

24   Erika Fischer-Lichte, Clemens Risi, Jens Roselt (Hg.), *Kunst der Aufführung – Aufführung der Kunst* (= Recherchen 18). Berlin: Theater der Zeit 2004. Erika Fischer-Lichte, Christoph Wulf (Hg.), *Theorien des Performativen* (Paragrana Bd. 10/1), 2001. Erika Fischer-Lichte, *Ästhetik des Performativen,* Frankfurt am Main 2004. Erika Fischer-Lichte, Christoph Wulf (Hg.) *Praktiken des Performativen* (Paragrana Bd. 13/1), 2004. Uwe Wirth, *Performanz. Zwischen Sprachphilosophie und Kulturwissenschaften.* Frankfurt am Main: Suhrkamp 2002. Hans-Thies Lehmann, *Das postdramatische Theater.* Frankfurt am Main: Suhrkamp 2002. Erika Fischer-Lichte, Doris Kolesch (Hg.), *Kulturen des Performativen* (Paragrana Bd. 7), 1998, Heft 1, Berlin: Akademie Verlag 1998.

25   Christoph Wulf, Jörg Zirfas (Hg.), *Die Kultur des Rituals. Inszenierungen. Praktiken. Symbole.* Paderborn: Wilhelm Fink Verlag 2004. Doris Bachmann-Medick, ‹Performative Turn›. In: D. B.-M., *Cultural Turns. Neuorientierungen in den Kulturwissenschaften,* 3. neu bearb. Aufl. Reinbek: Rowohlt 2009, S. 104–143. Jacques Derrida, ‹Signatur Ereignis Kontext›. In: Peter Engelmann (Hg.), *Randgänge der Philosophie,* Wien: Passagen Verlag 1988.

26   Angelika Nollert (Hg.), *Performative Installation.* Ausstellungskatalog. Köln: Snoeck 2003.

27   Diese Ausstellungsserie wurde auch für meine Überlegungen und kuratorischen Erfahrungen im Projekt *Bauch des Wals* zum zentralen Ausgangspunkt. Vgl. www.installaction.com.

28   Nollert 2003, S. 14.

29   Dorothea Rust, Mail an die Autorin vom 8. Juli 2011.

SKLAVEN DES RHYTHMUS

Die Performanz der Geselligkeit im Ausstellungskontext

Katya García-Antón

Was ist es nur, das die Performativität im Ausstellungskontext der letzten fünfzehn Jahre so faszinierend, so attraktiv gemacht hat?[1] Wurde die gleichermassen unerwartete wie fruchtbare Dynamik der Performativität zu ästhetischen Formen doppeldeutiger Geselligkeit verdichtet? Wie kam es, dass der konzeptuelle Impetus der 1960er und 1970er Jahre, den ästhetischen Prozess über die Zeit und den Ort hinweg auszudehnen, vom Atelier in den Galerieraum und darüber hinaus, in der Erstarrung des Prozesses und in seiner Kommerzialisierung zu einem performativen Event mündete? Diese und andere Fragen stehen im Mittelpunkt einer intensiven internen Auseinandersetzung unter Kuratoren über die Grenzen der Performativität im heutigen Ausstellungsbetrieb.

Die Faszination an der Performativität, die das Gewebe des Ausstellungswesens durchdringt, hat die Beziehung zwischen Künstler, Kurator und Publikum verändert. Diese Tendenz berührt nicht nur Ausstellungen, die Performances oder performative Installationen beinhalten, sondern auch kuratorische und künstlerische Projekte, die auf vielfältige Weise Konferenzen, Dialoge, Interviews, Debatten, Gespräche, ‹performierte Publikationen› sowie Bildungsprojekte und Lernevents zusammenführen. Offenbar ist die Performativität eine Kunst der Begegnung geworden, die im Hinblick auf das jeweilige Publikum, darunter Kunstfachleute, Geldgeber und Sammler, einen Raum für Geselligkeit bevorzugt. Tatsächlich gibt es viele Gemeinsamkeiten zwischen dem Performativen und dem, was sich in den letzten Jahren zur diskursiven und bildungsorientierten Wende in der kuratorischen Praxis entwickelt hat. Doch innerhalb welchen Kontexts operieren diese Entwicklungen? Zweifellos wird die Welle der Performativität in der Kunst heute durch den Zusammenhang zwischen der Idee der Gesellschaft als Spektakel und dem Auftauchen verschiedener Formen des ‹Erlebens› vorangetrieben. Ausserdem lassen sich die Auswirkungen einer von der Konsumdynamik gesteuerten Gesellschaft, in der Kunstwerke unter dem Druck leiden, möglichst leicht konsumierbar zu sein und ein Unterhaltungspotenzial haben zu müssen, auf die kreative Praxis nicht ignorieren. Darüber hinaus finden sich Kuratoren, die sich den wachsenden Forderungen nach einer Kapitalisierung des Wissens ausgesetzt sehen, in einer Position wieder, in der sie als diskursive Makler ihres eigenen Rufs agieren müssen, indem sie ihr intellektuelles Kapital territorialisieren und auf dem Feld des Erlebnismässigen miteinander konkurrieren.

Wie hat sich in einer Gesellschaft, in der sich der Staat schrittweise aus seiner kulturellen und sozialen Verantwortung zurückzieht, in einer Phase der Radikalisierung zwischen Besitzenden und Besitzlosen, die ursprüngliche Dynamik der Performativität verändert? Hat dies mit einer Kunstwelt zu tun, in der der Wert der Kreativität zunehmend von den Marktteilnehmern definiert wird, einer Kunstwelt, die politisch von der populistischen und demokratischen Agenda der

Regierung gesteuert und in sozialer Hinsicht von den Wohlhabenden in Beschlag genommen wird, um als ihr Privatspielplatz zu sein? Hat die Performativität weitgehend aufgehört, als ein radikaler Agent zu dienen, als Produzent ästhetischen Wissens und Überschreiter ästhetischer Grenzen? Wurde sie von der Dynamik des Konsensprinzips infiltriert und von der falschen Verheissung einer demokratischen Kunst vertuscht? Dieser Text wird deutlich machen, wie Verschiebungen innerhalb der Dreieckstruktur Kurator, Künstler und Publikum diese Praxis im neueren performativen Ausstellungsbetrieb haben problematisch werden lassen, und auf verschiedene Möglichkeiten hinweisen, Räume des Widerstands gegen diese schier ausweglose Situation zu erkunden.

Drei Modelle für eine Kunst
der Begegnung

Eines der verbreitetsten Kennzeichen eines heutigen performativen Kunstprojekts ist der Begriff der ‹Partizipation›, also der Teilhabe. Nirgendwo herrschte dieser in jüngerer Zeit stärker vor als in Nicolas Bourriauds 1998 erfolgter Theoretisierung einer Gruppe von Künstlern, deren Werke unter dem Oberbegriff der ‹relationalen Ästhetik› bekannt wurden.[2] Bourriaud, der die relationale Ästhetik als eine Kunstform des sozialen Austauschs begriff, war auch der Auffassung, sie sei eine Möglichkeit, «den Utopismus der historischen Avantgarde» zu überwinden, jedoch «nicht dadurch, dass man ihn einfach abschafft, sondern dadurch, dass man ihn durch die örtlich gebundene, kurzzeitige Herausbildung alternativer Lebensweisen verwirklicht».[3] Man hat die Gedanken des französischen Kritikers häufig als eine Kunsttheorie für die 1990er bezeichnet, und mit Sicherheit wurden sie im folgenden Jahrzehnt zu einem Mantra für zahlreiche Ausstellungen. Bourriaud zufolge wurden relationale Kunstwerke von einem breiten Spektrum von Künstlern wie etwa Rirkrit Tiravanija, Pierre Huyghe, Philippe Parreno und Carsten Höller mit dem Ziel produziert, eine grundlegende soziale Transformation der Bedingungen und des Begriffs der Kunst herbeizuführen. In Bourriauds Einleitung zu seinem Text zu diesem Thema heisst es: «Rirkrit Tiravanija organisiert ein Abendessen bei einem Sammler zu Hause und liefert ihm sämtliche Zutaten, deren es für die Herstellung einer Thaisuppe bedarf. Philippe Parreno lädt ein paar Leute ein, am 1. Mai an einem Fabrikfliessband ihren Lieblingshobbies nachzugehen … Christine Hill arbeitet als Kassenhilfe in einem Supermarkt und organisiert einen wöchentlichen Fitnessworkshop in einer Galerie.» Doch wie wir festellen werden, sollte sich die Konzentration auf die Theatralisierung als eine der Schwächen von Bourriauds Argument erweisen.

In einem gewissen Sinne werden relationale Kunstwerke in Bourriauds Vorstellung als selbstständige Gesellschaftsgruppen konzipiert, selbst wenn sie nur für einen Augenblick verwirklicht wurden. So bezeichnete etwa der Künstler Rirkrit Tiravanija das Projekt *The Land*, das er 1998 auf Reisfeldern ausserhalb von Chiang Mai in Thailand mitgründete, als ein Labor für nachhaltige Umwelt- und Kunstprojekte, als eine Art ökoästhetische Gemeinschaft. Der verwirklichte Utopismus eines solchen relationalen Projekts liess an die Entstehung verschiedener antikapitalistischer Bewegungen seit den 1990ern denken. Tatsächlich konnte man die Artikelserie, die in Bourriauds Buch *Relationale Ästhetik* versammelt wurde, in seinen eigenen Worten als ein Manifest ‹für eine neue politische Kunst› lesen, «eine mikropolitische Loslösung von dem kapitalistischen Austausch, durch die eine Handelsgemeinschaft geschaffen wird, die sich dem kapitalistischen Wirtschaftskontext entzieht»[4]. Eine solche Erklärung erinnerte auf beruhigende Weise an einen Grossteil des aktivistischen Hintergrunds der Performances der 1960er und 1970er Jahre und verlieh ihnen etwas Gravitätisches und eine Ahnentafel.

Doch in den letzten sechs Jahren haben verschiedene Kritiker die dunklere Seite der relationalen Münze und die umfassenderen sozioökonomischen Faktoren erkundet, die den Kontext ihrer nahtlosen Allgegenwart in der kuratorischen Praxis bilden. Stewart Martin und Claire Bishop versuchten in zwei unterschiedlichen Artikeln, *Critique of Relational Aesthetics* bzw. *Antagonism and Relational Aesthetics*, die Aufmerksamkeit auf die gravierenden Grenzen von Bourriauds problematischem Vorschlag zu lenken.[5] Sie diskutieren die Notwendigkeit, die Geschichte zurückzuerobern und die Idee der relationalen Ästhetik als einer ‹kritischen› Kunst des sozialen Austauschs zu rekonstruieren. Stewart bemerkt, dass die Anästhetisierung neuartiger Formen kapitalistischer Ausbeutung in den von Bourriauds erwähnten Werken «auf hilflose Weise zu einer Ästhetisierung des kapitalistischen Austauschs umgekehrt»[6] wird. Beide Autoren verweisen auf den Ausschluss relationaler Künstler, deren Werke Bourriauds Modell in Frage stellen und daher die Notwendigkeit hervorheben, diese Geschichte neu zu beurteilen. Vor allem Bishop schlägt den Begriff des ‹Antagonismus› als eine Form relationalen Widerstands vor, demzufolge relationale Kunst als eine immanente Kritik der Warenform *(commodity of form)* funktioniert. Ein herausragendes Beispiel für beide Kritiker ist das Werk Santiago Sierras, der, neben anderen Künstlern, denen man relationale Arbeit unterstellen darf, in *Relational Aesthetics* nicht diskutiert wird. Sierra schafft einfache Situationen, in denen Menschen, auf der Grundlage einer vertraglich vereinbarten Zahlung, angestellt werden, das Kunstwerk in einer Weise zu verkörpern, die ihre Kommodifizierung und Instrumentalisierung deutlich macht, und dadurch zugleich das Publikum in die Ethik derartiger Prozesse einzubinden. Dies war etwa bei der Arbeit *3 people*

paid to lay still inside three boxes during a party der Fall, die im Jahr 2000 während der Biennale von Havanna in Szene gesetzt wurde. Drei junge Frauen wurden angeheuert und erhielten jeweils 30 Dollar dafür, sich während einer Biennale-Kunstparty in je eine Holzkiste zu legen. Die eingeladenen Gäste wurden über den Inhalt der Kisten, die sie als Sitzgelegenheiten benutzten, nicht informiert. Sierra kaufte buchstäblich die Zeit dieser jungen Frauen, und die Gäste waren im Netz des Künstlers gefangen, da ihre Anwesenheit überhaupt erst die Motivation für die Schaffung dieses Werks gewesen war. Bourriauds Theorie zufolge ist ein Werk dieses Typs eine Anomalie: eine relationale Kunst, die keinen sozialen Raum abseits der Kommodifizierung postuliert, sondern hervorhebt, dass der soziale Austausch durch Geld vermittelt ist, und damit auf der Tradition der Institutionskritik der 1970er aufbaut.

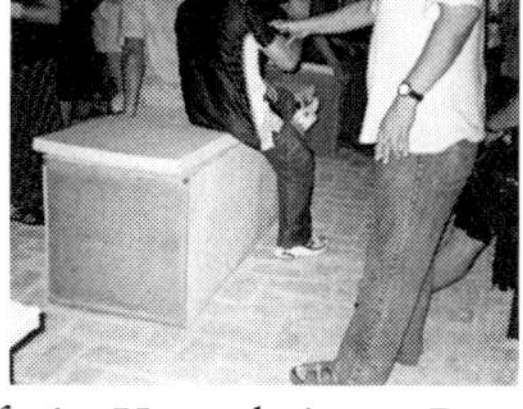

Bishops und Stewarts zentrale Argumente ähneln einander. Beide sind der Ansicht, Bourriauds gesellige Begegnungen seien nicht hinreichend antagonistisch, um als demokratisch gelten zu können, und drängen damit auf ein Korrektiv zu Bourriauds Ethik der Intersubjektivität. Dies wirft Fragen zur politischen Substanz der relationalen Kunst auf, da hier eine antagonistische (politische) statt einer geselligen (moralischen) Interpretation der sozialen Beziehungen der Kunst eingefordert wird. Aber es stimmt ebenfalls, dass auch diese alternative Theorie des Relationalen davon ausgeht, dass die Politik der Begegnung innerhalb des Werks gelöst werden muss. Problematisch daran ist, dass, wenn man dies zum wichtigsten Parameter des Werkes macht, andere Optionen vernachlässigt werden, bei denen sich die Hegemonie ebenfalls in Frage stellen liesse.

In Bezug auf Bourriauds Geselligkeit und die konfliktreicheren Beziehungen, die Bishop und Stewart bevorzugen, bringt Grant Kester ein drittes Modell in die Debatte ein, das soziale Begegnungen weder auf gesellige noch die politischen Antagonismen auf diejenigen beschränkt, die im Werk offen zutage treten. In seinem Buch *Conversation Pieces: Community and Communication in Modern Art* bietet Kester eine solide Darstellung der Beziehung zwischen partizipatorischen kulturellen Prozessen und der Hinwendung zu diskursiven Praktiken. Er vollzieht eine Reflexion nach, die, in seinen eigenen Worten, «zwischen der Kunst und der umfassenderen sozialen und politischen Welt» operiert.[7] Dieses Modell ist politisch aufgeladen: eine «neue Gattung von Kunst im öffentlichen Raum», die aus dem Gegensatz zwischen einer «bevormundenden Form von Tourismus» und «einem reziprokeren Prozess des Dialogs und der gegenseitigen Unterrichtung» eine Ethik für Künstler entwickelt.[8] Als Einführung in seine Ideen schlägt Kester vor, dass die traditionellen ästhetischen Strate-

gien und Kategorien sowohl der Moderne als auch der Postmoderne einander in der allgemeinen Übereinkunft darüber ähnelten, «dass das Kunstwerk gemeinsame diskursive Konventionen hinterfragen und unterminieren muss»[9]. Gemeinsame Merkmale dieser avantgardistischen Bezugssysteme sind für ihn die folgenden: Einerseits hätten sie ein reduktives Modell der diskursiven Interaktion bevorzugt, das auf dem traditionellen Gegensatz zwischen somatischer und kognitiver Erfahrung basierte, andererseits neigten sie dazu, die Definition der ästhetischen Erfahrung auf Augenblicke der unmittelbaren instinktiven Einsicht zu beschränken, und schliesslich beruhten sie auf einer im Wesentlichen solitären Interaktion zwischen einem Betrachter und einem physischen Objekt, das ein Begreifen kollektiver Prozesse in den Momenten der Produktion und Rezeption innerhalb der kreativen Praktiken nicht zuliesse.[10]

Im Gegensatz hierzu steht Kester ein anderes Bild des Künstlers vor Augen, nämlich das eines Künstlers, der an einem emanzipatorischen Modell der ‹dialogischen Interaktion› interessiert ist. Tatsächlich könnte man auch in Erwägung ziehen, dass seine Gedanken im weiteren Sinne zwangsläufig auch unser Verständnis einer performativen kuratorischen Praxis beeinflussen könnten. Die vorgeschlagene Direktive sieht einen seinen Betrachtern oder Mitarbeitern gegenüber offenen, aufgeschlossenen und verwundbaren Künstler vor. Die sozialen Modelle und Techniken, deren sich Kesters dialogische Künstler bedienen, sind in der Regel aus politischen Kontexten abgeleitet. Kester verfolgt sein Argument innerhalb existierender Praktiken, darunter das Werk von Stephen Willats, der seine künstlerische Praxis als offenes Werk betreibt, das auf Übereinkunft beruht. Willats Werk umfasst die Polemik und die Themen unserer zeitgenössischen Kultur und Gesellschaft als Mittel einer bewussten Untersuchung der Funktion und Bedeutung der Kunst in ihr. Das führt es zwangsläufig über die Normen und Konventionen einer objektbasierten Kunstwelt hinaus, da der Künstler es als eine Funktion seines Werks begreift, die Wahrnehmungen einer deterministischen Kultur von Objekten und Monumenten seitens der Menschen in jene Möglichkeiten zu verwandeln, die der Gemeinschaft zwischen den Menschen, dem Reichtum ihrer Komplexität und Selbstorganisation innewohnen. Das Kunstwerk spielt dabei eine dynamische, interaktive soziale Funktion. Für Willats sind diese Konzepte eine Konstante geblieben. So schrieb er bereits in den 1960ern:

«Ein Kunstwerk kann selbst einen gesellschaftlichen Zustand konstituieren, ein Modell zwischenmenschlicher Beziehungen.

Ein Kunstwerk kann aus einem Prozess in der Zeit bestehen, einem Lernsystem, mittels dessen man Zugang zu den Konzepten des sozialen Bildes, das in dem Werk übermittelt wird, haben und sie verinnerlichen kann.

Ein Kunstwerk muss den Relativismus anerkennen, der der Wahrnehmung und der Vergänglichkeit der Erfahrung innewohnt, da es kein Richtig oder Falsch gibt und es die Form eines Prozesses mit offenem Ende annimmt.

Ein Kunstwerk kann Menschen nur dadurch auf sinnvolle Weise einbinden und jedermann, der in seinen Bereich eintreten will, zur Verfügung stehen, indem es in seiner Präsentation die Mittel verkörpert, durch die Menschen imstande sind, die Sprache und die Verfahren zu erlernen, die notwendig sind, um seine Bedeutung zu verstehen und zu verinnerlichen.

Mein Werk vermittelt dem Publikum eine neue Art, Kunst in der Gesellschaft zu begegnen. Ich spreche nicht von einer Einwilligung, sondern von etwas Aktiverem, einem wechselseitigen Verständnis, einer Interaktion zwischen Menschen, ähnlich wie bei dem dynamischen Bild des Homöostats, bei dem alle Teile des Netzwerks gleich und gleichermassen miteinander verbunden sind.»[11]

In jüngerer Zeit hat die österreichische Gruppe WochenKlausur Projekte entwickelt, die unmittelbar in das soziale Gefüge eingreifen und mittelfristige infrastrukturelle, institutionelle, strategische Lösungen für immerwährende soziale Probleme wie Prostitution, Altenpflege, medizinische Versorgung Obdachloser, die Gestaltung von Klassenzimmern, Wahlsysteme, Einwanderung und gesellschaftliche Hürden etc. bereitstellen. Auf ihrer Webseite steht zu lesen: «Auf Einladung unterschiedlicher Kunstinstitutionen entwickelt die Gruppe kleine, aber sehr konkrete Vorschläge zur Veränderung gesellschaftspolitischer Defizite und setzt diese um. Künstlerische Kreativität wird dabei nicht mehr für formale Belange eingesetzt, sondern als Intervention in die Gesellschaft.»[12]

Das Problem besteht darin, dass Kesters Argument und die zitierten Beispiele für künstlerische Praktiken – man denke an die Formulierung gesellschaftspolitische Defizite in der Einleitung der Webseite von WochenKlausur – dadurch, dass sie ihr Augenmerk auf das Verhalten des Künstlers im Bezug auf eine Gemeinschaft richten, leicht zu einer moralisierenden Haltung verkommen können. Das wirft die Frage auf, ob derartiges Denken die Kunst der Begegnung (das Gesellschaftliche in der Kunst) auf das politische Feld einengt, und dieser problematische Aspekt wird von Kester nicht gelöst.

Nachdem wir nun drei Modelle von Geselligkeit innerhalb der Kunst der Begegnung betrachtet haben, wollen wir die umfassenderen Bedingungen in Betracht ziehen, unter denen sie operieren. Es handelt sich, das wollen wir nicht vergessen, um einen Kontext, in dem Kuratoren zunehmend unter dem Druck stehen, buchstäblich Räume der Gemeinschaftlichkeit in ihren Projekten zu performen, ein Kontext, nach dem das Publikum (oder die noch einflussreicheren privaten und öffentlichen Geldgeber?) zunehmend süchtig zu sein scheint (oder scheinen).

Eine kontextuelle Kritik
der Geselligkeit in der Kunst

Jan Verwoerts Text *Exhaustion and Exuberance. Ways to Defy the Pressure to Perform* befasst sich mit der finsteren Wende, mit der sich die heutigen, sich alle Mühe gebenden Kunst-Arbeiter konfrontiert sehen, vor allem dem Druck, ‹über Gebühr› performen zu müssen. Verwoert verfasste den Text während eines performativen Print-Projekts, das 2007 von Dexter Sinister am Centre d'Art Contemporain Genève initiiert wurde und im Rahmen dessen Heft 15 der Publikation *Dot Dot Dot* kompiliert und gedruckt wurde.[13] Diese Ausgabe untersuchte die Natur der zeitgenössischen Produktion, Überproduktion und Erschöpfung. Dexter Sinister zwang Verwoert, unter den Bedingungen, die er in einem früheren Text aus demselben Jahr mit dem Titel *Use me Up* in Frage gestellt hatte, zu arbeiten.[14] Dexter Sinister bemerkte dazu in der Einleitung: «Den Produzenten ganz buchstäblich zu zwingen, im unmittelbaren Raum seiner unmittelbar bevorstehenden Deadline zu arbeiten, die von der dräuenden Präsenz einer wartenden Druckmaschine symbolisiert wird. Im Verlauf zweier komprimierter Wochen entsteht dann der Rest des Heftes in Echtzeit auf der Grundlage dieser Voraussetzung.»[15]

Verwoert schreibt dazu in seinem performativen Text *Exhaustion and Exuberance* (Erschöpfung und Überschwang): «Nach dem Verschwinden der manuellen Arbeit aus dem Leben der meisten Menschen sind wir in eine Kultur eingetreten, in der wir nicht mehr einfach nur arbeiten, sondern performen. [Wir tun dies als, A. d. Übers.] eine ständig wachsende Gruppe kreativer Typen, die Jobs für sich selbst erfinden, indem wir unsere Talente erkunden und ausbeuten, um täglich kleine künstlerische und intellektuelle Wunder zu performen. Wir, die sozial Engagierten, schaffen gemeinschaftliche Räume für andere und uns selbst, indem wir als Agenten des gesellschaftlichen Wandels performen. Wenn wir performen, erzeugen wir Kommunikation und schaffen so Formen von Gemeinschaftlichkeit. Wenn wir performen, entwickeln wir Ideen und stellen so die Inhalte für eine Ökonomie bereit, die auf dem Zirkulieren einer anderen Währung basiert, nämlich der Information.»[16]

Verwoert gelangt zu dem Schluss, dass ‹wir› in einer extremen Performancekultur die Avantgarde, doch zugleich auch die Jobsklaven sind. Als Teil dieses ‹Wir› kommt man nicht umhin, auf dieser Stufe mit Verwoerts nachfolgender Beschreibung der Ähnlichkeiten zwischen der Welt der Kunst-Arbeiter und der Welt der Sex-Arbeiter zu

sympathisieren. ‹Wir› sind immer bereit zu performen, zu jeder Zeit, an jedem Ort in der Welt, und denken uns neue und kreative Möglichkeiten aus, um die Zufriedenheit unserer Kunden mit dem Erlebnis zu erhöhen und hoffentlich einen neuen Auftrag zu erhalten.

Tatsächlich scheint ‹Erlebnis› das Leitmotiv unserer Zeit zu sein. Lars Bang Larsen hat dies vor Kurzem in seinem Text *Zombies of Immaterial Labor: The Modern Monster and the Death of Death* sehr anschaulich gezeigt. Es geht darin um den Druck, den die Kapitalisierung der Kreativität im letzten Jahrzehnt auf die künstlerische Praxis und das künstlerische Denken ausgeübt hat, indem sie sie auf das Terrain des Erlebnismässigen und Konsensuellen gedrängt hat. Für Bang Larsen ist Kunst eine Norm geworden, und innerhalb der aktuellen ‹Erlebnisökonomie› besteht die normative Macht der Kunst in der Kommodifizierung einer herkömmlichen Idee oder der mythischen Andersheit der Kunst mit Blick auf die Reproduktion von Subjektivität und Ökonomie. Im Folgenden präsentiert Bang Larsen dann das Denken von James H. Gilmore und B. Joseph Pine II, die 1999 mit ihrem Buch *The Experience Economy: Work is Theatre and Every Business a Stage* den Begriff der Erlebnisökonomie in Umlauf gebracht haben.[17] Dieser Vorschlag beschreibt eine Wirtschaft, in der das Erlebnis eine neue Einkommensquelle ist, die man dadurch erschliesst, indem man etwas Einprägsames inszeniert.

«Produziert wird das Erlebnis durch das Publikum, und das Erlebnis wird durch ‹Authentizitätseffekte› erzeugt. In der Erlebnisökonomie sind es häufig die Kunst sowie ihre Authentizitätskennzeichen – Kreativität, Innovation, Provokation –, die den ökonomischen Status des Erlebnisses sicherstellen. [...] Entscheidend ist die psychologische Prämisse, in der Lage zu sein, das Wirklichkeitsgefühl der Konsumenten zu verändern. Gilmore und Pine heben die Profitabilität simulierter Situationen hervor. [...] Es ist klar, wie sich die Folgen der Erlebnisökonomie auf den Abbau künstlerischer und institutioneller Bedeutung ebenso wie sozialer Verbindungen auswirken können.»[18]

Im selben Artikel verweist Bang Larsen auf den anschaulichen Begriff des Eigenblutdopings, den sein Kritikerkollege Diedrich Diederichsen 2008 in seinem Buch *Eigenblutdoping: Selbstverwertung, Künstlerromantik, Partizipation* entfaltet hat.[19] Darin geht Diederichsen einen Schritt weiter als Bang Larsen, indem er sich mit der Sucht des Publikums befasst, das sich von Projekten angezogen fühlt, deren Erlebnisversprechen eines ist, bei dem es eigentlich nichts Neues einzuschreiben, keine einzigartige Identität beizutragen und auch keine Fertigkeit, mit der sich etwas Neues konstruieren liesse, gibt, sondern bei dem der Raum der Einschreibung einer der Vorhersagbarkeit, des Einvernehmens ist. Diederichsen vertritt die These, die traditionelle Macht der Kulturinstitution habe sich verschoben, wenn das Publikum eingeladen ist, in einer augenscheinlichen Demokratisierung der Kunst mitzuspielen und mitzutun. Aufgrund dieser falschen Prämisse

verliere das Publikum die Möglichkeit, seine jeweilige Subjektivität in irgendetwas ausserhalb seiner selbst einzuschreiben, und werde einer wichtigen Gelegenheit beraubt, dort, wo Kunst präsentiert wird, auf die Institution und den Ausstellungskomplex zu reagieren.

Die Überlegungen von Bourriaud, Bishop, Stewart, Verwoert, Bang Larsen, Diederichsen und anderer sind Ausdruck einer aufschlussreichen Diskussion der Faktoren, die den Begriff der Performativität heute schaffen und problematisieren. Doch es ist wichtig, die Debatte nicht auf die Kritik zu verengen. Wir wollen auch versuchen, uns einen Raum für eine Praxis des Widerstands für Kunst-Arbeiter innerhalb des performativen Szenarios vorzustellen. Was wären denn in der Tat solche anderen Möglichkeiten zu performen? Könnten wir uns ein ästhetisches Erleben vorstellen, das innerhalb des Feldes einer kollektiven Wirkung operiert, wo sich praktikable Formen des Widerstands ersinnen lassen?

Der Abbau des Sozialen durch Konflikte, Laxheit und Verbrechen

Eine Möglichkeit, in diese Diskussion einzusteigen, besteht darin, sich vorzustellen, wie man die Rolle des Publikums in einem performativen Feld in Frage stellen könnte. Auch wenn wir bislang Aufrufe vernommen haben, die Geschichte der künstlerischen Praxis wiederherzustellen oder den Energieaufwand innerhalb der Hochöfen der Kunstwelt wieder in Besitz zu nehmen, gilt es doch auch den operativen Raum des Publikums in dieser Auseinandersetzung zu bedenken. In der letzten Serie der Trilogie *The Nightmare of Participation* imaginiert Markus Miessen einen neuen Teilnehmertypus, der sich nicht den vorgegebenen Codes von Praxis und Produktion unterwirft, sondern ein nicht zu kontrollierender Irritationsfaktor ist.[20] Miessen geht dabei so weit, die Möglichkeit eines ‹konfliktträchtigen Teilnehmers› zu befürworten. Seiner Meinung nach ist der Begriff ‹Teilnahme› im letzten Jahrzehnt inflationär verwendet worden. Wenn jedermann sich in einen Teilnehmer verwandelt, dann wird der häufig unkritische, unschuldige und romantische Gebrauch des Begriffs auf beängstigende Weise inhaltsleer. Gestützt von einem wiederholtermassen nostalgischen Anstrich von Würdigkeit, unaufrichtiger Solidarität und politischer Korrektheit ist Partizipation ein Ausdruck für die Säumigkeit von Politikern geworden, die sich aus ihrer sozialen und kulturellen Verantwortung davonstehlen. Vergleichbar der Vorstellung von einem unabhängigen Politiker, der keiner spezifischen Partei angehört, unterstützt der dritte Teil von Miessens *Participation*-Trilogie die Rolle des von ihm so genannten ‹crossbench practitioner› (parteilosen Politikers), eines ‹interesselosen Aussenseiters› und ‹unaufgeforderten Teilnehmers›, der nicht durch vorhandene Protokolle eingeschränkt ist und die Arena mit nichts als krea-

tivem Verstand und dem Willen betritt, Veränderungen herbeizuführen. Vielleicht ist es diese Art Teilnehmer, die Charles Filch sucht. Filch, ‹der Bettler›, ist der sekundäre Nebendarsteller, der von der Künstlerin Dora García aufgefordert wurde, gelegentlich als Figur aus Bertolt Brechts Dreigroschenoper zu ‹entfliehen›. Die Künstlerin lud Filch erstmals anlässlich der *Skulptur Projekte Münster* 2007 ein, den Sommer dort zu verbringen und ein Tagebuch über seine Begegnungen mit der lokalen Bevölkerung und der internationalen Kunstszene zu führen (www.beggarsopera.org). Seine letzte ‹Eskapade› führte ihn in den spanischen Pavillon der Biennale von Venedig 2011, wo er in dem Projekt *L'Inadeguato,*

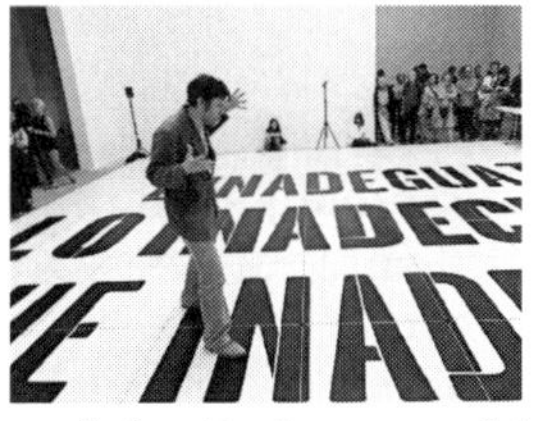

Lo Inadecuado, The Inadequate auf der Bühne erschien. Das Projekt liefert uns einen Grund, zum einen die unterschiedliche Art von Raum für das Publikum zu diskutieren – ein Miessens konfliktträchtigem Teilnehmer genehmer Aspekt – und zum anderen das Modell für einen prozessualen Typ von Performativität, der es vermeidet, zum Event zu erstarren.[21]

In einer diskursiven, erweiterten Performance, in welcher die Begriffe Abweichung, Radikalität, Aussenseiter, Exklusion, Zensur und Marginalität angeschnitten wurden, erhielten die Schauspieler Samir Kandil und Peter Aers, die diese Rolle entwickelten, kaum Anweisungen von García. In Venedig griffen sie zwangsläufig auf ihre Erfahrungen in Münster zurück, stützten sich aber auch auf die innere Logik ihres eigenen Werks. Ausserdem lebte die Performance aber auch von einzelnen ungezwungenen Mitgliedern des Publikums, die sich entschlossen mitzumachen oder die sie versuchten, zum Mitmachen zu animieren oder davon abzuhalten oder zu ignorieren. Für diesen Raum der (Nicht-)Einbindung (dis/engagement) gab es kein festgelegtes Protokoll, keine zu erledigende Aufgabe und keine Teilnehmergruppen, die vorher von einem Vermittler ausgesucht worden wurden, um das Werk möglich zu machen. Tatsächlich existiert Filch nicht eigens für das Publikum, ja seine Präsenz und seine Aktionen sind unabhängig davon, ob ein Publikum anwesend ist oder nicht. Es wurden dem Publikum in diesem Projekt auch nicht die üblichen ‹Einrichtungen› angeboten, sondern es handelte sich um ein unangemessenes Forum mit einer uneindeutigen Haltung gegenüber der Partizipation als solcher. Der Zuschauer war nicht als ein wesentlicher Teil des Werks an sich konzipiert, sondern als ein beiläufiger Passant. Und doch konnte die Einbindung in verschiedene Augenblicke von Filchs Prozess, ja in die Dynamik von *The Inadequate* die innere Struktur des Werks vorantreiben und auf immaterielle Weise seiner kreativen Dichte Vorschub leisten.

Und obgleich die Parameter von *The Inadequate* streng ausgearbeitet waren, blieb in jedem Moment dieser Performance eine Offenheit

der Form erhalten. In Filchs Fall provozierte uns diese Freiheit dazu, die Dichotomien freizulegen und zu hinterfragen, die García in eine Situation einfügte und die einen Grossteil ihrer künstlerischen Praxis kennzeichnen. Mit Filch umgeht die Künstlerin García das Konzept der Partizipation im Verständnis der ‹Relational Aesthetics›. Sie operiert jenseits der Modi des Einvernehmens und öffnet einen Raum für Miessens Idee der konfliktträchtigen Partizipation, die kein Prozess mehr ist, bei dem andere eingeladen werden, sondern ein Mittel, ohne Mandat zu handeln, als ungebetener Irritationsfaktor – ein erzwungener Zugang zu Wissensfeldern, die von einem Denken profitieren dürften, das von ausserhalb kommt. Wenn partizipatorische Kunst zum Leitkanal einer demokratischen Kunst fetischisiert wurde, dann muss Demokratie mitunter um jeden Preis vermieden werden. Tatsächlich kann man das Versprechen der Partizipation heute in performativen Ausstellungen auch als einen Raum der Pflichtversäumnis erleben, für den die Verantwortung zu übernehmen Politiker ablehnen. Die Demokratisierung der Kunst kann auch den stechenden Geruch ihrer Privatisierung aufweisen. Statt die nächste Generation konsensueller Erleichterer und Vermittler heranzuzüchten, könnte man Irritation als eine kreative Kraft begrüssen. Wenn in *The Inadequate* die prozessuale Diskursivität das Publikum von der Beschränkung der Partizipation befreite, dann schrieb das Projekt *A Crime against Art* das Publikum in die Performance ein, um ihm anschliessend Handlungsfreiheit zu geben. Ein hybrides Projekt, angesiedelt irgendwo zwischen Konferenz, kollektivem Workshop und Performance, bediente es sich im Wesentlichen der Diskursivität als eines Mittels, die Dreieckstruktur von Performativität, Spektakel und Partizipation zu untersuchen.

A Crime against Art erkundete die inhärenten Widersprüche und Komplexitäten in der Figur des Kurators, des Künstlers, des Kritikers und des Zuschauers innerhalb einer solchen performativen Anordnung.

Gedacht als ein inszenierter konzeptueller Prozess, der 2007 im Rahmen der Kunstmesse ARCO in Madrid stattfand, war *A Crime against Art* von den Scheinprozessen inspiriert, die avantgardistische Kunstströmungen (André Breton) in den 1920ern und 1930ern organisiert hatten. Diese Theatralität provozierte in der zeitgenössischen Kunstwelt eine Reihe polemischer Reaktionen.[22] Das Projekt, das wie ein Fernsehgerichtsdrama aufgebaut war und von vier Kamerateams gefilmt wurde, ging von der Vermutung aus, es sei ein Verbrechen begangen worden. Die Tatsache, dass der Prozess in Echtzeit und ohne Skript stattfand, war ein entscheidender Faktor für die anschliessende performative Diskussion. Die potenziellen Täter, sprich die Angeklagten, hatten sich selbst gestellt, doch die Natur des Verbrechens und die Beweise dafür waren vage, und es hatten sich auch keine Opfer gemeldet. Innerhalb dieser theatralischen Diskussion mit offenem Ausgang wurden die Zeugenaussagen und Kreuzverhöre zu einem

Versuch, der Natur des verstörenden ‹Verbrechens gegen die Kunst› auf die Spur zu kommen.

Die Anschuldigungen fassten die Problematik der Performance zusammen, um die es in diesem Essay geht, d. h. die Dichotomie zwischen der Schaffung eines Raums mit einem gewissen Wirkungsvermögen, aufgerechnet gegen das geheime Einverständnis mit der gigantischen Spektakel- und Konsummaschine, die eine Kunstmesse (oder Biennale, neben anderen Plattformen) charakterisiert als Ort, an dem sich performative Kunst produzieren lässt. Mit anderen Worten, *A Crime against Art* stellte die Frage, wie man eine Einladung akzeptieren kann, ein performatives Projekt in einem Raum wie einer Kunstmesse zu schaffen, und dennoch einen Raum der Unabhängigkeit aufrechterhalten, der die Moral einer Partizipation innerhalb des Systems hinterfragt. *A Crime against Art* integrierte einen Fragen stellenden Diskurs in ihren Aufgabenbereich und versuchte so zu vermeiden, zu einer vertanen Möglichkeit einer kritischen künstlerischen Wirkung zu werden: ein weiterer Unterhaltungsmoment, der zu einer weiteren Reduzierung des kleinen Raums beiträgt, der der zeitgenössischen Kunst als Vektor der Recherche verblieben ist. Diese Sackgasse wurde von der Sachverständigen und Kuratorin Maria Lind, die Auszüge aus einem Kunstbericht präsentierte, der die Kunstwelt der Zukunft betrifft, auf beredte Weise thematisiert. Dieser sah voraus, dass im Jahr 2015 Künstler – man könnte sagen, dass dies für alle Kunst-Arbeiter gilt –, «die sich weigern, an der Unterhaltungsindustrie teilzunehmen, zwangsläufig unter sich verschlechternden Bedingungen leben werden»[23].

Der Ausgang des Prozesses in *A Crime against Art,* sprich die Frage, ob die Angeklagten für unschuldig erklärt oder schuldig gesprochen wurden, war nicht wirklich der Punkt, um den es ging. Der Zweck des Ganzen bestand vielmehr in einer Diskussion und Inszenierung des Gebrauchs und Missbrauchs performativer Strukturen innerhalb des erotisch aufgeladenen und spektakelartigen Raums einer Kunstmesse. *A Crime against Art* versuchte, Performance als einen potenziellen Wert für den Wandel zu rekonfigurieren und auf diese Weise mehrere umstrittene Punkte in der heutigen Kunstszene offenzulegen. Darüber hinaus hinterfragte das Projekt die Idee der Verantwortung in einem Kunstwerk, vor allem dort, wo Performance und Partizipation betroffen sind, und es experimentierte mit verschiedenen Möglichkeiten, die performative Schaffung eines Kunstdiskurses zu verhandeln.

Ein rhythmisches NEIN

Die Performances von Charles Filch und *A Crime against Art* verweisen auf die Wichtigkeit der Diskursivität an verschiedenen Fronten. Sie tun dies einerseits, indem sie die natürliche Nähe der Performance zur öffentlichen Unterhaltung in der heutigen Konsumgesellschaft problematisieren, und andererseits, indem sie eine andere Dynamik für die Verbindung der Öffentlichkeit zum Kunstwerk und die Konstruktion desselben schaffen. Und schliesslich heben diese Werke auch den Wert der Diskursivität als interne Form der Kritik für Kunst-Arbeiter und -Denker hervor.

Vielleicht lässt sich aufgrund dieser heterogenen Genealogie von Zielen die seltsame Komplementarität und Synchronizität zwischen der Vorherrschaft der kuratorischen Geste (die immer mehr zum Schöpfer des Diskurses wird) und dem Eintreten für einen sprachlichen Austausch als Paradigma der Praxis verstehen. Hinzu kommt noch die allgegenwärtige Attraktivität des Begriffs ‹Diskurs› als ein Wort, mit dem sich Macht beschwören und ausüben lässt. Kurzum, die diskursive Wende, die in der Kunstwelt (Kuratoren und Künstler) vorherrscht… und damit das Dilemma der Performativität heute.

Doch dieser diskursiven Wende wohnt nichts Neues inne, jedenfalls nicht was die künstlerische Diskursivität betrifft. Man erinnere sich nur daran, wie der Konzeptualismus J.L. Austins *How to Do Things with Words* aufnahm, das erstmals 1962 veröffentlicht wurde.[24] Austins Ideen und das Versagen der Kritik zu jener Zeit veranlassten Künstler, die diskursive Lücke in der Selbstdarstellung mit Interviews und anderen Formaten zu füllen. Carl Andre, Donald Judd und Robert Morris etwa nahmen die Erklärung der Werke selbst in die Hand und benutzten veröffentlichte Gespräche als ein Genre, um dieses Ziel zu erreichen. Diese Künstler und andere verbanden das produktive Potenzial der Standardthesen ihrer experimentellen Kunstpraxis mit den Begleitkommentaren.

In jüngerer Zeit sind die buchstäblich ausgelegten Umsetzungen von Gesprächen über ihre Vorläufer im anglophonen Konzeptualismus der späten 1960er und frühen 1970er Jahre hinausgegangen. In diesen beiden Jahrzehnten war die Hinwendung zur Sprache in der Konzeptkunst noch keine unmittelbare Injektion von Sprache in die Kunst, sondern eine militante Bekräftigung der Tatsache, dass die Kunst Teil ihrer eigenen Vertriebs- und Werbestrukturen ist und sowohl eine Nähe zum Text aufweist als auch an diesem beteiligt ist. Die Wende zum Diskursiven wird also als ein reflexives Beachten der Bedingungen der Möglichkeit reproduziert – im Kunstsystem und als solches. In den späten 1980ern und 1990ern beobachtet man dann eine daran anschliessende Korrelation zwischen der Hinwendung zum Diskursiven und der expliziten Thematisierung der infrastrukturellen Prozesse und Rollen der Kunstwelt. Dies verdeutlicht eine grosse Vielfalt künstlerischer Praktiken, von Hans Haackes Sozialerhebungen

bis hin zu Tino Sehgals theatralisch-spielerischem Umgang mit den Prozessen des Kunstmarkts und Dora Garcías Problematisierung der Rolle der Institution und des Betrachters im Kunstwerk in den letzten Jahren.

Neuartiger hingegen ist die immer weiter wachsende Bedeutung der Rolle des Kurators, etwa in künstlerischen Projekten wie *A Crime against Art*. Diese Veränderung ist teilweise ähnlichen Umständen geschuldet wie den weiter oben erwähnten, nämlich dem Versagen der Kritiker, einen hinreichend starken Diskurs bereitzustellen. Doch diese Veränderung hat auch mit der neuen Dynamik der Territorialisierung und des Handels mit Wissen zu tun, die in unserer Zeit gang und gäbe sind. Carolyn Christov-Bakargiev hat unlängst die Fallstricke beschrieben, die mit der Kommodifizierung des Prozesses und des Wissens verbunden sind. In ihrem Notizbuch zur *dOCUMENTA13* schreibt sie, «dieser überholte Gegenstand des 20. Jahrhunderts, die Ausstellung» habe «eine Art Manierismus herausgebildet», sodass gelegentlich spezifische Inhalte entkörperlicht würden und spezifische Kunstwerke mit ihrem Mangel an Transzendenz fast durchsichtig geworden seien.[25] Christov-Bakargiev fährt fort: «Ich bin der Ansicht, dass Verfahrensfragen ebenso aussagekräftig, wenn nicht aussagekräftiger sind als der sogenannte Inhalt oder das Thema eines künstlerischen Produkts – wie man Wirkung erzielt und wie man sich zu anderen verhält, wie man als Künstler vorgeht oder wie man als Teil des Publikums agiert.» Im Folgenden betont sie besonders die Gefahren, die in dem Versuch lauern, den Prozess der künstlerischen Kreativität zu einem kommerziellen Paket zu schnüren. «Auch wenn der zur Erzielung eines Ergebnisses genutzte Prozess möglicherweise ein ‹kreativer› ist, erscheint es mir wichtig, diesen Prozess nicht selbst in ein Produkt zu verwandeln. Folglich bin ich keine grosse Verfechterin der sich abzeichnenden dominanten unkritischen Ideologie der Kreativität. […] Wir sollten uns heute daher sehr genau mit dem Problem befassen, wie Künstler, Kulturproduzenten und Intellektuelle innerhalb der sich auf der Grundlage des Austauschs von Wissensprodukten entwickelnden Ökonomie und Hegemonie verfahren können.»[26]

Was immer man mit dieser Lektüre von Querbeziehungen anfangen mag, klar ist, dass das Diskursive im performativen Kunstwerk oder im kuratorischen Bestreben als einem seiner vielen Momente mit dem Prozess einhergegangen ist, die verschiedenen Beziehungen zwischen den Kunstschaffenden, dem Publikum und institutionellen Prozessen neu zu formulieren. Projekte wie Dora Garcías *Charles Filch* und *A Crime against Art* erinnern uns an diese Militanz, indem sie die Möglichkeit problematisieren, in eine Form gestischer, kristallisierter Performativität statt einer prozessualen, quecksilbrigen Performativität zu verfallen.

Angesichts der Tatsache, dass die kreativen Prozesse von Performance und Performativität auf eine einzigartige Weise zu Unterhaltungs-

paketen erstarrt sind und das Publikum in von vornherein festgelegte Formateinhaltsleerer Partizipation getrieben wurde, stellt sich heute die Frage, wie man die Praxis und ihr Publikum hinsichtlich dieser belastenden Imperative erleichtern kann. Vor über einem Jahrhundert beschloss Robert Walser, eine ‹reizende kugelrunde Null› zu werden, um in seiner literarischen Laufbahn einem ähnlichen Druck wie dem von uns beschriebenen zu entfliehen. Nachdem er in Berlin ein erfolgreicher Schriftsteller gewesen war, kehrte Walser in seine schweizerische Heimat zurück, um sich unter dem ‹akzeptierten› Niveau der Sprache seiner Zeit wegzuducken. Zu diesem ‹Wegducken› gehört auch die von ihm geschaffene Serie der Mikrogramme, die für das normale Auge nicht zu entziffern und scheinbar die Frucht unsinnigen Verhaltens sind. Die Gesellschaft betrachtete Walsers NEIN als eine Form der Marginalisierung – antithetisch heroisch in ihrer Geringfügigkeit. Heute würden selbst solche kleinen und doch zugleich grossen Gesten von den Märkten und Diskursen vereinnahmt.

Da wir beim Thema Worte sind, ist es möglicherweise passend – als ein offenes Fenster auf unsere Sackgasse und als ein zeitweiliger Abschluss dieser Diskussion –, eine weitere literarische Figur und einen Meister des NEIN zu betrachten. Ich denke dabei an die vielen Erscheinungsformen Bartlebys, die Enrique Vila-Matas in seinem meisterhaften Roman *Bartleby & Co.* schildert.[27] Diese Kompilation von Fussnoten, die die traditionelle narrative Struktur und Fortentwicklung meidet, greift Herman Melvilles Figur des Bartleby auf, die der Inbegriff einer verneinenden Existenz ist und deren Standardantwort auf jedes an sie herangetragene Ersuchen lautet: «Ich würde es vorziehen, es nicht zu tun.» Vila-Matas schildert die zahlreichen Verkörperungen Bartlebys in der modernen Kultur, vor allem in der Literatur. Der Schriftsteller teilt uns mit: «Nur aus dem negativen Drang, aus dem Labyrinth des Nein, kann die Literatur der Zukunft hervorgehen.»[28] Mit dieser Haltung im Hinterkopf gilt es, um dem versklavenden Rhythmus unserer performativen Zeit zu entkommen, eine (künstlerische oder kuratorische) Praxis in Erwägung zu ziehen, die eine Möglichkeit darstellt, es vorzuziehen, etwas nicht zu tun, eine Art Ausweichmanöver der Kunstschaffenden, das nicht versucht, das System frontal anzugehen, sondern das einen Raum neben diesem schafft: eine Form der Unbestimmtheit mit offenem Ausgang, hinreichend weit entfernt von einer absorbierbaren Wirklichkeit. Ob diese Position dann über die vielen Kanäle von Nebenaktionen entwickelt wird, die uns zur Verfügung stehen, etwa heimtückische Scharlatanerie, gaunerhafte Betrügerei oder verruchtes Pokern, um den kreativen Prozess nicht offenzulegen, bleibt unserem kollektiven Vorstellungsvermögen überlassen. Wessen es hier bedarf, wurde (in einem anderen Kontext, nämlich einem aktuellen philosophischen Aufsatz von Chus Martínez, den ich jedoch für das Feld der Performativität besonders relevant finde) als die Möglichkeit beschrieben, unterschiedliche

Arten des Denkens zu schaffen: eine Logik, die imstande ist, uns mit dem Wesen der Kunst zu verschmelzen, statt uns auf kritischem (und zudem konsumierbarem, wie ich meine) Abstand zu halten.[29]

1   Hierbei handelt es sich um einen Verweis auf das Plakat *Just what is it that makes today's homes so different so appealing,* das Richard Hamilton 1956 für die Ausstellung *This is Tomorrow* in der Whitechapel Gallery, London, entwarf. Das Werk sollte emblematisch für die amerikanische Konsumgesellschaft der 1950er Jahre werden.

2   Nicolas Bourriaud, *Relational Aesthetics* (1998), Dijon: Les Presses du Réel, 2002.

3   Stewart Martin, ‹Critique of Relational Aesthetics›, in: *Third Text,* Bd. 21, Nr. 4, Juli 2007, S. 371.

4   Bourriaud, a.a.O., S.42.

5   Martin, a.a.O.; Claire Bishop, ‹Antagonism and Relational Aesthetics›, in: *October,* Nr. 110, Herbst 2004, S. 51–79.

6   Martin, a.a.O., S.371.

7   Grant Kester, *Conversation Pieces: Community and Communication in Modern Art,* Berkeley, Los Angeles, London: University of California Press, 2004.

8   Ebd., S.151.

9   Ebd., S.88.

10   Ebd., S.88f.

11   Steven Willats. Aufgerufen am 7.5.2012. http://stephenwillats.com/context

12   Wochenklausur. Aufgerufen am 7.5.2012. http://www.wochenklausur.at/projekte/menu_en.htm

13   Jan Verwoert, ‹Exhaustion and Exuberance. Ways to Defy the Pressure to Perform›, in: *Dot Dot Dot 15,* 15. Dezember 2007, produziert im Centre d'Art Contemporain Genève, Schweiz, für *Dot Dot Dot Magazine,* New York, 2007. *Dot Dot Dot Issue 15* wurde von Mai Abu ElDahab, Stuart Bailey, Walead Beshty, Sarah Crowner, Joyce Guley, Will Holder, Anthony Huberman, Polona Kuzman, David Reinfurt, Joke Robaard, Jan Verwoert und Jan Dirk de Wilde zwischen dem 24. Oktober und dem 7. November 2007 vor Ort im Centre d'Art Contemporain Genève produziert und auf Ricoh TC2, Rico JP 8500 und Riso V8000-Schablonendruckmaschinen in einer Auflage von 3000 Stück gedruckt. Dieses Projekt war Teil der Ausstellung *Wouldn't it be Nice… Wishful Thinking in Art and Design,* Centre d'Art Contemporain Genève, Schweiz, 2007 (kuratiert von Emily King und Katya García-Antón).

14   Jan Verwoert, ‹Use Me Up›, in: *Metropolis M,* Nr. 1, Februar 2007.

15   Dexter Sinister. Aufgerufen am 7. 5. 2012. http:/www.dextersinister.org/index.html?id=123

16   Jan Verwoert, ‹Exhaustion and Exuberance…›, a. a. O., S. 90.

17   James H. Gilmore, B. Joseph Pine II, *The Experience Economy: Work is Theatre and Every Business a Stage,* Cambridge, Ma.: Harvard Business School, 1999.

18   Lars Bang Larsen, ‹Zombies of Immaterial Labor: The Modern Monster and the Death of Death›, in: *e-flux journal, Are You Working too Much? Post-Fordisms, Precarity and the Labor of Art,* London: Sternberg Press, 2001, S. 86.

19   Diedrich Diederichsen, *Eigenblutdoping: Selbstverwertung, Künstlerromantik, Partizipation,* Köln: Kiepenheuer & Witsch, 2008.

20   Markus Miessen, *The Nightmare of Participation (Crossbench Praxis as a Mode of Criticality),* London: Sternberg Press, 2010.

21   Die erweiterte Performance *L'Inadeguato, Lo Inadecuado, The Inadequate* fand im spanischen Pavillon auf der 54. Biennale von Venedig statt. Ich war die Kuratorin des Pavillons. Eine detaillierte Aufzeichnung des Projekts findet sich auf www.theinadequate.net. Versionen der Publikation auf Spanisch, Englisch und Italienisch können von dieser Webseite heruntergeladen werden.

22   Auf der Grundlage von *The Trial,* das Anton Vidokle und Tirdad Zolghadr im Februar 2007 organisiert hatten, wurde *A Crime against Art* von Eric Menard und Hila Peleg 2007 als Video ediert und vom Bureau des vidéos, Paris, produziert.

23   Maria Lind, 2005. ‹European Cultural Policies 2015. A Report with Scenarios on the Future of Public Funding for Contemporary Art in Europe›. *European Institute for Progressive Cultural Policies,* http:/eipcp.netpolicies/2015lind/en. Aufgerufen am 13. 5. 2012.

24   J. L. Austin, *How to Do Things with Words,* Oxford: Clarendon Press, 1962 (dt.: *Zur Theorie der Sprechakte,* Stuttgart: Reclam, 1972).

25   Carolyn Christov-Barkagiev, ‹Brief an einen Freund›, in: *100 Notizen – 100 Gedanken,* Nr. 003, Ostfildern: Hatje Cantz, 2011.

26   Ebd.

27   Enrique Vila-Matas, *Bartleby & Co* (2000), London: Vintage, 2005.

28   Ebd., S. 2.

29   Chus Martínez, ‹As little time on the ground as possible. First attempt on the possibility of artistic significance beyond philosophy of history›, in: *Mousse Magazine,* Nr. 30, Oktober/ November 2011, S. 102.

AUFDECKUNG, ÜBERRESTE, ‹TOTE DINGE› UND DIE ZEIT DAZWISCHEN

Anmerkungen zum Ausstellen von Performances

Federica Martini

Zwischen 1970 und 1986 besuchte Joseph Beuys regelmässig das Hessische Landesmuseum Darmstadt, um dort den sogenannten *Beuys-Block,* eine auf sieben Räume verteilte Installation von

Werken, Gegenständen aus seinem Leben und Requisiten aus seinen Performances, neu zu ordnen. Nach seinem Tod blieb die Installation als alternde Spur ehemaliger Aktionen unverändert in den Museumsräumen. Für mehr als zwanzig Jahre eingefroren unter dem Zauber der musealen Konservierungsstandards, stand der *Beuys-Block* vor Kurzem infolge der Renovierungspläne des Landesmuseums im Zentrum einer heftigen Debatte: Wird der *Beuys-Block* noch derselbe sein, wenn der Boden und die Wände dieser ortsspezifischen, ursprünglich performativen, aber heute statischen Installation sich verändert haben? Was war die Absicht des Künstlers? Hat sich Beuys' Geste nicht in eine Dokumentation oder eine bedeutende Sammlung verwandelt, nachdem die reguläre Neuordnung der Räume seitens des Künstlers beendet war?

Beuys' frühes Experiment hinsichtlich der (Über-)setzung von Performancerequisiten und -ephemera in einen Museumsraum verweist auf eines der Hauptthemen bei der Ausstellung von Performances, nämlich den Verlust und die Unzugänglichkeit des Live-Acts. Auf diesen Verlust reagiert das Format der Ausstellung traditionell, indem es die Performance mittels ihrer Spuren und Objekte präsentiert, etwa Fotografien, Videos, Requisiten, Anmerkungen, Skizzen und mündliche Interviews, die versuchen, die Absicht der Künstlerinnen und Künstler und den jeweiligen historischen und ästhetischen Kontext zu rekonstruieren.[2] Es handelt sich dabei um einen vermittelten Blick auf die Performance, der teilweise auf der Annahme beruht, dass das Publikum beim Live-Act durch die Präsenz des Künstlers/der Künstlerin einen «direkten, unmittelbaren Zugang» zu Informationen hat.[3]

Wie Thomas MacEvilley in einem Text über James Lee Byars hervorhebt, war der direkte, unmittelbare Zugang für viele Performancekünstlerinnen und -künstler durch ihre Selbst-Ausstellung gewährleistet.[4] Als Byars 1969 eingeladen wurde, in der Antwerpener Galerie Wide White Space auszustellen, «sass er in einem weissen Anzug, einer weissen Maske und einem weissen Hut in einem stuhlartigen Arrangement, mit rotem Samt drapiert in einer ansonsten leeren weissen Galerie» und unterhielt sich auf der Grundlage von Fragen mit den Besuchern. Wie eine Erklärung Byars' von 1978 zeigt, galten seine Präsenz und seine Arbeit als nicht voneinander zu trennen: «Der Tod tilgt alle meine Werke, stellen Sie sie nie wieder aus.»

Dennoch werden Byars' Performances in Ausstellungen heute mit Hilfe dessen gezeigt, was von den historischen ‹Akten› übrig ist, wie dies in der 2009 in Detroit, Milton Keynes und Bern ausgerichte-

ten Retrospektive *I'm Full of Byars* geschah, wo Objekte, Texte und Videos zusammengestellt wurden, um sein Werk zu illustrieren. Doch während es aus kunsthistorischer Sicht verständlich ist, zu versuchen, den Kontext und die Rezeption früherer Performances zu rekonstruieren, ist der Versuch, die Dokumente als einen Ersatz für ‹das eigentliche Werk› zu installieren, eher fragwürdig. Aus dieser letzteren Sicht spielt die Performance jene Rolle, die der Leichnam in Detektivgeschichten spielt, bei denen die Erzählung beginnt, nachdem das Verbrechen bereits begangen wurde. Doch wie Gertrude Stein so geistreich nahelegt, dürfte zwischen der Trauer und der Ermittlung der Tod der Heldin/des Helden die produktivste narrative Quelle sein, wenn wir die Überreste des Verbrechens – des Akts – nicht einfach als Beweise für eine unzugängliche Vergangenheit betrachten, sondern als Werkzeuge für die performative Realisierung der Gegenwart des Romans.[5]

Übertragen auf die Bedingungen des Ausstellens von Performances, beeinflusst diese ‹detektivische Haltung› die Art und Weise, wie wir den Status des Performance-Dokuments betrachten. Wie die Kunsthistorikerin Sophie Delpeux schreibt, ist die Fotografie einer Performance nicht zwangsläufig nur ein Dokument oder eine ‹mise-en-image› einer Geste, sondern selbst ein autonomes Bild.[6] Delpeux verfolgt diese Position ins Jahr 1966 zurück, als Allan Kaprows Performance-Fotografien nicht als ‹Dokumente von Ereignissen› veröffentlicht wurden, sondern als Werkzeuge, um die Einbildungskraft der Betrachter zu steigern.[7]

Darüber hinaus impliziert die Dokumentation von Performances auch das Inszenieren, wie Babette Mangolte im Hinblick auf ihre Zusammenarbeit mit der Tänzerin Trisha Brown schreibt: «Als Filmemacherin wusste ich, dass Tanz und Schnitte nicht zusammenpassen und dass eine ununterbrochene Kamerabewegung die einzige Möglichkeit war, das Vier-Minuten-Solo zu filmen. Das hatte ich gelernt, indem ich mir Fred Astaires und Gene Kellys Tanznummern ansah. Irgendwie muss die Filmkamera den hypnotischen Blick und die völlige Konzentration des faszinierten Betrachters evozieren, und wenn man das Solo in kleine, aus verschiedenen Kamerapositionen aufgenommene Abschnitte zerlegen würde, würde dies die Konzentration und die Ehrfurcht des Zuschauers unterbrechen.»[8]

Das jedoch impliziert, dass die Fotografien der Performances «als (oder vielleicht durch) die Performance produziert werden können (statt [als Fotografien] von der Performance)»[9]. Dieses Anliegen animierte Vito Acconcis *Photo-Piece* (1969), das aus einem Spaziergang in der Stadt bestand, bei dem er eine Kamera in den Händen hielt, jedes Mal, wenn er mit den Augen blinzelte, ein Bild machte und auf diese Weise Bilder produzierte, die gleichzeitig ein Beweis für den Akt und der Akt selbst sind.[10]

Sowohl Mangoltes hypnotische Kamerabewegungen als auch Acconcis Aufnahmen als Reaktion auf seinen blinzelnden Blick gehen über eine einfache Aufzeichnung einer Geste hinaus, da die Aufzeich-

nungsmedien und die Positionen, die sie gegenüber dem Akt einnehmen, eine nicht ganz getreue Übersetzung desselben darstellen. Sie zeigen fast dieselbe Sache, fast denselben Akt, aber in diesem Bruchteil zwischen der ursprünglichen Geste und ihrer (Wieder-)herstellung durch Video und Fotografie produzieren sie neue, autonome Bilder.

In der vom Künstler Mike Kelley kuratierten Ausstellung *Playing with Dead Things* (1993, Arnheim, neuinszeniert 2004 in der Tate Modern, London) verdichtete sich dieses Gefühl eines flüchtigen Erkennens und eines mehrdeutigen Status in der Idee des Unheimlichen, welches impliziert, dass vergangene Erinnerungen von einer aktuellen Begegnung und der Unsicherheit darüber ausgelöst werden, ob der Gegenstand belebt oder unbelebt ist. Eine ähnliche Ungewissheit angesichts der Objekte und Bilder, die Performances dokumentieren, wurde 2008 durch die Ausstellung *Not to Play with Dead Things* in der Villa Arson in Nizza auf die Probe gestellt. Die Ausstellung stellte die Abhängigkeit der Requisiten von performativen Akten in Frage, indem sie sie im Ausstellungsraum dekontextualisierte.[11] Die kuratorische Strategie konzentrierte sich auf eine Neulektüre von John Bocks Einzelausstellung im FRAC Provence-Alpes-Côte d'Azur (2005), wo die Inszenierung und der Inhalt der Ausstellung von den Überresten der Performance bestimmt wurden, die dort während der Eröffnung des Kunstzentrums stattgefunden hatte. Auf der Grundlage der Annahme, dass Performance ein gewisses Mass an ‹Aktualisieren, Umschreiben und Neuinszenieren›[12] beinhaltet, ging es bei *Not to Play with Dead Things* um eine Diskussion der ästhetischen Position von Performance-Gegenständen ‹nach dem Akt›. «Sind sie bedeutungslose Gespenster?», fragt Kokurator Eric Mangion. Sollen sie «die Energie der Aktion wiederherstellen, aus der sie hervorgegangen sind»? Widersprechen sie der Unmittelbarkeit der Performance?[13]

Ausser mit der Hypothese, Performance-Objekte seien autonom oder etwas zwischen Performance und Objekten Angesiedeltes, arbeitete *Not to Play with Dead Things* auch mit «der missbräuchlichen Verwendung historischer Performance-Dokumente als kreative[m] Prozess». Wie die Kunsthistorikerin Amelia Jones bemerkt hat, werden Performances auch immer «durch den Filter der Erinnerung» betrachtet. Der begrenzte Zugang zum Live-Act impliziert zwei Formen von Wissen: Beteiligung für die Zeugen und, später einmal, die Interpretation anhand von Dokumenten und der Oral History für die Historiker.[14] Das Wissen der Zeugen und das der Historiker sind für Jones gleichermassen legitim, auch aufgrund der Art und Weise, wie Spuren von Performances aufbewahrt werden, nämlich, schreibt Jessica Santone, als «etwas, das erneut gespielt, gelesen oder interpretiert werden muss, um erlebt zu werden»[15]. Indem sie Performance nicht nur als einen einzigartigen Live-Act begriffen, sondern als ein Event, das dazu einlädt, wiederholt und re-präsentiert zu werden, schlugen Künstlerinnen wie Tania Bruguera und Catherine Sullivan Werke vor, die auf der Verschiebung historischer Dokumentationen in verschiedenen zeit- und ortsspezifischen Situationen beruhen.[16]

Diese Position wurde 2001 in der von Jens Hoffmann kuratierten Ausstellung *A Little Bit of History Repeated* in den Berliner Kunst-Werken zu einem kuratorischen Statement. Die Ausstellung versammelte Performances aus den 1960ern und 1970ern – Re-Enactments von historischen Präsentationen, die von Künstlerinnen und Künstlern aus jüngeren Generationen neu interpretiert wurden oder ihnen als Inspirationsquelle für neue Werke dienten.[17] Das auf einige Tage konzentrierte Projekt historisierte nicht die ausgewählten Performances, sondern eine bestimmte Art, den Ausstellungsraum performativ zu nutzen, etwa die, die man in der *Between*-Serie in der Kunsthalle Düsseldorf von 1969 bis 1973 erleben konnte.[18] Dieses von Karl Ruhrberg und Jürgen Harten konzipierte und geleitete Projekt der Kunsthalle bestand aus einer Reihe von Einladungen an Künstler wie Tony Morgan, den Ausstellungsraum zwischen den Ausstellungen zu nutzen, die offizieller Bestandteil des Programms dieser Institution waren.

Während Jens Hoffmanns Ausstellung auf einer Gegenüberstellung von Dokumenten und ihren performativen Interpretationen beruhte, hinterfragte die *Between*-Serie die Möglichkeit, durch eine Störung des räumlichen institutionellen Diskurses und Zeitrahmens einen Raum für Performance zu schaffen. Betrachtet man *Between* als eine Form kultureller Produktion und schreibt diese Serie in eine kuratorische Perspektive ein, so wirft die Performance Fragen hinsichtlich der Zeitlichkeit der Ausstellung auf, jenseits der blossen Positionierung von Gesten, Objekten und Bildern in ein historisches Vor und Nach dem Akt und jenseits der Dauer. Die Gewohnheit, Performances im Rückblick zu zeigen, wird hier durch die Idee konterkariert, Performance als tatsächliche Präsenz im Ausstellungsraum zu konstruieren.

Eine Reaktion hierauf ist die zunehmende Verbreitung des Festivalformats in Ausstellungsräumen, um eine Plattform zu schaffen, bei der das Publikum sich an dem Live-Act beteiligen kann und die performative Geste in einer ortsspezifischen Situation ein Enactment oder Reenactment erfahren kann. Nichtsdestotrotz bleiben auf diese Weise die Performance-Szene und das Ausstellen von Dokumenten überwiegend getrennt voneinander. Zwei neuere Ausstellungsprojekte versuchten über diese Unterscheidung hinauszugehen, indem sie sich auf den Zusammenhang zwischen dem Dokumentieren und der kuratorischen Praxis innerhalb des Ausstellungsraums konzentrierten.

2011 präsentierte das Mamco (Musée d'art moderne et contemporain de Genève) *Hôtel Sarkis'* eine ‹paradoxe Retrospektive›, die eine Auswahl von Sarkis, Werken zeigte, welche eine Hommage darstellte und Schriftsteller, Maler, Musiker und andere Kulturvertreter aus der Vergangenheit evozierte oder sich offen von ihnen inspirieren liess.[19] Die meisten davon sind posthume Interpretationen, die auf Sarkis' Enttäuschung angesichts der Ausstellungen von Künstlern wie Marcel Broodthaers und Joseph Beuys nach ihrem Tod zurückgehen. Diese Enttäuschung inspirierte ihn dazu, Christian Bernard, den Kurator

und Mamco-Direktor, in seiner Abwesenheit eine retrospektive Deutung seines Werks vornehmen zu lassen und seine Ausstellung erst am Tag vor der Eröffnung zu ‹entdecken›.[20] Christian Bernard stellte sich vor, sein Museum sei ein Hotel oder eine Unterkunft für Werke, die zuvor international in verschiedenen Ausstellungskontexten installiert gewesen waren, und präsentierte die Werke in der Ausstellung auf eine Weise, die Sarkis’ Prozess des «Evozierens, Umschreibens, Aktualisierens und Neuinszenierens» ähnelte. Gedacht als mögliche Aufführung von Sarkis’ Originalpartitur, entwarf die Ausstellung die Museumswände mit plötzlichen ‹Farbbeulen› neu, die aus Gemälden stammten, auf die er in seinen Werken Bezug nahm. Ein roter Faden durchzog und organisierte den chromatischen Raum der Ausstellung, wo sich die kuratorische Hauptstrategie durch die Verwendung von Wiederholung und Synchronizität aus einem sorgfältigen Umgang mit Rück- und Vorausblicken entwickelte, eine Entscheidung, die sowohl den Erinnerungsaspekt der Werke verwirklichte als auch diese und ihre unterschiedlichen Zeitlichkeiten durch die Ausstellungslinse heraufbeschwor. Statt einen Verlust zu dokumentieren, wie dies so viele Retrospektiven tun, setzte sich *Hôtel Sarkis* mit der Idee auseinander, dass Erinnerung performativ ist, und produzierte letztlich (kuratorisches) Wissen, statt an die Vergangenheit zu erinnern.

Eine andere Methode, dies zu tun, besteht darin, «archivarische Forschung mit der Praxis zu verbinden», wie etwa in *If I Can’t Dance I Don’t Want to Be Part of Your Revolution*, einer Plattform, die 2005 von den Kuratorinnen Frederique Bergholtz, Annie Fletcher und Tanja Elstgeest gegründet wurde, um «die Entwicklung und Typologie von Performance und Performativität in der zeitgenössischen Kunst» zu erkunden.[21] Im Rückgriff auf Hanne Darbovens Definition ihres Werks als Kontemplation, unterbrochen von Aktion, basiert *If I Can’t Dance* auf einer Kombination von Forschung und Produktion von Zweijahresprogrammen, die in öffentlichen Situationen präsentiert werden, welche sich «genau durch ihre Durchführung bei dem jeweiligen Ereignis und an dem jeweiligen Ort» entwickeln. Alle Stadien in dem Programm, Forschung, der Akt des Einrichtens der Szene, die Einbeziehung des Publikums und die Wissensproduktion, befinden sich gleichermassen auf den Agenden der Künstler, Forscher und Kuratoren. Im Mittelpunkt des Interesses stehen hier nicht mehr der Status von Live-Acts, miteinander verbundene Dokumente und Objekte, sondern die Umstände, die es einem kuratorischen Projekt ermöglichen, eine Plattform der Kulturproduktion zu werden. Die Übersetzung visueller Poesie, ein Akt, der die Transposition des Textes unter den Gesichtspunkten Form und Bedeutung verhandelt, verlangt ebenfalls diese Art der Positionierung zwischen einer Beachtung des visuellen Formats (wie man übersetzen soll) und der Auswahl der Bedeutungen, die sowohl den Worten als auch den Formen zugrunde liegen (was man übersetzen soll), die die Präsentation der Performance in

einem Ausstellungskontext prägen. Sowohl Lyrik-Übersetzung als auch Performance-Ausstellungen setzen sich mit dieser Idee auseinander, wie viel Verlust die ursprüngliche künstlerische oder poetische Geste verkraften kann, um Zeugnis von dem vergangenen Ereignis abzulegen.

Die andere Option, so schlägt es das Projekt *If I Can't Dance* vor, besteht darin, sich die Performance-Ausstellung als eine Situation vorzustellen, an der man teilnehmen kann. In dieser Hinsicht wird Dokumentation eines der Elemente in der Ausstellung/Situation, wo Wissen nicht nur repräsentiert, sondern produziert wird. Dies erinnert irgendwie an Marshall McLuhans Überzeugung, aufgezeichneter Jazz sei so schal wie die Zeitungen von gestern.[22] Dieses Statement erklärt die schwierige Versöhnung Rückschau haltender und vorausschauender Blicke in einer einzigartigen Präsenz. Gleichwohl produzieren die Zeitungen von gestern per definitionem ein zeitspezifisches Wissen, das, so die Annahme, für die Dauer eines spezifischen Tages gelten soll. In diesem besonderen Zeitrahmen ist das Hauptziel keine Historisierung, sondern das Performen von Geschichte in einer begrenzten Gegenwart, innerhalb eines fortgesetzten, nichtlinearen Diskurses, der dazu bestimmt ist, sein Format am nächsten Tag einmal mehr neu zu verhandeln.

1   Gertrude Stein, ‹What Are Masterpieces and Why Are There So Few of Them› (1940), in: Lawrence S. Rainey (Hg.), *Modernism: An Anthology*, London: Blackwell Publishing, 2005, S. 413.

2   Siehe Barbara Clausen (Hg.), *After the Act: The (Re)presentation of Performance Art*, Ausst.-Kat., Wien: MUMOK, 2005.

3   Amelia Jones, ‹Presence in Absentia›: Experiencing Performance as Documentation, in: *Art Journal*, Bd. 56, Nr. 4, 1997, S. 11–18.

4   Thomas MacEvilley, ‹James Lee Byars – A Study of Posterity›, in: Susanne Friedli, Matthias Frehner (Hg.), in: *I'm Full of Byars – A Homage*, Ausst.-Kat., Bielefeld: Kerber Verlag, 2009, S. 105.

5   G. Stein, a. a. O.

6   Sophie Delpeux, *Le corps-caméra. Le performer et son image*, Paris, Editions Textuel, 2010, S. 17.

7   Ebd. Siehe auch Allan Kaprow, *Assemblages, Environments and Happenings*, New York: Harry N. Abrams, Inc., 1966.

8   Babette Mangolte, ‹On the Making of Water Motor, A Dance by Trisha Brown filmed by Babette Mangolte›, unveröffentlichter Aufsatz, 2003.

9   Philip Auslander, ‹The Performativity of Performance Documentation›, in: *Performance Art Journal*, Nr. 84, 2006, S. 1–10.

10   Siehe auch Delpeux, a. a. O.

11   Eric Mangion, Marie de Brugerolle (Hg.), *Not to Play with Dead Things*, Ausst.-Kat., Zürich: JRP Ringier, 2009.

12   Richard Martel, ‹Performance›, in: Eric Mangion, Marie de Brugerolle, a. a. O., S. 14.

13   Ebd.

14   Jones, a. a. O.

15   Jessica Santone, ‹Marina Abramovićs Seven Easy Pieces: Critical Documentation Strategies for Preserving Art's History›, in: *Leonardo*, Bd. 41, Nr. 2, 2008, S. 147–151.

16   Siehe Tania Bruguera, *Tribute to Ana Mendieta* (1985–1996); Catherine Sullivan, *'Tis a Pity She's a Fluxus Whore* (2003).

17   Jens Hoffmann (Hg.), *A Little Bit of History Repeated*, Ausst.-Kat., Paris: Editions Valerio, 2001.

18   Renate Buschmann (Hg.), *Chronik einer Nicht-Ausstellung. Between 1969–73 in der Kunsthalle Düsseldorf*, Berlin: Dietrich Reimer Verlag, 2007.

19   Siehe Christian Bernard, *Hôtel Sarkis*, 2011. Aufgerufen im Januar 2012. http://www.mamco.ch

20   Samuel Schellenberg, ‹Sarkis, chambres avec vue›, in: *Le Courrier*, 19. Februar 2011. Aufgerufen im Januar 2012. www.lecourrier.ch

21   http://www.ificantdance.org/. Aufgerufen im Januar 2012.

22   Marshall McLuhan, *Understanding Media*, New York: McGraw-Hill, 1964 (dt.: *Die magischen Kanäle*, Dresden, Basel: Verlag der Kunst, 1994).

STIMMEN IN DER AUSSTELLUNG

Barnaby Drabble

In einer Szene von Woody Allens Film *Play It Again, Sam* besucht Allan Felix, die Hauptfigur (von Woody Allen selbst gespielt), im verzweifelten Bemühen, Frauen zu treffen, ein Kunstmuseum. Vor einem Gemälde von Jackson Pollock bleibt er stehen und fängt nervös ein Gespräch mit einer jungen Frau an, die das Bild betrachtet.

Felix: Ist das nicht ein schöner Jackson Pollock?

Junge Frau: Ja.

Felix: Was sagt Ihnen das Bild?

Junge Frau: Es stellt erneut die Negativität des Universums dar, die widerliche, einsame Leere der Existenz. Das Nichts. Das Dilemma des Menschen, der gezwungen ist, in einer öden, gottverlassenen Ewigkeit zu leben wie eine winzige flackernde Flamme in einer ungeheuren Leere, in der es nichts gibt als Verfall, Grauen und Erniedrigung. All das ist eine unnütze, trostlose Zwangsjacke in einem schwarzen, absurden Kosmos.

Felix: Was machen Sie am Samstagabend?

Junge Frau: Mich umbringen.

Felix: Und am Freitagabend?

Ein zentrales Motiv in dem über 200-jährigen Nachdenken über das Verhältnis von Kunst und Betrachter ist die Frage nach der Möglichkeit von Bildinhalten – «Was sagt Ihnen das Bild?» –, geht sie doch von der Prämisse aus, dass Kunstwerke und die Ausstellungen, in denen sie zu sehen sind, uns etwas zu sagen haben. Im Laufe dieser Geschichte hat sich die Erwartung ausgebildet, dass sich die Kunsterfahrung von unserer Alltagserfahrung deutlich unterscheide. In anderen Zusammenhängen schauen wir Dinge an und akzeptieren sie als stumm. Funktionale oder natürliche Objekte sind nämlich von dieser Art des Umgangs mit ihnen ausgenommen – wir würden nicht einen Milchkarton anschauen und sagen: «Ich verstehe ihn nicht», oder beim Betrachten eines Baums die Frage äussern: «Was bedeutet er nur?» Wir können somit feststellen, dass die Ausstellung einen transformativen Prozess einleitet, innerhalb dessen Dinge Bedeutungen erhalten, und dass dieser Prozess mit einer bezeichnenden und pädagogischen Funktion verknüpft ist, die sich im Laufe einer langen Geschichte herausgebildet hat. Die Ausstellung ist also ein Ort, an dem wir zur Teilnahme an einem mentalen Spiel aufgefordert werden, bei dem wir uns vorstellen, dass Objekte zu uns sprechen.

Insbesondere in den letzten fünfzig Jahren wurden die physischen Eigenschaften des Ausstellungsraums dahingehend entwickelt, dass sie diesem ungewöhnlichen Zweck noch konsequenter dienen: Der ritualisierte Raum der Ausstellung – ein heller, ruhiger, weisser Raum mit getrennt voneinander präsentierten Objekten an den Wänden und auf dem Boden – fungiert als Bühne für einen stummen Austausch.[1] Natürlich ist der Begriff des sprechenden Objekts bloss eine metaphorische Redewendung, aber eine aufschlussreiche, wenn wir uns klarmachen, wie wichtig er für unser Verständnis unserer Rolle

als Betrachter in Kunstausstellungen ist. Nehmen wir das Faktum, dass Ausstellungen im buchstäblichen Sinn des Wortes nicht sprechen können, und konfrontieren es mit der Tatsache, dass wir uns dennoch angesprochen fühlen, dann stehen wir vor einem interessanten Dilemma, das die Frage aufwirft: Wessen Stimmen hören wir eigentlich in der Ausstellung?

Diese Frage steht im Mittelpunkt einer seit Langem in der Kunstwelt geführten Debatte über die Machtverhältnisse zwischen Künstlern, Institutionen, Kritikern und Kuratoren. Jeder dieser Akteure ist auf verschiedenen Ebenen an der Produktion, Vermarktung und Vermittlung einer Ausstellung beteiligt. Doch so wie sich die Vorstellungen von Kunst und ihre ökonomischen Bedingungen verändert haben, so haben sich auch diese Verhältnisse geändert. Angesichts dieser Machtverschiebungen stellen sich nun die Fragen: Wer spricht für wen, und wessen Stimme ist die lauteste?

Auf dem Höhepunkt der Moderne wurden grosse Kunstwerke als selbstbezüglich und autonom verstanden und von einer Kunstkritik begleitet, die ihren künstlerischen Wert ausschliesslich auf die stilistischen und formalen Qualitäten zurückführte.[2] Grosse Künstler wurden als intuitive und genialische Schöpfer verstanden, die sich weit über der Ebene der profanen Dinge des Alltags bewegten und eben durch ihre Werke sprachen. Wenn wir das unbesehen glauben, dann sind die Stimmen in der Ausstellung *per se* die der Künstler.

Doch die Künstler selbst, ebenso wie Kritiker und in letzter Zeit auch Kuratoren, wandten sich schliesslich gegen diese Vorstellung. Darunter waren jene, die eine Verbindung von Kunst und Leben anstrebten und für die die Produktion von Kunst Teil einer breiteren gesellschaftlichen und politischen Wirklichkeit ist und wiederum auf diese einwirkt. Eine Folge dieses Einstellungswandels war, dass die Kunstinstitutionen genauer untersucht und ihre angeblich neutrale Rolle in Frage gestellt wurde. Blickt man auf die Museen des 19. Jahrhunderts mit ihren pädagogischen und kanonisierenden Imperativen[3] und auf die des 20. Jahrhunderts mit ihren kaum kaschierten Verbindungen zum Kunstmarkt, liegt es auf der Hand, danach zu fragen, inwieweit heutige Kunstmuseen und Galerien immer noch unseren Geschmack kontrollieren und unsere Ansichten über das gesellschaftlich Akzeptable prägen. Manche Theoretiker meinen hierzu, dass die Ausstellung als die Stimme der Institution verstanden werden kann[4] und dass diese Stimme in den meisten Fällen eher disziplinierend denn emanzipatorisch wirkt.[5]

Im Mittelpunkt dieser Debatten stehen Überlegungen zur veränderten Rolle des Kurators. Diese zuvor eher unbedeutende Figur teilt sich inzwischen mit dem Künstler die Bühne des Geschehens. Die bekanntesten Kuratoren werden als grosse Persönlichkeiten und Königsmacher in der Kunstwelt betrachtet; ihre Gesichter erscheinen auf den Titelblättern der Kunstzeitschriften, ihre Meinungen über Kunst

werden öffentlich debattiert, ihre Auswahl der Werke für Ausstellungen wirkt sich auf die Verkäufe der Künstler aus und beeinflusst die Sammler. Manche Kommentatoren sind der Meinung, dass die Kuratoren inzwischen wichtiger geworden sind als die Kritiker, die früher die Definitionsmacht über die Kunst ihrer Zeit besassen. Andere gehen noch weiter und behaupten, der Kurator habe sogar dem Künstler seine Bedeutung entwendet und die Kunstwerke in Ausstellungen würden zunehmend zur blossen Illustration der bevorzugten Themen und Theorien des Kurators benutzt.[6]

Für viele lässt sich der Wendepunkt zu dieser Entwicklung Ende der 1960er Jahre festmachen, als sich mit Harald Szeemanns *When Attitudes Become Form* in der Kunsthalle Bern oder Seth Siegelaubs *January Show* in New York, die beide neue Richtungen in der Konzeptkunst beleuchteten, experimentelle Ausstellungen durchzusetzen begannen. Bei diesen Beispielen, in denen sich die Kunst der Zeit widerspiegelt, war die Konzeption der Ausstellung ebenso wichtig für das Verständnis der Kunst wie die Kunst selbst. Die Folgen dieser Entwicklung sind offensichtlich: Wo der Kurator eine kreative Rolle einnimmt, erlangt die Ausstellung den Status eines Metakunstwerks. In solchen Situationen gesellt sich die Stimme des Kurators zum wachsenden Chor der Stimmen in der Ausstellung und vermag im Extremfall – bei mangelndem Feingespür – die anderen Stimmen zu übertönen.

Angesichts all dieser angesprochenen Entwicklungen lässt sich die Frage, wessen Stimme wir eigentlich beim Besuch der Ausstellung hören, nicht leicht beantworten. Und noch schwerer erscheint eine Beantwortung der Frage, was eine gute Ausstellung ausmacht und welchen Tonfall sie annehmen könnte. Und zwar deshalb, weil Ausstellungen wie gesagt mehrstimmig aufgebaut sind und nicht nur die Objekte sprechen, sondern auch ihr jeweiliges Umfeld spricht. Ausserdem kommen zu den Stimmen der Künstler diejenigen der Kuratoren und der Institutionen hinzu, in denen sie arbeiten. Insofern können Ausstellungen von Harmonien oder Misstönen geprägt sein, und die Beurteilung ihrer Qualität erfordert genaues Hinhören; man muss ein Ohr dafür haben, wie sie zusammenklingen, sich gegenseitig ergänzen, erweitern oder widersprechen. Wenn wir genau genug hinhören, nehmen wir eine andauernde Folge sich überschneidender Debatten wahr. Die Sensibilität eines Künstlers für die Stimme der Institution kann ihn zu einem kritischen Widerspruch oder einem spielerischen Echo bewegen. Kuratorische Entscheidungen können künstlerische Positionen miteinander in Dialog bringen oder die Prozesse hinter den Objekten mittels paralleler Kommentierung deutlich machen.

Doch die Vorstellung einer allzu grossen kritischen Distanz zu den Stimmen, die wir in der Ausstellung hören, können wir uns nicht erlauben. Schliesslich erinnert uns die Frage «Was sagt das Bild *Ihnen?*» daran, dass wir ebenfalls präsent sind. Wenn wir uns entschliessen, diese Frage zu beantworten, selbst im Stillen und nur für uns, dann ist

eine der Stimmen in der Ausstellung unsere eigene. Ob wir eine Ausstellung allein besuchen oder mit anderen, die Gespräche während des Besuchs oder danach haben eine besondere Qualität, da wir erschliessen wollen, was uns zu den Schlussfolgerungen über das Gesehene führt. Wenn wir unsere Meinung zur Kunst begründen, auch uns selbst gegenüber, dann beschäftigen wir uns im Zeichen der persönlichen Ästhetik plötzlich mit einem viel grösseren Thema. Wir fangen nämlich an, unsere Subjektivität zu trainieren; wir konstruieren und verteidigen eine eigene, besondere Rolle gegenüber dem im Museum Erlebten. Und zwar deshalb, weil man bei der Beantwortung der Frage «Was sagt Ihnen das Bild?» mindestens ebenso viel über sich selbst sagt wie über die zur Diskussion stehenden Kunstwerke.

Von den vielen Stimmen in der Ausstellung wird zurzeit am wenigsten über diejenige des Publikums diskutiert. Wenn aber das vergangene Jahrzehnt als das goldene Zeitalter des Kurators erscheint, dann mag das nächste dem Ausstellungsbesucher gehören. Diese Prognose mag als weiterer Schritt weg von einer Anerkennung der Schlüsselrolle des Künstlers verstanden oder als ein Ruf nach Populismus missverstanden werden. Solche Risiken bestehen, ändern aber nichts an der Tatsache, dass eine echte Anerkennung der Fähigkeit des Publikums zu sprechen und nicht bloss zuzuhören radikaler ist, als es auf den ersten Blick erscheinen mag. Weit davon entfernt, die Bedeutung der Künstler zu schmälern, unterstützt sie letztlich sogar die Bedeutung ihrer Werke. Das Kunstwerk bleibt der entscheidende Faktor für die Qualität sowohl der Ausstellung als auch des Gesprächs über sie, gerade weil die besten Werke, auch wenn sie erklärtermassen etwas zu sagen haben und hierfür neue Sprachen einführen, es doch bewusst vermeiden, alles offenzulegen oder sich selbst auszudeuten. Genau aus diesem Grund wird zeitgenössischer Kunst so oft ein elitäres Denken oder absichtliche Unverständlichkeit unterstellt, was auf einem elementaren Missverständnis beruht.

Es ist verständlich, dass die Leute die Dinge gerne erklärt bekommen und dass Kunst manchmal das frustrierende Gefühl provozieren kann, nicht zu wissen, was etwas bedeuten *soll*. Doch sollte dies nur als Kritik an einer Ausstellung gelten dürfen, deren erklärtes Ziel es ist, Wissen oder Fachkompetenz direkt zu vermitteln. «Warum hat Ihnen die Ausstellung nicht gefallen?», fragt jemand. «Ich habe nicht verstanden, was der Künstler sagen wollte», kommt als Antwort. «Warum hat sie Ihnen gefallen?» – «Weil ich das Gefühl hatte, dass sie mir etwas zu sagen hat.» Wortwechsel dieser Art mögen auf die Bedeutung jenes Spiels zurückweisen, auf das wir uns im Umfeld des Museums oder der Galerie freiwillig einlassen: Wir stellen uns vor, dass Objekte zu uns sprechen. Dieses Spiel gut zu spielen heisst, in erster Linie in Gefühle zu investieren, in assoziative Vorstellungen, und eine Bereitschaft aufzubauen, auf Bedeutungen zu spekulieren, die sich als nützlich und schliesslich auch lehrreich erweisen können.

Wenn wir die Rolle des Kurators im Lichte dieser Vorstellungen betrachten, wird einerseits deutlich, dass die Ausstellung als Meta-kunstwerk ein ganzes Feld interessanter Parameter bietet, mit denen das Spiel der sprechenden Objekte aufgebaut und experimentell weiterentwickelt werden kann. Andererseits liegt im darin enthaltenen Konzept des Kurators als Autor auch eine Gefahr, denn die Vorstellung, dass die kuratorische Konzeption ein Werkzeug zum Verständnis der Ausstellung sei, ist genauso fragwürdig wie die Prämisse, dass die Intention des Künstlers das Kunstwerk erkläre. All dies sind Stimmen in der Ausstellung, doch die ganze Breite ihres Beutungsspektrums wird eingeschränkt, wenn eine behauptet, mit grösserer Autorität zu sprechen als die anderen. In der Anerkennung der Stimme des Publikums steckt daher das Potenzial, gerade das Gegenteil einer Minderung der Kunsterfahrung zu bewirken. Verlangt ist eine Anerkennung der Komplexität der Erfahrung von Kunst und der Notwendigkeit, auf vorgefasste Meinungen zu verzichten. Auf Ausstellungen bezogen heisst das: Vermittlung versteht sich am besten als die Aufgabe, der Stimme des Publikums Geltung zu verschaffen.[7]

Gekürtzte Fassung. Erstveröffentlichung: *Swiss Exhibition Award 2009*. Hg. Bundesamt für Kultur/Julius Bär Stiftung, Bern 2010.

1   Brian O'Doherty, *Inside the White Cube: The Ideology of the Gallery Space*, Santa Monica: Lapis Press 1976 (dt.: Brian O'Doherty, *In der weißen Zelle. Inside the White Cube*, hg. und mit einem Nachwort versehen von Markus Bruederlin, Berlin: Merve Verlag 1996).

2   Prominent vertreten u. a. von Clement Greenberg. Vgl. Clement Greenberg (1939), ‹Avantgarde and Kitsch›, in: *Art and Culture: Collected Essays*, Boston: Beacon Press 1961, S. 3–21.

3   Tony Bennett, *The Birth of the Museum. History, Theory, Politics*. London: Routledge 1995.

4   Bruce Ferguson, ‹Exhibition Rhetorics: Material speech and utter sense›, in: Greenberg, R. Ferguson, B., und Nairne, S. (Hg.), *Thinking about Exhibitions*, London: Routledge 1996, S. 175–191.

5   Oliver Marchart, ‹Die Institution spricht›, in: Jaschke, B., Martinz-Turek, C., und Sternfeld, N. Hg. *Wer spricht? Autorität und Autorschaft in Ausstellungen*. Wien: Verlag Turia + Kant 2005, S. 34–58.

6   Rebecca Gordon Nesbitt, ‹Harnessing the means of production›, in: Ekeberg, J. (Hg.), *New Institutionalism, Verksted no. 1*. Oslo: Office for Contemporary Art Norway 2003, S. 59–88.

7   Die Schwierigkeiten, die damit verbunden sind, liegen auf der Hand. Oliver Marchart geht so weit, diesen Aspekt des Kuratierens als ‹Organisation des Unmöglichen› zu bezeichnen. Vgl. Oliver Marchart, ‹The Curatorial Function – Organizing the Ex/position›, in: Drabble, B., und Richter, D. (Hg.), *Curating Critique*, www.on-curating.org, issue 09/11, S. 43–47.

WENN DER WAHRHEITS-DISKURS AUF DAS SPEKTAKEL TRIFFT

Dorothee Richter

Dieser Essay wird einige der historischen Perspektiven, die heutige Kulturpraktiken beeinflussen, einer erneuten Betrachtung unterziehen und dabei die Frage stellen: Woher rührt der Konflikt zwischen den bildenden Künsten und dem Theater, und in welche Richtung bewegt er sich?

Was Präsentationsfragen betrifft, fand in jüngerer Zeit eine zunehmende wechselseitige Angleichung von Theater- und Ausstellungspraktiken statt. Belege hierfür sind die Einbeziehung von Szenografie und Theaterkulissen in Ausstellungen und Installationen und die von Videoprojektionen in Theaterproduktionen. Dies führte in beiden Fällen zu einem weitgehenden Verschwinden dessen, was man als eine strenge Narration bezeichnen könnte. Nach einigen theoretischen Anmerkungen werde ich hierfür vier Beispiele als Fallstudien heranziehen: erstens die Arbeit der Fluxuskünstler, zweitens diejenige Christoph Schlingensiefs, drittens die von Spartacus Chetwynd und schließlich eine in die Ausstellung *Spill the Beans* integrierte Theaterszene von Renata Burckhardt.

Zur Skizzierung der theoretischen Prinzipien beziehe ich mich auf die Unterschiede, die Kant zwischen verschiedenen Gebieten in den Künsten festgestellt hat. Kant setzte sich nicht nur ausführlich mit den Künsten auseinander, sondern präsentierte sie auch in einem ganz neuen Licht. Aus Terry Eagletons Sicht lieferte Kants Theorie den ideologischen Hintergrund für das im Entstehen begriffene Bürgertum. Er tat dies nicht nur, indem er das Sinnliche vom Rationalen trennte und so eine Reibung institutionalisierte oder benannte, die der modernen Subjektivität zugrunde liegt, sondern auch mit seiner Definition des Subjekts im absoluten Gegensatz zum Objekt, durch die er das Subjekt von seiner materiellen Existenz entfremdete. Nach diesem Konzept ist das Subjekt autonom und bleibt auf seltsame Weise allein: Das Subjekt ist kein Phänomen in der Welt, sondern eine transzendentale Perspektive auf sie.[1] In den Worten Terry Eagletons: «Wenn die Freiheit aufblühen und das Subjekt sich erweitern soll, indem es die Herrschaft über die Dinge ausübt und ihnen seine unauslöschliche Präsenz aufprägt, dann ist die systematische Kenntnis der Welt von entscheidender Bedeutung, und diese muss auch die Kenntnis anderer Subjekte umfassen.»[2]

Doch dadurch wird das Subjekt in eine einsame Position versetzt, und interessanterweise ist es der Bereich der Ästhetik, der diesen entfremdeten Subjekten eine Form von Gemeinschaft bietet. Um nochmals Eagleton zu zitieren: «Was uns als Subjekte zusammenbringt, ist nicht Wissen, sondern eine unbeschreibliche Wechselseitigkeit des Gefühls, und dies ist sicher einer der Hauptgründe dafür, dass *das Ästhetische* im bürgerlichen Denken solch eine zentrale Rolle spielt. Denn die alarmierende Wahrheit ist, dass in einer sozialen Ordnung, die durch Klassenunterschiede und Wettbewerb gekennzeichnet ist, Menschen schließlich hier, und zwar nur hier, in einer intimen Gemeinschaft zusammengehören können.»[3]

Außerdem war das Konzept des künstlerischen Genies in Kants Sicht an die Subjektivität gebunden, da er den Geniebegriff aus den

Fähigkeiten eines ewigen Schöpfers herleitet, ihn jedoch in seiner Darstellung zur Funktion des künstlerischen Subjekts werden lässt. Diese Kreativität lässt sich auch auf die Erfordernisse für einen unabhängigen Unternehmergeist zurückführen. Kant sah die Existenz eines wichtigen Bruchs in der Subjektivität: das Sinnliche, das mit den Künsten und dem Körper zusammenhängt, und das Vernünftige, das mit dem Rationalen und dem Geist zusammenhängt. Dieser Widerspruch wurde später von Adorno und Horkheimer problematisiert, die darauf hinwiesen, dass sich der Geist aus dieser Sicht stets im Widerspruch zur Existenz des Körpers befinden und diesen einsperren werde.[4]

Dieser sehr kurze theoretische Exkurs wird als Hintergrund fungieren, der zeigt, wie und auf welche Weise die bildenden Künste und das Theater seit der Aufklärung schon durch ihr historisches Konzept verortet sind. Kant zufolge gehören beide zum Sinnlichen, doch es ist offenkundig, dass die bildenden Künste dem Konzept einer mimetischen rationalen Wahrheit näher stehen und das Theater den sinnlichen und verdrängten Vergnügungen und Lüsten des Körpers. In der bürgerlichen Gesellschaft kam Theaterstücken die starke pädagogische Funktion zu, diese verstörenden Lüste des Körpers zu unterdrücken, und dies impliziert, dass man die *Moral* aus Theaterstücken lernen muss. So betrachtet stehen also zwei Prinzipien, nämlich jenes des Theaters und jenes der bildenden Künste, auf dem Spiel, wenn wir den Konflikt zwischen Theaterpraktiken und bildenden Künsten seit den 1960ern diskutieren. Oder um es noch drastischer auszudrücken: Was passiert, wenn das Spektakel auf den Wahrheitsdiskurs trifft? Selbst wenn die Praktiken, die sich im Theater und in den bildenden Künsten manifestieren, fast dieselben zu sein scheinen, haben sie doch einen unterschiedlichen Kontext, und dies wiederum impliziert, dass es mehr Unterschiede gibt, als es auf den ersten Blick scheinen mag.

Die folgende vereinfachte Matrix skizziert diese Unterschiede ausgehend von einer historischen Aufklärungsperspektive wie derjenigen Kants. Sie nimmt sich außerdem die Freiheit, Peter Bürgers Kategorien aus seiner berühmten *Theorie der Avantgarde* (Rezeption, Produktion und Gebrauch) auf das Gebiet der Gattungen des Theaters und der bildenden Kunst zu übertragen.[5] Die dritte Kategorie wurde von mir für diesen spezifischen Kontext geändert, sie versucht, den Modus der Ansprache der Öffentlichkeit, sprich die zugrunde liegende Pädagogik, zu beschreiben.

	THEATER	BILDENDE KÜNSTE
	Bezogen auf das Sinnliche	Bezogen auf das Vernünftige
ÖFFENTLICHKEIT	Gruppe in einem dunklen Raum	Individuum in einer Überblickssituation, kann sich frei bewegen
PRODUKTION	Hierarchische Gruppe	Individuelles Genie
ZUGRUNDE LIEGENDE PÄDAGOGIK	Moral von Leben, Liebe und Krieg	Verhalten, Kontrolle im Inneren des Subjekts verankern

Nach den Katastrophen des Zweiten Weltkriegs war das Theater im Europa der 1950er ein Ort, der die Ober- und Mittelschicht mit informativen und zeitlosen Werten versorgte; zumindest war dies die gängige Ideologie, wie ein Theaterstück zu sein hatte. Wie Richard Sennett angemerkt hat, saß das Publikum damals mehr oder weniger unbeweglich auf seinen Plätzen und sah sich an, was man ihm auf der Bühne darbot.[6] Damit unterschied sich die Situation deutlich von der im Europa vor der Französischen Revolution, als die – reichen – Adeligen sich im Theater frei bewegten, miteinander plauderten und das Bühnengeschehen kommentierten. Auch in den Museen und Galerien der westlichen Städte der Nachkriegszeit waren die Menschen angehalten, sich die Exponate schweigend anzusehen und von spontanen, lauten oder expressiven Bekundungen abzusehen.[7] In allen Kulturstätten verhielt sich das Publikum auf äußerst gehemmte Art, da das Subjekt selbst die Kontrollinstanz inzwischen verinnerlicht hatte. Es kontrollierte sich in einer Umgebung des totalen Überblicks und der totalen Sichtbarkeit (Öffentlichkeit). Wie in der Matrix oben skizziert, ging man davon aus, das Theater werde in einem Arbeitsprozess von einer großen, hierarchisch organisierten Gruppe produziert, während die bildenden Künste das Produkt der Genialität und der geschickten Hände eines Einzelnen (Produktion) seien.

Mit den in den 1960ern übernommenen Praktiken wurden die Kategorien des Theaters und der bildenden Künste zwar hinfällig, aber dennoch weiterhin von den Institutionen, den Museen und Galerien für die bildenden Künste einerseits und dem Theater andererseits, definiert und gerahmt.

Der Begriff der Performativität, der in unserem Kontext verwendet werden kann, um verschiedene bild- und theaterbasierte Praktiken zu diskutieren, lässt sich auf einen weiten Begriff des Performativen zurückführen. 2002 beschrieb dies das Team des Münchner Kunstvereins im Hinblick auf seinen kuratorischen Ansatz: «Das Konzept der Performanz geht auf die Sprachphilosophie der 1950er zurück, die sie als konzeptionellen Gegensatz zur Kompetenz definierte. Performanz charakterisiert hier den konkreten Gebrauch von Sprache und bedeutet die Realisierung von Ausdrücken in einer spezifischen Situation durch einen individuellen Sprecher, die angewendete und verkörperte Sprache. Kompetenz hingegen ist die ideale Idee eines Sprechers, der aus einer begrenzten Zahl sprachlicher Elemente eine unbegrenzte Zahl von Ausdrücken bildet. Diese implizite Metaebene der Kompetenz wurde innerhalb des Konzepts der Performanz von Noam Chomsky und J. L. Austin geleugnet. Austins Sprechakttheorie in *How to Do Things with Words* impliziert, dass Sprache nicht nur eine referenzielle Funktion hat, sondern auch eine performative.»[8] Laut Austins Definition verwirklicht das Performative auch das, was es charakterisiert – einen sogenannten Sprechakt. Gemeint ist hier der Zusammenhang zwischen Handlung und Sprache, etwa der Zusam-

menhang zwischen den Worten «Ich gratuliere dir» und der Handlung des Händeschüttelns oder Aussagen wie «Ich schwöre» oder «Ich wette», bei denen die Handlung als solche bereits impliziert ist. Das entscheidende wertende Urteil performativer Ausdrücke ist dementsprechend nicht ihr Wahrheitsniveau, sondern vielmehr der relative Erfolg oder das relative Scheitern der von ihnen intendierten Bedeutung. «Unter performativ versteht man also die Konstituierung einer Bedeutung durch einen Akt oder eine bestimmte Praxis.»[9]

Der Text des Teams des Kunstvereins München überträgt die Sprechakttheorie auf ähnliche Weise auf die bildenden Künste, und zwar vor allem auf das Kuratieren, wie dies Dorothea von Hantelmann in ihrer Publikation *How to Do Things With Art* mit ihrer Übertragung der Sprechakttheorie auf die Kunst tat.[10] Man kann beide Ansätze als eine Paraphrase von Judith Butlers Idee der sozialen Praktiken auffassen, die immer wieder geäußert / performiert werden müssen, um wirksam zu werden. Nach diesem Verständnis hängt ‹das Performative› jedweder Äußerung, ob einer künstlerischen, kuratorischen oder theaterbasierten, mit ihren Wirkungen zusammen.

Fluxus

Im Fall von Fluxus wurde der Zusammenbruch der Gattungen Dichtung, bildende Künste, Theater insofern durch Musik vermittelt, als Fluxusereignisse als musikalische Partituren notiert waren. Durch diese Verfremdung ließ sich alles unter dem Aspekt der Notation aufzeichnen und überall von jedermann anhand dieser Notation oder Partitur reproduzieren. Ein gutes Beispiel für die Ablehnung eines bildlich orientierten Kunstkonzepts ist La Monte Youngs Fluxusevent *Composition 5:* «Die Aktion beschränkt sich darauf, einen oder mehrere Schmetterlinge im Aufführungsraum fliegen zu lassen und dabei Sorge zu tragen, daß es allen Tieren möglich ist, in die Freiheit zu fliegen.»[11] Musikpartituren stellten also eine Metasprache bereit, die eine Nivellierung aller Handlungsmöglichkeiten mit schriftlichen und visuellen Objekten und Subjekten ermöglichte.

Für George Maciunas, den ‹Vorsitzenden› von Fluxus, war es wichtig, dass man Fluxus und Happening auseinanderhielt. Er führte das Happening auf das Theater und das barocke Ballett am Hof von Versailles zurück, während Fluxus sich gegen die elitäre ‹Hochkunst› wandte und kollektive Lebensstile favorisierte, worunter ein fließender Übergang zwischen Kunst und Leben oder deren Vereinigung verstanden wurde. Die Fluxusaktionen selbst verweigerten sich daher der Künstlichkeit oder einer Trennung vom Alltagsleben. Selbst jene Objekte, die später als Fluxuseditionen bekannt wurden, begannen ihre Existenz als Verkörperungen von Aktionspartituren, Ephemera, die jederzeit von jedermann aktiviert und performt werden konnten, mit

der einzigen Einschränkung, dass sie bei einer öffentlichen Aufführung als Fluxus bezeichnet werden mussten. Der Wahrheitsdiskurs der bildenden Künste wird in dem Konzept sichtbar, dass Fluxus Verstellung vermeiden und weder dramatisch noch kunstfertig sein sollte. Fluxus-Kunst-Amüsement soll, in den Worten von Emmett Williams, «einfach, unterhaltend und anspruchslos sein, sich mit Belanglosigkeiten beschäftigen, weder besondere Fähigkeiten noch zahllose Proben erfordern, weder handelbar noch institutionalisierbar sein.»[12]

Vor allem die letzte Anforderung sollte sich als unmögliche Aufgabe erweisen. Um den Preis einer Verleugnung eines Teils seiner Ziele und Produktionsprozesse wurde Fluxus handelbar und institutionalisiert. So ist etwa die multiple Urheberschaft vieler Fluxus-Produktionen, vor allem bei den Editionen und Filmen, heute in Vergessenheit geraten, weil Fluxus wieder Teil des Feldes der bildenden Kunst und daher wieder auf die Zuschreibung einer ganz spezifischen Autorschaft reduziert wurde. Die folgende Matrix fasst einige der Hauptpunkte der Produktion und Rezeption des traditionellen Theaters im Verhältnis zur neoavantgardistischen Fluxusbewegung zusammen:

	THEATER	BILDENDE KÜNSTE	FLUXUS
	Bezogen auf das Sinnliche	Bezogen auf das Rationale	Bezogen auf Zufallsoperationen
ÖFFENTLICHKEIT	Gruppe in einem dunklen Raum	Individuum in einer Überblickssituation	In einer Gemeinschaft – das Publikum kann Teil einer Partitur sein oder kann eine Partitur neu interpretieren
PRODUKTION	Hierarchisch	Individuelles Genie	In einer Gruppe Gruppenurheberschaft unklar – Produktion ist motiviert durch musikalische Partituren
ZUGRUNDE LIEGENDE PÄDAGOGIK	Moral von Leben, Liebe und Krieg	Sich benehmen, Kontrolle im Inneren des Subjekts verankern	Neubewertung des Alltagslebens – Politisches Bewusstsein antibürgerlich

In unserem Kontext ist es wichtig, darauf hinzuweisen, dass die verschiedenen Produktionen und die multiple Urheberschaft eng miteinander verbunden waren. Die Events wurden auf die Bühne gebracht, und die Partitur des Events entstand manchmal erst danach. Die Eventpartitur bestand aus grundsätzlichen Anweisungen, die auf ganz unterschiedliche Weise umgesetzt werden konnten. Viele Fluxuseditionen enthalten Konglomerate dieser Anweisungen oder schlagen vor, durch bestimmte Aktionen von ihnen Gebrauch zu machen. Der Objektcharakter, der heutige Präsentationen von Fluxus-‹Werken› kennzeichnet, ist also sehr fragwürdig. So wurden etwa die Reste von Nam June Paiks Interpretation von La Monte Youngs Fluxuseventpartitur *draw a straight line* später sowohl von der Kunstgeschichte als auch vom Kunstmarkt als selbstständiges Kunstobjekt behandelt.

Kunst/Leben:
Christoph Schlingensief

Im Mittelpunkt der künstlerischen Praxis des verstorbenen Christoph Schlingensief standen die Prozesse der Umgestaltung der Konzepte von ‹Kunst› und ‹Leben› und die Frage nach der Repräsentation des Persönlichen. Schlingensief griff auf Quellenmaterial aus seiner persönlichen Geschichte und chaotische Lebensereignisse zurück und widmete seine verletzte Persönlichkeit mit totaler Hingabe der Ansammlung der von ihm gewählten Medien: «Die Praxis von Christoph Schlingensief (1960–2010) stellt einen Streifzug durch verschiedene Arten der künstlerischen Auseinandersetzung dar: vom Filmemachen zum Aktivismus, vom Schauspielen zur Regie, von der Malerei zum Journalismus. Die Vielfalt der Materialien, die dies impliziert, hat nicht nur die Grenzen zwischen traditionellen künstlerischen Kategorien verwischt, sondern einer Dekonstruktion und Rekonstruktion der visuellen Welten nach sich gezogen. Indem es alles absorbiert und sich der Linearität und klassischen Narration verweigert, verlangt das Werk den sensorischen Fähigkeiten des Betrachters sehr viel ab. In dem Bemühen, Schlingensiefs Aktivitäten zusammenzufassen, ist man versucht, den Begriff ‹universell› zu gebrauchen.»[13]

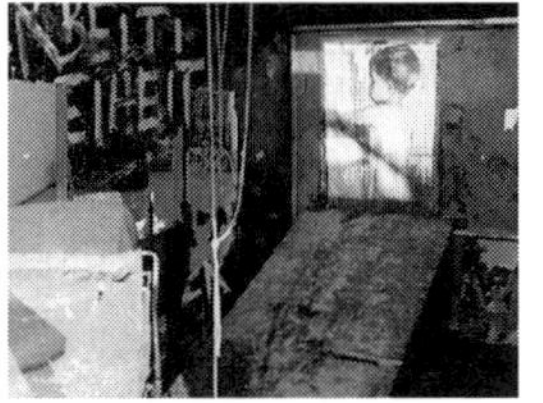

Dieses Zitat stammt aus der Presseerklärung zu Schlingensiefs Ausstellung *Kaprow City*, die von November 2007 bis Februar 2008 im Migros Museum Zürich gezeigt wurde. Raphael Gygax, der Kurator der Ausstellung, weist darauf hin, dass die Ausstellung in ihrer ersten Erscheinungsform ein begehbares Bühnenbild war, das in der Berliner Volksbühne von Schauspielern genutzt und erst später in eine Installation für das Museum transformiert wurde. Diese Bilder vermitteln eine Ahnung von dem runden Bühnenbild, das im Museum statisch war. Die ursprüngliche Drehbühne wurde in eine Filminstallation verwandelt. Der Hauptfilm mit dem Titel *Fremdverstümmelung* war ursprünglich für Moritz Eggerts Oper *FREAX* produziert worden. Die Installation im Migros Museum bestand außerdem aus zwei Filmen, die Schlingensiefs Vater gedreht hatte, sowie aus einem ‹Waschvideo›. Im ersten Raum wurden verschiedene mit den Überwachungskameras der Theaterfassung aufgenommene Videos gezeigt.

Mit seiner Überführung aus dem Theater in den Ausstellungsraum verwandelte sich das Material aus einem atmosphärischen Bühnenbild (Hintergrund) in ein skulpturales Kunstobjekt (Vordergrund). Während Theater traditionell innerhalb einer hierarchischen Gruppe produziert wird, die aus Regisseur, Bühnenbildner, Schauspielern,

Technikern, Beleuchtern, den für Spezial- und Toneffekte zuständigen Mitarbeitern, Musikern, Filmemachern usw. besteht, wird im Kontext all diese Arbeit unter dem Namen eines einzigen Urhebers subsumiert, in diesem Fall Schlingensief. Infiziert vom Umfeld der bildenden Künste, erlangt das Material automatisch den Wert eines Kunstwerks und verliert die nutz- und greifbaren Merkmale des Bühnenbilds. Die Sehnsucht nach körperlichem Vergnügen, die im Kontext des Theaters gegenwärtiger ist, wird daher zugunsten des distanzierteren Gefühls des Visuellen zum Schweigen gebracht. Auch für das Publikum haben sich die Zugangsbedingungen geändert; während das Material im Theater betreten werden konnte, ist dies im Ausstellungsraum nur teilweise der Fall. Die Installation ist also durch die Voraussetzungen der Paradigmen der bildenden Kunst beeinflusst. Indem das zur Schau gestellte Künstlersubjekt als durch seine Familiengeschichte verletztes positioniert wird, wird die Begegnung noch weiter von irgendwelchen sozialen oder politischen Bedingungen entfernt. Die Installation führt die Sehnsucht nach einer körperlichen Überschreitung des zum Verstummen gebrachten Besuchersubjekts ein, doch es gelingt ihr nicht, dies zuzulassen, indem sie jeglichen theatralischen Zugang zum Objekt blockiert. Die Medienkritik, die man in den verschwommenen Videos sehen konnte, ließ sich kaum von ihrer Affirmation unterscheiden. Auch wenn der Transformationsversuch interessant war, war die daraus resultierende festgelegte Attitüde eindeutig der Übertragung aus dem Theaterkontext in den Ausstellungsraum zu verdanken. Diese Festlegung spiegelte auch die Rückkehr des (männlichen) Urhebersubjekts als Genie wider.

	Schlingensiefs Werk im Bereich THEATER		Schlingensiefs Werk im Bereich BILDENDE KÜNSTE
	Bezogen auf das Sinnliche	→	Bezogen auf das Irrationale
ÖFFENTLICHKEIT (REZEPTION)	Gruppe in einem dunklen Raum	→	Individuum in einer verwirrenden Situation, kann sich frei bewegen
PRODUKTION	Hierarchische Gruppe		Individuelles Genie, verletzt durch seine Familiengeschichte
ZUGRUNDE LIEGENDE PÄDAGOGIK	Moral von Leben, Liebe und Krieg		Sich benehmen, Kontrolle und Selbstdisziplin im Inneren des Subjekts verankern

Spartacus Chetwynd

Schlingensiefs Installation war nur ein Teil der fortgesetzten Untersuchung der Überschneidungen von Theater und bildender Kunst seitens des Migros Museums. Eine weitere Ausstellung in dem Museum widmete sich dem Werk der britischen Künstlerin Spartacus Chetwynd,[14] in deren Performances Materialien recycelt werden; dies geschieht inmitten von Bühnenbildelementen, die passenderweise wirken, als seien sie aus Abfällen hergestellt. In einem Artikel für die Zeitschrift *Frieze* beschreibt Tom Morton ihr Werk folgendermaßen: «In den letzten Jahren hat Chetwynd mit Hilfe einer flexiblen Truppe von etwa 20 Freunden und Familienmitgliedern eine Reihe von Performances aufgeführt, die auf alles Mögliche zurückgriffen: von *Conan der Barbar* (1982) bis zu *Der unglaubliche Hulk* (2008), von den Performances Yves Kleins bis zu Hokusais erotischen Druckgrafiken. Obwohl sie sorgfältig produziert sind, scheinen diese Spektakel immer kurz davor, in eine fröhliche Anarchie überzugehen: Die Darsteller schlürfen Bier, improvisieren Textzeilen und checken zerstreut ihre SMS, als ginge es hier nicht darum, das Publikum davon zu überzeugen, seine Ungläubigkeit eine Weile außer Kraft zu setzen, sondern stattdessen ein karnevaleskes Element in den Alltag einzuführen. Mir drängt sich zwangsläufig der Gedanke auf, dass ihre Werke genauso von der BBC-Kinderfernsehserie *Why Don't You?* (1973–1995) mit ihrer Lasst-uns-gleich-hier-mit-der-Show-loslegen-Kinder!-Haltung beeinflusst sind.»[15]

Chetwynds Charaktere agieren als Subjekte, die einen Anspruch auf kulturelles Material erheben und es neu lesen können, gemäß ihren eigenen Bedürfnissen, gegen den Strich. Für ihr Werk *The Fall of Man* (2006) etwa präsentierte Chetwynd Abschnitte aus der Genesis, Miltons *Paradise Lost* und Karl Marx' und Friedrich Engels' *Deutscher Ideologie*

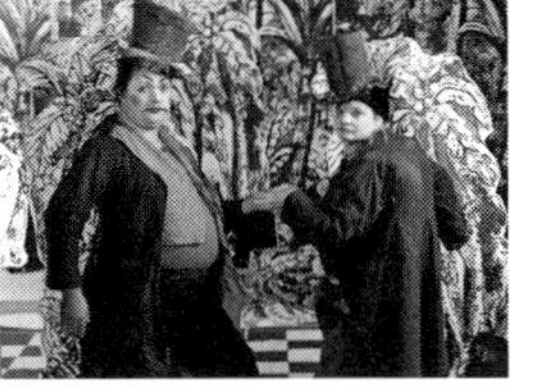

als Puppenspiel. Die aus Kartoffeln angefertigten Marionetten wurden von ihren als Clowns verkleideten Darstellern auf improvisierten Pappkartonbühnen zum Leben erweckt. In diesem absurden Kontext wurden die normalerweise mit Geschichte und Bedeutung aufgeladenen Texte ganz gleichgültig behandelt, so als seien sie untereinander oder gegen jeden beliebigen anderen Text austauschbar. Durch die Einbeziehung alltäglicher Verhaltensweisen seitens der Schauspieler, die etwa mit ihren Handys herumspielten, entsteht eine Spannung, bei der die Unterscheidung zwischen Schauspielern und Publikum jeden Moment zusammenzubrechen droht. Doch andererseits scheinen erstere das Publikum durch ihr unbekümmertes Verhalten und ihren Mangel an sichtbaren Fähigkeiten auch aufzufordern, sich ihnen anzu-

schließen, als ob sich ihre absonderlichen sexuellen Darbietungen innerhalb einer Minute kopieren ließen. Bei vielen ihrer Performances lässt Chetwynd das Publikum auf derselben Ebene wie die Schauspieler Platz nehmen, und die Trennung zwischen beiden besteht dann häufig ausschließlich aus einem Installationselement wie etwa einem Tisch.

	THEATER	BILDENDE KUNSTE	CHETWYND
	Bezogen auf das Sinnliche	Bezogen auf das Rationale	Bezogen auf Kinderspiele und das Absurde
ÖFFENTLICHKEIT (REZEPTION)	Gruppe in einem dunklen Raum	Individuum in einer Überblickssituation	In einer Gemeinschaft – das Publikum wird durch die Darbietung affiziert und seine Anwesenheit wird gewissermaßen anerkannt
PRODUKTION	Hierarchische Gruppe	Individuelles Genie	In einer Gruppe Gruppenurheberschaft unklar – Urheberschaft unklar, wird aber letztlich unter dem Namen eines Künstlers subsumiert. Die Produktion wird durch eine spielerische Do-it-yourself-Haltung motiviert
ZUGRUNDE LIEGENDE PÄDAGOGIK	Moral von Leben, Liebe und Krieg	Sich benehmen, Kontrolle im Inneren des Subjekts verankern	Neubewertung der Kulturgeschichte und Medienzugang möglich – möglicher Spaß trotz der Absurdität der sogenannten Wirklichkeit

Im Ruckgriff auf Dorothea von Hantelmanns *How to Do Things With Art* [16] könnte man die Meinung vertreten, dass nicht nur, wie Austin dies ausführlich dargelegt hat, das gesprochene Wort, sondern auch das Spiel der Zeichen in der bildenden Kunst sich auf Handlungen bezieht und ein Geschehen auslöst. Die Übertragung des Bühnenbilds in den Ausstellungsraum bringt dieselben Probleme mit sich, denen wir bereits bei Fluxus und Schlingensief begegnet sind. Das Material wird dahingehend transformiert, dass aus dem Zubehör einer Handlung eine festgelegte Situation und damit sofort ein Kunstwerk wird. Auch das anarchische Element des Live-Acts wird durch diese Transformation unterdrückt; die Begegnung mit einem Ereignis, bei dem sich die Möglichkeiten nie vollständig kontrollieren lassen, geht verloren.

Renata Burckhardt:
Eine theatralische Szene in einer Ausstellung

Das letzte hier zitierte Beispiel ist die Szene mit dem Titel *Inclusion/exclusion – acteurs in the art system*. Diese fand in dem Ausstellungsprojekt *Spill the Beans* statt, das im Februar 2010 von Andrea Roca, Zoë Meyer und Renata Burckhardt kuratiert wurde. Wie die Organisatoren im Pressematerial erklärten, konzentrierte sich die Ausstellung auf die existierenden Strukturen sowie Ökonomie und Politik der heutigen Kunstwelt und zeigte verschiedene Werke von Künstlern, die diese Strukturen und Mechanismen hervorheben und kritisieren und die Kontrolle der Prozesse der Anerkennung in der Kunstwelt unterwandern oder sie offensiv für ihre eigenen Zwecke ausbeuten.[17] Zwischen stärker objektbasierten Kunstwerken wurde im Ausstellungsraum ein Setting von der Szenografin Melanie Mock gestaltet. Es bestand aus einer zentralen erhöhten Plattform, die an die auf Handels- und Kunstmessen üblichen Präsentationsbühnen erinnerte. Die Kuratoren benutzten die Plattform für eine Reihe von Interventionen, die die Dynamik des zeitgenössischen Kunstgeschäfts erkundeten.

Die Schriftstellerin Renata Burckhardt schrieb eine Szene für die Ausstellung. Darin traten Schauspieler, die verschiedene Kunstwelttypen porträtierten, auf und führten im Publikum einen Dialog miteinander, der jedoch nicht sofort als Inszenierung zu erkennen war. Die beiden Protagonisten begannen mit einer typischen Situation aus dem Kunstfeld: Eine relativ unbekannte, nicht mehr junge Künstlerin zeigt einem jungen, hippen Kurator Werke, der auf eine gönnerhafte Weise darauf reagiert. Allmählich finden sich die beiden auf der erhöhten Plattform in dem Raum wieder und ‹setzen› die von ihnen repräsentierten Machtverhältnisse buchstäblich ‹in Szene›. Im Verlauf des Gesprächs macht die weibliche Protagonistin klar, dass ihr Partner ein einflussreicher Galerist ist, und übernimmt nach und nach das Kommando über das Geschehen. Diese Narration wurde durch teilweise mit Megafonen übermittelte Überlegungen über den Realraum («Es ist kalt hier») und die tatsächliche Situation der Schauspieler unterbrochen. Selbst wenn die Botschaft möglicherweise eine eher schlichte war, nämlich dass Geld definitiv Einfluss auf Kunstinstitutionen und ihr Ausstellungsprogramm hat, verstanden sich die Darsteller ausgezeichnet darauf, die Machtverhältnisse untereinander durch subtile Änderungen ihrer Attitüden und Verhaltensmuster zum Ausdruck zu bringen.

Mit genau solchen Bedeutungsnuancen hatten alle im Raum Anwesenden schon einmal zu tun. Auch die in der Szene vorkommenden Verweise auf den spezifischen Raum, in dem sich das Geschehen abspielte (die Tür war nicht geschlossen), bezogen die Zuschauer zusätz-

lich in diese ein. Die Botschaft der theatralischen Intervention führte dazu, dass man plötzlich die eigene Position innerhalb der Kunstwelt erkannte. Die Zugangsbedingungen zu ihr wurden sichtbar.

	THEATER	BILDENDE KÜNSTE	Szene in einer Ausstellung von RENATA BURCKHARDT
	Bezogen auf das Sinnliche	Bezogen auf das Rationale	Bezogen auf Kinderspiele und das Absurde
ÖFFENTLICHKEIT (REZEPTION)	Gruppe in einem dunklen Raum	Individuum in einer Überblickssituation	In einer Gemeinschaft – das Publikum wird durch die Darbietung affiziert
PRODUKTION	Hierarchische Gruppe	Individuelles Genie	Hierarchisch in einer Gruppe, aber auch auf der Grundlage einer langfristigen Vorproduktion
ZUGRUNDE LIEGENDE PÄDAGOGIK	Moral von Leben, Liebe und Krieg	Sich benehmen, Kontrolle im Inneren des Subjekts verankern	Selbstbewusstheit

In diesem Beispiel wird auch das Problem des statischen Kunstwerks erkennbar. In unserer spektakulären Medienwelt wäre es wohl nicht genug, es einfach nur zu sehen. Doch das Publikum überwältigenden Emotionen auszusetzen, wie das in den Massenmedien ebenfalls häufig der Fall ist, ist ebenfalls keine Option. Aufklärung bedeutet immer, jemandem seine oder ihre Position bewusst zu machen und eine mögliche Handlung, einen Schritt in Richtung Selbstermächtigung vorzuschlagen. Sämtliche Kategorien der Rezeption, der Produktion und der Pädagogik/des Gebrauchs, sprich der zugrunde liegenden Aussagen, können (auf-)gelöst werden und zielen auf eine Botschaft ab, die über das Gegebene hinausgeht.

Man könnte hieraus die Schlussfolgerung ziehen, dass es heute einen Konflikt zwischen Theater und bildender Kunst gibt, der die Kategorien im Kant'schen Sinne hinfällig werden lässt. Doch dieses Thema wird nicht nur durch ein ideologisches Verlangen vorangetrieben, sondern es ist auch Teil einer gewissen Hilflosigkeit der Position der sogenannten ‹Hochkunst›, die heutzutage in der Gesellschaft und seitens der Politik weniger Unterstützung erfährt. Der Aspekt der Bildung insgesamt ist für Politiker nicht von großem Interesse, solange die Massen nicht in den Prozess einbezogen sind (aus diesem Grund ist die Idee der Kunsterziehung in dieser Hinsicht problematisch). Derweil scheinen Vertreter des Feldes der bildenden Künste unter dem Aspekt ideologischer Bedürfnisse zu versuchen, das Ausstellungsformat in etwas Spektakuläreres zu verwandeln. Die Bewegung von den Kant'schen festgelegten Gattungen zu dieser neueren Überschneidung führt zu einer Situation, in der die Urheberschaft des Einzelnen immer mehr hinter eine postfordistische Idee neuer freier Kombinationen ersetzbarer und austauschbarer Teile zurücktritt. In solchen

Zeiten ist die Frage danach, wie die Besucher-Subjekte angesprochen werden, schwierig, und die Antwort kann auch in scheinbar ähnlichen Projekten sehr unterschiedlich ausfallen. Eindeutig aber ist, dass man das, was ich als ‹zugrunde liegende Pädagogik› bezeichnet habe, nie als etwas Selbstverständliches betrachten, sondern in jedem Fall sorgfältig diskutieren sollte.

1   Vgl. Terry Eagleton, *The Ideology of the Aesthetics,* Oxford: Blackwell 1990, S. 72.

2   Ebd., S. 73.

3   Ebd., S. 75.

4   Theodor Adorno, Max Horkheimer, *Dialektik der Aufklärung. Philosophische Fragmente,* Amsterdam: Querido 1947.

5   Siehe Peter Bürger, *Theorie der Avantgarde,* Frankfurt am Main: Suhrkamp 1974.

6   Siehe Richard Sennett, *Verfall und Ende des öffentlichen Lebens. Die Tyrannei der Intimität,* Frankfurt am Main: Fischer Verlag 2004.

7   Siehe Tony Bennett, *The Birth of the Museum, History, Theory, Politics,* London: Routledge 1995.

8   J. L. Austin, *How To Do Things with Words,* Oxford. Clarendon Press 1962.

9   Søren Grammel, Maria Lind, Katharina Schlieben, 2002, «Curating Per-Form: Reflections on the Concept of the Performative», in: Maria Lind, Søren Grammel, Katharina Schlieben, Judith Schwarzbart, Ana Paula Cohen, Julienne Lorz, Tessa Praun, Gesammelte Drucksachen / Collected Newsletters, München 2004, deutsch/englisch, 6 Ausgaben von 2002–2004. Hg. von Revolver und Kunstverein München.

10   Dorothea von Hantelmann, *How to Do Things With Art: The Meaning of Art's Performativity,* Zürich, Berlin: JRP Ringier 2002.

11   Siehe Jürgen Schilling, *Aktionskunst. Identität von Kunst und Leben? Eine Dokumentation,* Luzern, Frankfurt am Main: C. J. Bucher Verlag 1978, S. 81.

12   Emmett Williams, «St George und der Fluxus-Drachen», in: Klaus Schrenk (Hg.), *Aufbrüche, Manifeste, Manifestationen. Positionen in der bildenden Kunst zu Beginn der 60er Jahre in Berlin / Düsseldorf und München,* Köln: DuMont 1984, S. 33.

13   Vgl. die Presseerklärung des Migros Museums zur Ausstellung.

14   Raphael Gygax, Heike Munder (Hg.), *Spartacus Chetwynd,* Ausst.-Kat., Zürich, Berlin: JRP Ringier 2007.

15   Tom Morton, Mai 2007, «Spartacus Chetwynd», in: *Frieze,* Nr. 107, http://www.frieze.com/issue/article/spartacus_chetwynd/. Aufgerufen am 13.5.2012.

16   Hantelmann, a. a. O.

17   Andrea Roca, Zoë Meyer, Renata Burckhardt, Master Project for the Postgraduate Program in Curating, *Spill the Beans,* http://www.curating./org/index.php/master_projects/spill-the-beans. Aufgerufen am 13.5.2012.

WIE PERFORMT MAN DIE STADT?

Sally De Kunst

Das Belluard Bollwerk International ist ein kleines grosses Kunstfestival, das jedes Jahr zum Sommeranfang in Fribourg (CH) stattfindet. Es ist dafür bekannt, eine eigene Sicht aktueller künstlerischer Trends zu haben und Werke lokaler und internationaler Künstlerinnen und Künstler in einem sozialen Kontext zu prä-

Dies ist eine sehr persönliche Anleitung. Es gibt keine verbindliche Gebrauchsanweisung für das Belluard Bollwerk International. Im besten Falle hat ein Kunstfestival in einer kleinen Stadt in der Schweiz kein Profil, sondern besteht aus einer Reihe von Miniprofilen. Es konzentriert sich auf jedes Projekt, jeden Künstler, jede Künstlerin und bewahrt die künstlerische Autonomie im Verhaltnis zum gegebenen Kontext. Die tatsachliche Kunst definiert die Vielfalt eines Festivals und offenbart das heterogene Profil seines Standorts. Festival Belluard Bollwerk International, www.belluard.ch

sentieren. Die verschiedenen Erscheinungsformen, die wir produzieren oder präsentieren, lassen sich nur schwer auf einen Nenner bringen. Es heisst, wir seien irgendwie ‹dazwischen›. Das ist gleichzeitig komplex, herausfordernd und aufregend. Unser oberstes Ziel ist es, ein gutes Gleichgewicht zwischen künstlerischer Autonomie einerseits und der Verbindung zwischen dem Künstler und seiner sozialen Umgebung andererseits, zwischen Kunst und Gesellschaft sowie zwischen einem Kunstfestival und seiner sozialen Funktion in einer Stadt zu finden. Dies bedeutet jedoch nicht, dass wir soziokulturelle Arbeit leisten. Vielmehr untersucht das Festival auf unterschiedliche Weise ‹Performativität›: Handlungen oder Äusserungen, die kraft ihrer Performanz die Situation oder die Machtbeziehungen innerhalb der gegebenen Begegnung oder des gegebenen Kontexts verändern.

Der folgende Beitrag ist meine persönliche, aus zehn Schritten bestehende Anleitung, wie man das Belluard Festival organisiert. Sie beruht auf meiner langjährigen Erfahrung in Fribourg.

1. Lernen Sie
Ihr Umfeld kennen

Fribourg ist eine kleine Stadt im Bundesstaat Schweiz, einem dezentralisierten Land mit vier offiziellen Sprachen, 26 Kantonen und ebenso vielen Mentalitäten und Kulturen. Auch wenn sie sich geografisch im Mittelpunkt Europas befindet, scheint die Schweiz ihr Augenmerk – in den darstellenden (etwas weniger in den visuellen) Künsten – sehr stark auf die lokale Produktion zu legen, was häufig mit der Kulturpolitik und den Förderinstitutionen zusammenhängt. In der deutschsprachigen Schweiz bedeutet ‹Internationalismus› vor allem den Austausch mit Deutschland und Österreich. In der französischsprachigen Romandie gibt es eine enge Verbindung zu Frankreich. Fribourg ist eine katholische Stadt

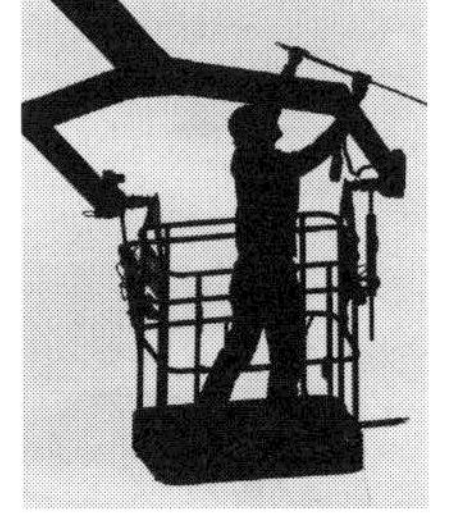

(mit 34 000 Einwohnern, davon ein Drittel Ausländer) mit einer renommierten Universität (10 000 Student/Innen), und es liegt an der Sprach- und Kulturgrenze. In dieser Stadt gibt es ein hohes Mass an abergläubischen Praktiken, sie hat die höchste Dichte an Einkaufszentren pro Einwohner in Europa, und es finden sich dort sieben Tattoo-Läden für die 34 000 Ortsansässigen. Diese komplexe Kombination verleiht der Stadt etwas ‹Kosmopolitisches›, eine gewisse Offenheit und Neugierde. Wir scheinen uns an einem ziemlich bemerkenswerten Ort zu befinden, der sich als idealer Kontext erweist, da die Leitung eines Festivals wie jene des Belluard Bollwerks impliziert, dass man nie innehält und ständig weitergeht, um am Puls der Zeit zu bleiben.

NB: Häufig dringt man mittels künstlerischer Projekte unter die Oberfläche eines lokalen Kontexts vor. Im Jahr 2010 behandelte der deutsche Künstler Thomas Bratzke ein Gebäude mit Akupunktur. Bei den Recherchen zur Performance-Installation *Building Therapy* zeigte sich, dass Fribourg das Mekka der alternativen Therapie und des Aberglaubens ist. Ein Beispiel hierfür ist die Praxis der ‹faiseurs de secret›, Menschen, die über die Gabe verfügen, andere Menschen via Telefon zu heilen.

2. Global denken,
lokal handeln

Unsere Arbeit am Belluard Bollwerk Festival ist mit dem Risiko behaftet, inhaltlich oder formal atypische Projekte zu realisieren und zu präsentieren. Innerhalb der gegebenen kulturpolitischen Situation, die wie erwähnt stark auf das Geschehen vor Ort fixiert ist, bleibt es Jahr für Jahr eine Herausforderung, ein aussergewöhnliches internationales Festival zu organisieren, das in Fribourg verankert sein möchte. Dies bedeutet jedoch nicht, ich würde hier für eine Rückkehr zur kulturpolitischen Nabelschau plädieren. Eine Folge der Globalisierung ist, dass die romantische Idee der kulturellen Herkunft oder der lokalen Wurzeln mehr oder weniger an Bedeutung verloren hat. Authentizität bezieht sich nicht mehr auf die Herkunft, sondern vielmehr auf die erfolgreiche Ankunft einer kulturellen Praxis in einer neuen Umgebung, im Idealfall mit einem eigenen, eigensinnigen Flair. In diesem Sinne wird das Lokale für ein Festival wie das Belluard Bollwerk International interessant, insofern es internationale Kunstwerke hervorbringt, die eine interaktive Beziehung zu einem lokalen Kontext herstellen und diesen hinterfragen: indem es örtliche Künstlerinnen und Künstler

anregt, beschränktes Denken durch das Ausprobieren neuer Formate zu überwinden. Indem es einen Wettbewerb mit einem Leitmotiv organisiert, der Künstler und Fachleute aus anderen Gebieten herausfordert und der einen betreuten Aufenthalt anbietet, mittels dessen man die Stadt und die lokale Gesellschaft kennenlernen kann. Indem man die örtlichen Besucher auf aktive Weise dadurch einbindet, dass man sie zu Performern oder zu Teilnehmern an einem künstlerischen Projekt macht. Indem man andere Orte in der Stadt nutzt und Passanten als Publikum gewinnt. Indem man sich aktiv an örtlichen und umfassenderen künstlerischen Aktivitäten beteiligt.

NB: Häufig realisieren wir Projekte, die Lizenzproduktionen oder schöpferisches Gemeingut sind, wie etwa den *Complaints Choir* [Chor der Beschwerden] (2008) oder die *Human Library* [Menschliche Bibliothek] (2010). Damals inszenierte Sylviane Tille, die Direktorin des Theaters von Fribourg, *The Great Public Sale of Brilliant but Unrealized Ideas*© [Der grosse öffentliche Verkauf brillanter, aber nicht realisierter Ideen©], eine Auktion von Kunstideen statt Kunstwerken. Siebzehn Ideen internationaler und lokaler Künstler wie Santiago Sierra, Miranda July, San Keller, Jean-Damien Fleury und anderer wurden von Experten geschätzt und vom Auktionator Bernard Piguet vom Hôtel des Ventes in Genf für Geld oder ‹kreatives Kapital› (künstlerische Ideen) verkauft. Der Abend artete auf brillante Weise in Anarchie und in einer aktiven Beteiligung des Fribourger Publikums aus.

3. Zuschauen, zuhören und reden, reden, reden

Konkret gesagt ist die Art, wie Entscheidungen getroffen werden, damit das Festival jedes Jahr zustande kommt, sehr intuitiv: Ich lasse mich von dem leiten, was ich sehe, höre, lese, von den Diskussionen, die ich mit 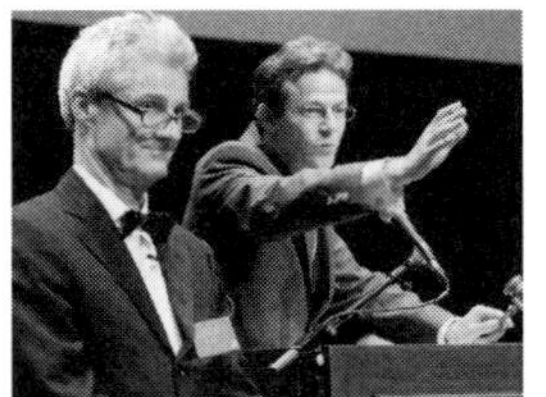 Künstlern habe, und von dem die Gesellschaft betreffenden Fragen, mit denen sie sich befassen. Wechselseitiges Interesse ist sehr wichtig. Ausserdem sollten sich Künstler für die Praxis und die Wirklichkeit interessieren. Beim Zusammenstellen des Programms stehe ich häufig im Dialog mit vielen unterschiedlichen Menschen: den Künstlerinnen und Künstlern, aber auch meinem Team, den Mitgliedern unseres Verbands, Politikern, Stiftungen, Sponsoren, Kollegen auf dem Gebiet der nationalen und internationalen Kunst, Journalisten, lokalen

Behörden, Fachleuten auf verschiedenen Gebieten, mit den Eigentü-
mern bestimmter Orte in Fribourg, die wir nutzen wollen, dem Publikum ... Ich betrachte meine Praxis als Direktorin eines Kunstfestivals
als einen konstanten Fluss von Dialogen mit vielen Leuten.

NB:　Bei einer informellen Diskussion mit der Bibliothekarin Madeleine Dietrich in Fribourg erfuhr ich von dem schöpferischen Gemeingut *Human Library*. Ich lud Sylviane Tille ein, ihre Fassung
2010 in der Staats- und Universitätsbibliothek Fribourg zu organisieren. Der Katalog enthielt 60 menschliche Bücher – Personen mit einer speziellen Fertigkeit oder bestimmten Kenntnissen
– und 15 Wörterbücher (mit Simultandolmetschern). Das Projekt
kam bei den Festival- und Bibliotheksbesuchern sehr gut an.

4. Arbeiten
‹à la tête du client›

Obwohl sich das Festival demons-
trativ in der Stadt ausbreitet, haben wir einen Hauptspielort: Das
Belluard (oder Bollwerk) ist eine
alte Festung aus dem Mittelalter
mit Anklängen an Shakespeares
Globe Theatre. Es ist zur Hälfte
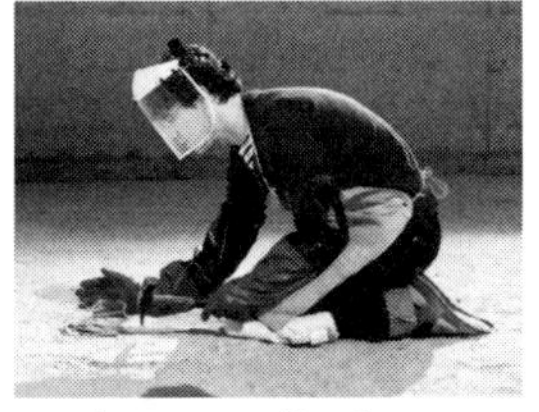
ein Freilufttheater und besitzt eine Schauspielbühne. Der Ort wurde
1983 von Künstlern besetzt, die das Belluard Bollwerk International
gegründet haben, und es bildet seither jedes Jahr den Mittelpunkt des
Festivals. Es ist ein Hingucker, prachtvoll, aber auch ein sehr domi-
nantes Gebäude, in dem man nicht einfach jede Performance oder jedes Kunstprojekt präsentieren kann. Der Raum trägt also massgeblich
zu den Entscheidungen bei. Im Belluard präsentieren wir eher ‹konven-
tionelle› Projekte, nicht in inhaltlicher, sondern in formaler Hinsicht,
wie Konzerte und Darbietungen. Manchmal nutzen Künstler den Ort
auf andere Weise. Im Jahr 2011 zum Beispiel haben die Musiker/Kom-
ponisten Antoine Chessex, Valerio Tricoli und Jérôme Noetinger die
Festungsarchitektur für die Klangarbeit *Espèce d'Espace* genutzt. So
hatte man das Belluard noch nie ‹gehört›. Gleichwohl finden dort auch
Theaterstücke wie die Produktion *Tomorrow's Parties* von Forced Entertainment oder *External* (2011) der jungen britischen Theatertruppe
GETINTHEBACKOFTHEVAN statt.
　　　Ein anderer Ort, den wir häufig nutzen, ist das Theatre Nouveau Monde im Ancienne Gare. Es handelt sich um eine klassische
Black Box, die es uns ermöglicht, Performances, szenische Lesungen, Filme oder andere kleinere Bühnenprojekte wie *L'effet de Serge*
von Philippe Quesne (2008) zu präsentieren. Der Raum eignet sich

aber auch für andere Formen, wie zum Beispiel das *Mundkino* [wirvwar] der schweizerischen Künstler Gilles Aubry & Stéphane Montavon (2010), bei dem sich das Publikum auf Kissen legen und mit geschlossenen Augen einer Klanglandschaft lauschen konnte, die auf Feldaufnahmen aus Fribourg und von anderen Orten beruhte. Neben diesen ‹klassischeren› Bühnen produziert das Belluard Bollwerk Festival viele Arbeiten, die in einem Bezug zur Stadt und zu ihren Einwohnern stehen. Viele Projekte finden im öffentlichen Raum oder an anderen Stellen oder in anderen Gebäuden in Fribourg statt. Wir haben Projekte in der Universität, in Einkaufszentren, in einer Bibliothek, in alten Lagerhäusern, in einem Gerichtshof, in städtischen Gärten, auf der Strasse, in einem Freibad, hinter der Kathedrale und an anderen Orten gemacht. Für diese ortsspezifischen Werke und für die Bühnenwerke arbeiten wir ‹à la tête du client›: Jeder Künstler, jede Künstlerin schlägt ein Konzept oder ein Projekt vor, und gemeinsam mit ihm oder ihr suchen wir nach dem richtigen Schauplatz für das Projekt (nie andersherum).

NB: Es erweist sich als sehr konstruktiv, sich die Zeit für einen langen Spaziergang durch die Stadt mit einem Künstler / einer Künstlerin zu nehmen und ihm / ihr verschiedene Stellen und Plätze zu zeigen. Häufig liefert ein Raum die Inspiration zum ersten künstlerischen Vorschlag. Die britische Künstlerin Sheila Ghelani etwa modifizierte ihre Performance-Installation *Covet Me, Care For Me,* bei der die Besucher ein geblasenes Glasherz zerbrechen können, nachdem sie beschlossen hatte, ihre Arbeit im Werkhof zu präsentieren, einem schönen, teilrenovierten alten Bootsdepot in Fribourg.

5. Locken Sie Künstler
mit einem Leitmotiv

Um dem künstlerischen Input als Ausgangspunkt stärkere Beachtung zu schenken, wurden die Regeln für den ein Jahr lang gültigen Aufruf, Vorschläge für das Belluard Bollwerk International – ein traditionelles Fenster im Festivalprogramm – einzureichen, 2008 geändert. Jedes Jahr wählten wir ab diesem Zeitpunkt, häufig im Dialog mit anderen Kunstfachleuten, ein ‹Leitmotiv›: 2008 *Mis-Guided* mit Wrights & Sites, einer Gruppe von Künstlern/Forschern aus Grossbritannien; 2009 *KITCHEN* – eine Neuerfindung unseres Festivalzentrums – mit Oliver Schmid, Patrick Aumann und Adrian Kramp, drei Architekten aus drei unterschiedlichen

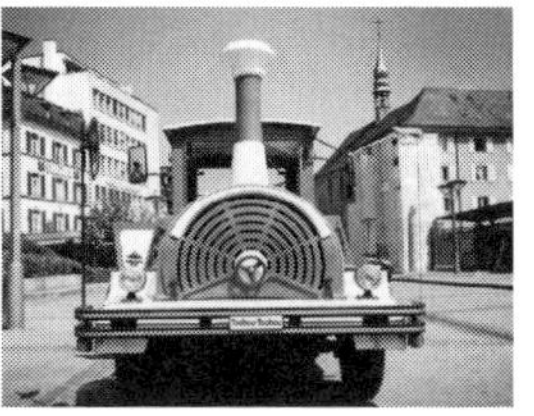

Büros in Fribourg; 2010 *Urban Myth* in Zusammenarbeit mit dem Belluard-Büroteam; 2011 *Hope* mit Elke Van Campenhout, einer Dramaturgin aus Belgien. Diese Leute wurden eingeladen, weil sie an einem Thema arbeiteten, das für uns zu diesem Zeitpunkt von Belang war: entweder weil es das Festival als eine Gemeinschaft und einen Treffpunkt *(KITCHEN)* betraf oder weil es sich um eine Frage handelte, die sowohl in Fribourg als auch global omnipräsent war *(Urban Myth)*, oder weil viele Künstler sich damit befassten und es sich um eine aktuelle politische Thematik handelte *(Hope)*. Diese Stichwörter sind keine thematischen Vorgaben, sondern vielmehr eine Art Brille, durch die man das tatsächliche Geschehen auf dem Gebiet der Kunst betrachten kann. Im Übrigen beherrscht das Leitmotiv nicht die gesamte Kommunikation des Festivals.

Da Fribourg eine Stadt im ständigen Wandel ist, in der urbane Veränderungen sowohl kritisiert als auch begrüsst werden, berücksichtigte der erste Aufruf 2008 diese Alltagswirklichkeit. Unter der Überschrift *Mis-Guided* und der Kodirektion des englischen Kollektivs Wrights & Sites wurden für das Festival sechs Interventionen im öffentlichen Raum realisiert. Diese Projekte führten die Besucher nicht zu historischen oder malerischen Teilen der Stadt, sondern zeigten ihnen eher deren ‹Rückseite›: die Gewerbegebiete, die sich ändernden und expandierenden Viertel. Auf spielerische Weise hinterfragten die sechs Projekte die städtische Gesellschaft, und dies ohne den kleinsten Anflug von Nostalgie, sondern aus einer subtilen, kritischen Perspektive heraus.

NB:	Die *Mis-Guided*-Projekte 2008 betrafen nicht nur die Festivalbesucher, sondern zogen auch die Aufmerksamkeit von Passanten und Touristen auf sich. Zu unserer angenehmen Überraschung wurden zwei der Projekte, nämlich *Tschou-Tschou* von Alexander Hana (eine alternative Tour mit dem Touristenzug von Fribourg in die gewerblichen Aussenbezirke der Stadt) und *Hier, aujourd'hui, demain* von Robert Walker (eine geführte Tour mit 3-D-Brillen durch das sich ständig verändernde Viertel Pérolles) nach dem Festival vom Tourismusbüro Fribourg in dessen Sommerprogramm 2009 übernommen.

6. Gehen Sie
Risiken ein

Eine aus acht Personen bestehende Jury (halb lokal, halb international besetzt, etwa mit Architekten, Grafikdesignern, Künstlern, Kuratoren auf dem Gebiet der bildenden Kunst, Programmgestaltern im Bereich der darstellenden Künste, Dramaturgen und mir) wählt aus den durchschnittlich 250 bis 550 Bewerbungen, die wir jedes Jahr

erhalten, zwischen – je nach Art des Aufrufs und der Projekte – einem bis neun Vorschläge aus. Die endgültige Auswahl dauert zwei Tage und besteht aus langen Diskussionen sowie einer Darstellung der ausgewählten 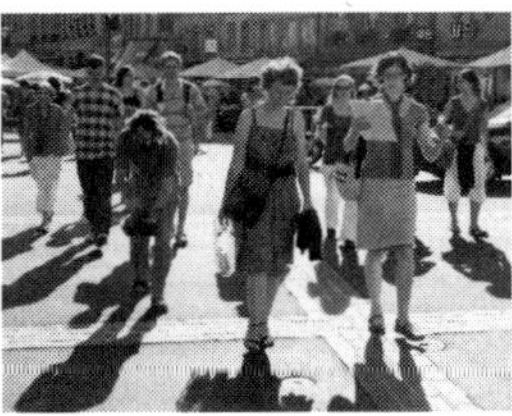 Projekte. Dieser Teil der Festivalpraxis ist sehr wichtig, da er meine Entscheidungen als Programmgestalterin beeinflusst. Erstens erhalten wir viele Vorschläge von Künstlern oder anderen Kunstfachleuten, die ich nicht kenne und denen ich in meinen normalen Netzwerken nicht begegnen würde, obwohl ich versuche, aus diesen herauszutreten. Zweitens haben diese Künstler eine völlig andere Sicht auf das Leitmotiv. Es ist wie mit einem Stein, den wir ins Wasser werfen, woraufhin dieses sich in verschiedenen Richtungen zu kräuseln beginnt. Drittens ist die endgültige Auswahl das Ergebnis einer richtig harten Auseinandersetzung. Einige der Projekte, die so Teil des Programms werden, hätte ich so, für mich persönlich, nicht gewählt. Doch durch die Diskussion in der Gruppe stelle ich fest, dass ich vieles aus einem anderen Blickwinkel sehe und neue Sichtweisen in das Festival hineingetragen werden, was sehr erfrischend ist.

NB: 2010 entschied sich die Jury für das Projekt Anonymous, einen Künstler, der seine Identität geheim halten wollte, und einen Plan, der das Festival als Institution aufs Spiel setzte. Wir konnten keinen Vertrag mit einem anonymen Künstler schliessen, kein Geld auf sein Konto überweisen, nichts versichern ... Während des Festivals machte Anonymous verschiedene unangekündigte Interventionen, und das Bemühen, seine Identität aufzudecken, entwickelte sich in Fribourg zu einem regelrechten Sport. In philosophischer Hinsicht setzte sich dieses Projekt mit verschiedenen Fragen zu Urheberschaft und Kunst auseinander.

7. Bleiben Sie
auf dem Laufenden

Auch wenn wir uns, nach 28 Jahren, als Institution etabliert haben, betrachten wir uns immer noch gerne als ein ‹kleines grosses Festival›, das auf gesellschaftlicher und künstlerischer Ebene Tuchfühlung mit dem Zeitgeschehen hält. Jedes Jahr ermöglicht uns das Programm des Festivals, eine neue Künstlergeneration und damit auch neue Ideen zu empfangen. Während es sich 2008 mehr auf die städtische Situation allgemein konzentrierte, wurde das Festival 2009 stark von der ökonomischen Krise und dem Thema des Kunstkonsums beeinflusst. Laut *La Liberté* vom 28. April 2009 hat die Zahl leerer Schaufenster in Fribourg zuge-

nommen, ein Phänomen, das auch in anderen Städten zu beobachten ist. Vor diesem Hintergrund lud das Belluard Festival 2009 drei Künstler und zwei Künstlerduos ein, für einen Zeitraum von zehn Tagen einen Laden in Fribourg zu eröffnen. Ihre Projekte stellten eine Reflexion über Konsum, wirtschaftliche Transaktionen und die wirtschaftliche Stellung von Künstlern dar.

2010 war das Jahr ‹urbaner Mythen› (siehe Punkt 5), eine Ausgabe, bei der auch viele Nord-Süd-Fragen in das Programm einsickerten. Als das Belluard Festival im Mai 2010 unter dem Titel *Hoffnung* den Aufruf zu Vorschlägen für 2011 startete, schien es uns erforderlich, ein zeitgenössisches Verständnis zu diesem Begriff zu entwickeln. Wir waren der Ansicht, Hoffnung verorte sich jetzt ganz in der Ewigkeit, als eine subtile spaltende Kraft in jedweder Situation, Beziehung und ethischen Konstellation, statt in einem Traum einer blutigen Revolution. Ein Jahr später, im Juni 2011, zur Zeit des Festivals, hatte sich die Welt völlig verändert … Dennoch glauben wir, dass Hoffnung genau das ist, etwas, das sich die ganze Zeit ändert, nicht greifbar ist und Handlungen, Revolutionen und Bewegung impliziert. Für uns heisst ‹hoffnungsvoll sein› nicht, die einfache Stimmigkeit einer aktivistischen Position zu akzeptieren. Wir ziehen es vor, auf der nicht so leicht definierbaren Ebene einer ungelösten Poetik und ungelöster Befragungen zu bleiben, die uns von verschiedenen Künstlern mit einem jeweils anderen Hintergrund vorgeschlagen werden.

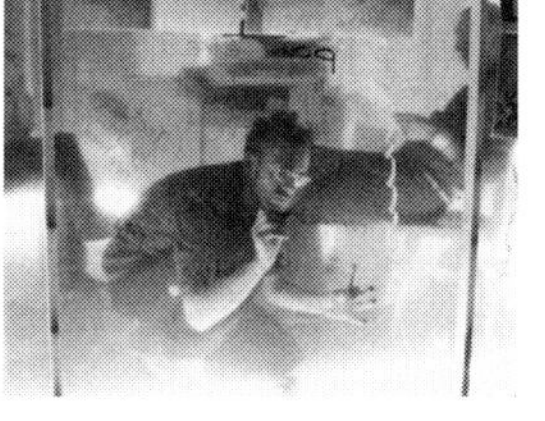

NB: Sehr häufig überholt die Wirklichkeit die Kunst. Als 2010 die Künstler Nicolas Galeazzi (CH) & Joel Verwimp (B) vorschlugen, in ihrem performativen Copyshop *Coyotl: Imprimerie des mythes* die Verbindung zwischen Oberst Gaddafi & Damien Hirst zu untersuchen, und dies einer der ‹Mythen› war, die unser Grafikdesigner René Walker für seine Werbekampagne mit anonymen Plakaten auswählte, konnten wir den grossen Medienskandal nicht voraussehen, der damit zum Zeitpunkt unserer Pressekonferenz ausgelöst werden sollte. Von allen Schweizer Medien fand ausgerechnet die *Tribune de Genève* heraus, dass die Urheberschaft an einem der Plakate, auf dem es hiess «Gaddafi nach Fribourg eingeladen», bei Belluard Bollwerk International lag, und dies genau zu der Zeit, als eine der beiden Schweizer Geiseln von der libyschen Regierung befreit werden sollte. Einige Schweizer Zeitungen schrieben, das Belluard Festival gefährde das Leben der Geisel, was eine heftige Diskussion in den Medien und eine politische Auseinandersetzung über unsere Kampagnen und unser Festival auslöste, die bis zur Freilassung der Geisel andauerten.

8. Sorgen Sie für Aufsehen

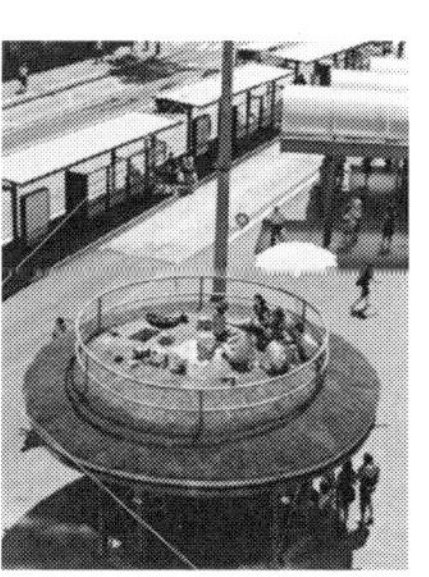

Das Festival Belluard Bollwerk International hat eine Geschichte der Produktion und Präsentation von Kunstwerken, die in manchen Fällen Skandale verursacht, aber auf jeden Fall immer für Aufsehen gesorgt haben. Viele durch Mundpropaganda bekannt gewordene Projekte der letzten 28 Jahre führen inzwischen ein häufig entstelltes, übertriebenes oder boulevardmässig aufbereitetes Eigenleben. Vor allem Gerüchte verbreiten sich unbeabsichtigt. Doch 2010 lancierte das Festival den Aufruf *Mythos der Stadt* in der gezielten Absicht, für Aufsehen zu sorgen. Bei manchen der realisierten Projekte entstand der ‹Mythos› nicht durch eine Handlung. Mehrere Projekte wurden nicht vom Festival angekündigt, und ihre Performativität existierte eher in der Mund-zu-Mund-Propaganda und der Suggestivität dessen, was noch kommen könnte, oder in der Nacherzählung dessen, was geschehen war.

NB: Obwohl das Festival mit einer spielerischen, deutlichen Kommunikation arbeitet, sind es häufig die Projekte im urbanen Raum, die die Aufmerksamkeit der Passanten wecken und zu einer unkonventionellen Werbung werden. Eines der auffälligsten Beispiele war *Die Insel* (2008) des deutschen Künstlers Christian Hasucha, eine grasbedeckte Insel auf einem Gerüst vor dem Bahnhof, somit auf einem der belebtesten Plätze von Fribourg. Man konnte die Insel in Zeitfenstern von drei Stunden Länge gratis anmieten. Auf einer Plattform, die im städtischen Raum das Territorium in Frage stellt, waren die Mieter Betrachter und Performer zugleich.

9. Arbeiten Sie mit einer Community of Practice (CoP)

Die Projekte *Human Library* und *The Great Public Sale of Brilliant but Unrealized Ideas*© (siehe Punkt 2) sind Beispiele für eine ‹Community of Practice› (CoP). Dabei handelt es sich den Kognitionsanthropologen Jean Lave und Etienne Wenger zufolge um eine Gruppe von Leuten, die ein Interesse, eine Praxis und/oder einen Beruf miteinander teilen. Die Gruppe kann sich selbst entwickeln, indem sie Wissen und Erfahrungen austauscht.

Die Gruppe kann aber auch in der Absicht gebildet werden, Wissen über ein bestimmtes Gebiet in Erfahrung zu bringen. Zeitgenössische Künstler wenden sich an Spezialisten, damit diese ihnen bei der Entwicklung ihrer Werke helfen. Dabei kann es sich um eine künstlerische Unterstützung handeln, häufiger geht es aber auch um einen Wissensaustausch mit Spezialisten auf einem anderen Gebiet: Ingenieuren, Wissenschaftlern, Architekten, Schamanen, Köchen, Politikern und anderen. Die ausgewählten Künstler werden zu einem gemeinsamen Aufenthalt in Fribourg eingeladen. Sie erhalten die Gelegenheit, sich untereinander und das Team kennenzulernen, die Stadt zu besuchen und Spezialisten zu treffen, die ihnen dabei helfen können, ihr Projekt zu entwickeln und zu produzieren. Da wir keinen festen Veranstaltungsort und kein Atelier haben, sind diese Aufenthaltsstipendien entscheidend für die Vorbereitung des Festivals und die Zusammenarbeit mit den Künstlern und anderer Personen in Fribourg in dem jeweiligen Jahr. Alle diese Spezialisten oder Teilnehmer und ihre Kollegen, Freunde und Verwandten sind daher Teil der *Community of Artistic Practice*. Der Wissensaustausch, der während eines Festivals oder in dessen Entstehungsphase stattfindet, ist somit eine Form der gemeinsamen Teilhabe an einem heimlichen Wissen, einem Wissen, das nicht greifbar und explizit ist, sondern eher durch künstlerische Projekte zwischen verschiedenen Bereichen und Menschen weitergegeben werden kann. Alle Mitglieder einer solchen Gemeinschaft werden durch das, was sie gemeinsam erzeugen, stimuliert: Gemeinsames Wissen eröffnet neue Perspektiven, neue Formen, neue Kunst für eine sich wandelnde Gesellschaft.

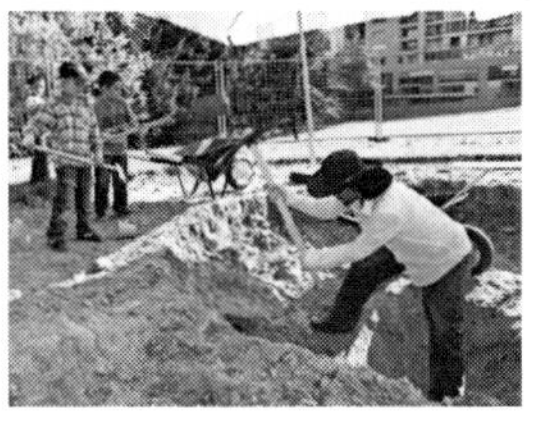

NB: Häufig stellen die einfachsten Konzepte die grösste Herausforderung dar und können daher zur grössten Teilnehmergemeinschaft führen. *The Digging Project* der in Brüssel ansässigen Künstler Kosi Hidama & Gosie Vervloessem (2011) etwa war ein poetisches Projekt, das jedoch logistisch sehr schwer zu realisieren war und darin bestand, in einem öffentlichen Garten mitten in Fribourg zehn Tage lang ein Loch zu graben. Der Stadtarchitekt, die städtischen Ingenieure, der archäologische Dienst des Kantons Fribourg, ein Geobiologe und ein Magnetiseur waren nur einige der Experten, die für die Recherchen und die Produktion herangezogen wurden.

10. Seien Sie
ein guter Gastgeber

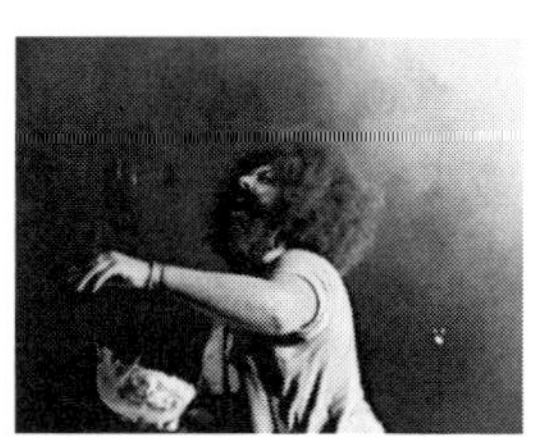

Ein wichtiger Aspekt des Festivals ist Gastfreundschaft. Ein innovatives künstlerisches Programm kann besser in einer geselligen Atmosphäre gedeihen, in der sich ein breites Publikum (oder eine breite *Gemeinschaft* [community]) willkommen fühlt. Diese Gastfreundschaft lässt sich ganz konkret bewerkstelligen, indem man einen Zeit-Raum schafft, in dem man Menschen trifft und mit ihnen isst, trinkt, diskutiert. Im Hinblick auf die Idee des Festivals als eine Gemeinschaft auf Zeit, als Ort, der zwei Wochen lang sowohl ein professionelles Umfeld für starke Arbeiten internationaler Künstler als auch einen geselligen Rahmen für den Austausch zwischen Künstlern, Ortsansässigen, Besuchern und Profis bietet, lancierte das Belluard Bollwerk International einen Aufruf für Vorschläge für eine ‹Küche› für seine Ausgabe 2009. Denn im Mittelpunkt jedes künstlerischen Prozesses befindet sich stets eine Küche: eine Kochstelle, ein Ort, wo man etwas essen und sich treffen kann, ein Platz, der kreative Diskussionen fördert. Und ohnehin finden die interessantesten Begegnungen immer in der Küche statt …

Um diese Idee des sozialen Miteinanders zu verstärken und zu fördern, entwarfen Antonio Louro (PT) & Benedetta Maxia (IT) ein auf Tischen basierendes Modulsystem namens *KITCHAIN*, das die Leute dazu einlud, durch ihre Handlungen das gesamte Arsenal (ein altes Zeughaus neben dem Belluard) in eine riesige Küche zu verwandeln. Das Publikum konnte sich zwischen einer aktiven oder einer passiven Rolle entscheiden: aktiv, weil man wirklich seine eigene Mahlzeit in einer der Kochnischen zubereitete, passiv, indem man den professionellen Köchen Jean Piguet, Arnaud Nicod und Maïté Collin bei der Arbeit zusehen und ihre köstlichen Mahlzeiten probieren konnte. Daneben umfasste *KITCHAIN* eine Bar und bot Raum für kleinere Projekte und Partys. Aufgrund seiner Flexibilität konnte das Festival den Raum unterschiedlich gestalten und das Küchen-Raum-Konzept jedes Jahr erneuern. *KITCHAIN* hat sich als grosser Erfolg erwiesen und zieht seit seiner Eröffnung 2009 ein immer grösseres Publikum an (Blog: www.kitchain.net).

NB: Ein Festival ist seinem Wesen nach ein ‹Fest›, sollte also auch festlich sein. Partys gehören unbedingt dazu. Ein musikalischer Höhepunkt der letzten Jahre war die umwerfend komische, brillante und unberechenbare Performance des amerikanischen Musikers-Komikers-Beatboxers Reggie Watts im Jahr 2010.

EASTSIDE PROJECTS MANUAL
DRAFT #2

Gavin Wade

Dies ist eine Anleitung für Eastside Projects. Sie erläutert, woraus der Kunstraum besteht, wie er angelegt wurde, für wen er gedacht ist, wie man ihn nutzen kann und was er zu bieten hat. Räume gehen selten mit Gebrauchsanweisungen einher. Eastside Projects wurde auf der Grundlage von Erfahrungen und im Hinblick auf das allfällige zukünftige Publikum, mögliche Bewohner und Bearbeiter des Raums gestaltet, um seinen spezifischen Kontext zu präsentieren und zu seinem Gebrauch einzuladen. Wie bei einer Maschine oder beim Erlernen einer Fertigkeit dürfte eine Anleitung sinnvoll sein, um die Gebrauchsmöglichkeiten von Eastside Projects voll ausschöpfen zu können. Auf diese Weise möchten wir Eastside Projects für neue Formen der Auseinandersetzung öffnen.

Situation

Eastside Projects ist ein von Künstlerinnen und Künstlern geleiteter Raum, eine öffentliche Galerie für die Stadt Birmingham und die Welt. Organisiert wird er von einem Gründungskollektiv, das aus Simon und Tom Bloor, Céline Condorelli, Ruth Claxton, James Langdon und Gavin Wade besteht, der den Raum als Erster konzipierte und jetzt leitet.

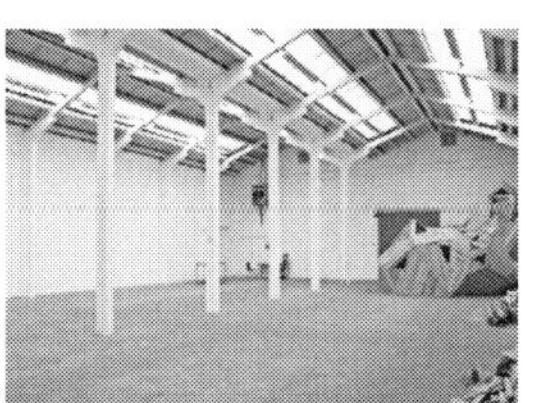

Eastside Projects versucht, die Rolle und Funktion von Kunst im städtischen Kontext zu hinterfragen, indem diese Einrichtung experimentelle zeitgenössische Kunstpraktiken einlädt und präsentiert und sich sowohl nach innen als auch nach aussen intensiv an den kulturellen Aktivitäten der Stadt beteiligt und diese unterstützt. Eastside Projects steht der Öffentlichkeit zur Verfügung und ist offen für vielfältige Formen der Beteiligung von Künstlerinnen, Künstlern und anderen in diesem Bereich Tätigen.

Eastside Projects soll ein integraler Bestandteil der Struktur der Stadt und Teil des öffentlichen, von der Regierung subventionierten Bereichs sein. Dies ist ein richtiger und angemessener Teil des Kampfes, das Monopol von kultureller Hegemonie in Schach zu halten, und trägt dazu bei, den von Künstlerinnen und Künstlern geleiteten Raum als ein öffentliches Gut zu etablieren.

Eastside Projects ist eine Non-Profit-Organisation und arbeitet mit der Birmingham City University zusammen; finanziell wird Eastside Projects vom Arts Council England West Midlands unterstützt.

Eastside Projects befindet sich in einem Industriegebäude – einer ehemaligen Tischlerei – im Zentrum der Eastside von Birmingham und in unmittelbarer Nähe zu anderen Kunstproduktions- und Aus-

stellungsstätten wie Ikon Eastside, Custard Factory und VIVID. Das Gebäude wurde mit Mitteln des Arts Council England West Midlands renoviert und umfasst einen 225 Quadratmeter grossen Ausstellungsraum, einen zweiten, kleineren, der 70 Quadratmeter gross und für Videoprojektionen ausgestattet ist, sowie ein Atelier für Künstlerinnen und Künstler mit einem Aufenthaltsstipendium. Ausserdem befinden sich vor Ort Büros und Studios für die Bild- und Tonbearbeitung der Visualisation Research Unit (VRU) der Birmingham City University. Die Renovierung und die Erschliessung des Ausstellungsraums erfolgten durch Support Structure: Céline Condorelli und Gavin Wade.

Zweck

Während herkömmliche Galeriestrukturen dazu neigen, die Benutzer zur Passivität zu verleiten, verlangt Eastside Projects durch sein Design, dass man sich aktiv verhält. Diese Aktivität ist das Stichwort für weitere Arbeiten jenseits des öffentlichen Raums der Galerie für und in die Öffentlichkeit. Das sollte der Zweck der Galerie sein.

Präsentationsformen

Der Ausstellungsraum wurde auf der Grundlage der folgenden Fragen entwickelt: Wie unterstützen Architektur und Design das Kunstmachen parallel zum Prozess des Kuratierens? Können Architektur und Design als eine Form des Kuratierens als Teil eines Galerieprogramms genutzt werden? Können wir uns einen Kontext vorstellen, der auf aktive und explizite Weise Ausstellungen und Kunst produziert, statt beides zu verkörpern oder zu repräsentieren? Können Ausstellungen auch die Mittel, Beziehungen und zugrunde liegenden Ideologien bei der Repräsentation des Raums zur Schau stellen?

Die Galerie wird zu einer Projektmaschine, der von Künstlerinnen und Künstlern geleitete Raum ist ein Produktionsraum, d.h. ein Raum für Sensibilität, für Ausstellungen und für ein spezifisches Verständnis für Objekte, Kontext und Erfahrung. Dadurch wird der Ausstellungsraum Teil eines Diskurses über Performativität, mit einem gebauten Kontext, der sich mit seinem Gegenstand auseinandersetzt, statt ihn lediglich zum Konsum anzubieten. Eastside Projects ist eine Präsentationseinrichtung, die mit einem speziellen Programm entworfen wurde und parallel dazu als eine offengelegte Form des Kuratierens funktionieren soll, wobei die Design- und Architektursprache diesen Prozess unterstützt.

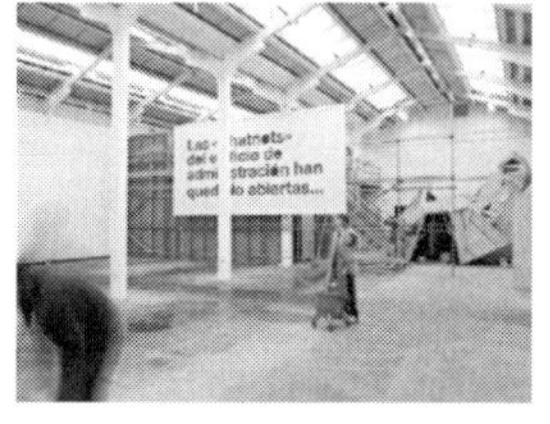

Unserer Vorstellung nach soll ein solcher Kunstraum kritische Fragen zur Produktion von Kunst, zu ihrer Wahrnehmung, zu ihrem Konsum und zu möglichen Auseinandersetzungen durch das räumliche Display des Kunstraums aufwerfen.

Kunstwerke als vorhandene Bedingungen

Eastside Projects betrachtet Design, Organisationsstrukturen und Architektur als integralen Bestandteil seines Programms; jeder Aspekt der Galerie ist Teil eines Prozesses und entwickelt sich ständig weiter. Die vorhandenen Bedingungen werden durch das Ausstellungsprogramm und mit diesem konstruiert. Die Künstlerinnen und Künstler sind eingeladen, die vorhandenen Bedingungen für die Galerie zu bestimmen. Werke können dort installiert bleiben, und man kann auf vorhandene Werke reagieren. Die erste Ausstellung, *This is the Gallery and the Gallery is Many Things,* lieferte die erste Reaktion auf den Ort und ändert erstmals die vorhandenen Bedingungen, indem sie das vorhandene Gebäude mit einer ganz dünnen und fragilen Schicht, einer Verkleidung, einer temporären Ad-hoc-Ästhetik überzog. Dabei handelt es sich eindeutig um eine Ergänzung des Gebäudes, gleich einem Gerüst, und bot damit zusätzliche Möglichkeiten für Veränderungen. Um Erfahrungen zu sammeln und das Gebäude einem Lernprozess zu unterziehen, sollten einige Spuren von dem übrig bleiben, was dort früher geschah. Die Galerie ist eine Sammlung. Die Galerie ist selbst ein Kunstwerk.

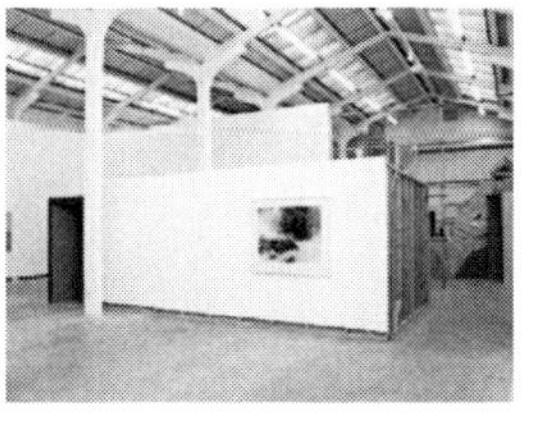

Bleibende Installationen

Das Eastside Projects-Büro ist das Kunstwerk *Pleasure Island* von Heather und Ivan Morison. Der Bau wurde aus dem Holz von Redwood-Bäumen aus einem Wald in Wales errichtet, der den Künstlerinnen und Künstlern gehört. Das ursprünglich für den walisischen Pavillon auf der 52. Biennale von Venedig 2007 in Auftrag gegebene Gebäude wurde für Eastside Projects in einer langfristigen Verbindlichheithinsichtlich der Erkundung der Natur von Kunstwerken im Raum angepasst. Zu den neuen Bestandteilen innerhalb des Gebäudes zählen eine Küche, Schreibtische, Regale und ein grösserer Eingang. Das Künstlerpaar hat als Teil des Galerieprogramms innerhalb des *Pleasure Island* eine Reihe von Puppentheater-Vorstellungen präsentiert. Die erste Vorstellung anlässlich der Eröffnung von Eastside

Projects am 26. September 2008 trug den Titel *I Love You Pleasure Island* und wurde von Owen Davies und Suzy Kemp aufgeführt.

Andere bleibende Werke wurden von den Künstlerinnen und Künstlern Matthew Harrison, Peter Fend, Mark Titchner, Lawrence Weiner, ISAN, Barbara Holub, Scott Myles und Susan Collins erarbeitet.

Verweise auf
vorhandene Bedingungen

Drei historisch wichtige Vorläuferausstellungen lieferten Verweise und ein zugrunde liegendes Ethos für die erste Ausstellung und die andauernde Entwicklung der Galerie als ein fortgesetztes Kunstwerk.

1. El Lissitzkys *Abstraktes Kabinett* (1926/30) auf der Internationalen Kunstausstellung Dresden und in der Niedersächsischen Landesgalerie Hannover stand für ein deutliches und radikales Auftreten des Künstler-Kurators, der ein eigens hierfür errichtetes Environment für Kunstwerke von Piet Mondrian, Naum Gabo und Lissitzky erschuf. Es funktionierte selbst als Kunstwerk und ging mit der Auswahl und der Integration der Werke anderer Künstlerinnen und Künstler einher. Das *Abstrakte Kabinett* kann als Modell eines Kunstraums verwendet werden, als eine Präsentationsvorrichtung, die so gestaltet ist, dass sie verschiedene Richtungen in einem Programm unterstützt. Wir denken dabei weniger an El Lissitzkys Ästhetik als an seinen Ansatz in puncto Raumdesign als eine Form des Kuratierens, bei der das Gebäude und die Grafik den kuratorischen Prozess unterstützen und produzieren.
2. Ein weiteres wichtiges Referenzbeispiel liefert die Peter Nadin Gallery (1978/79), New York, die von Peter Nadin, Christopher d'Arcangelo und Nick Lawson gegründet wurde. Dort gab es eine Dauerausstellung mit dem Titel *The work shown in this space is a response to the existing conditions and/or work previously shown within the space* (Das in diesem Raum gezeigte Werk ist eine Reaktion auf die existierenden Bedingungen und/oder Werke, die vorher in dem Raum gezeigt wurden). Zu den Künstlerinnen und Künstlern zählten Daniel Buren, Peter Fend, Dan Graham, Louise Lawler, Sean Scully und Lawrence Weiner. Die Künstlerinnen und Künstler reagierten direkt auf die Werke der jeweils anderen und entwickelten so ein kumulatives Environment. Das Projekt von Nadin, d'Arcangelo und Lawson begann mit dem Text: «Wir haben uns zusammengetan, um als ein Mittel des Überlebens in einer

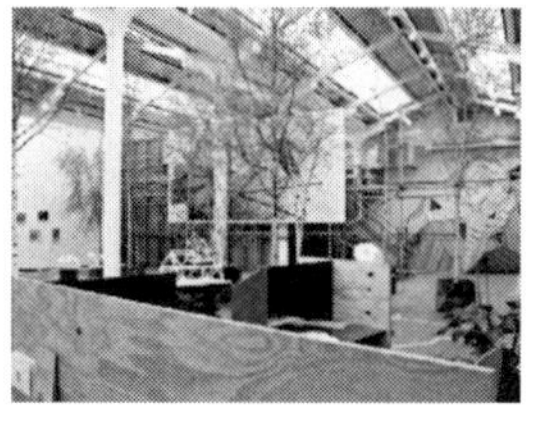

kapitalistischen Ökonomie funktionale Konstruktionen zu realisieren und um existierende Strukturen zu ändern oder auf Vordermann zu bringen.» Der Text bildet den Ausgangspunkt für die Galeriepolitik und -strategie. Auf die Ausstellung von Nadin mit dem ‹leeren› Galerieraum folgte *This is the Gallery and the Gallery is Many Things* mit einer Analyse der Funktion, der Gestaltung und der Ausführung durch die Fachleute, welche das Fundament der Galerie und ihrer Künstlerinnen und Künstler bilden.

Zwei der Künstler (Fend und Weiner) trugen semipermanente Werke zu der ersten Ausstellung bei Eastside Projects in Birmingham bei.

3. *This is the Show and the Show is Many Things,* 1994, im Museum van Hedendaagse Kunst, Gent, kuratiert von Bart de Baere, bildet den letzten Referenzpunkt für unser Projekt. Die Ausstellung umfasste Künstlerinnen und Künstler wie Honoré d'O, Fabrice Hybert, Louise Bourgeois, Suchan Kinoshita, Jason Rhoades und Luc Tuymans. Die Ausstellung wurde kollektiv als ein Gemeinschaftsprojekt geplant. Die Beziehungen untereinander definierten bestimmte Funktionen des Museumsraums neu. Der Titel der ersten Ausstellung bei Eastside Projects, *This is the Gallery and the Gallery is Many Things* (Dies ist die Galerie und die Galerie ist viele Dinge), bezieht sich auf diese Ausstellung und funktioniert auch als Strategie und Slogan.

Erstveröffentlichung: Celine Condorelli, James Langdon & Gavin Wade (hg.), *Eastside Projects Manual Draft 2, Support Structures,* Berlin, New York: Sternberg Press 2009.

BAUCH DES WALS

Sibylle Omlin

Das breite Untersuchungsfeld der Performance-Installation wurde im Projekt *Bauch des Wals* (2010/11) zur Ausgangslage[1]. Für das Ausstellungsprojekt wurde ein eigenes Veranstaltungsformat angelegt: die Verkettung von möglichen Ereignissen.

Beteiligt waren siebzehn Kunstschaffende mit unterschiedlichen Performancepraktiken an fünf Ausstellungsorten mit je spezifischen Gegebenheiten: einem White cube, einem Offspace, einem experimentellen Ausstellungsraum mit Schaufenstercharakter, einem Landschaftspark sowie dem öffentlichen Raum. Der Wechsel vom einem zum anderen, von der Performance zur Installation, von einem Raumdispositiv ins andere bildete den Forschungskern dieses Projekts. Die Verkettung von Möglichkeiten innerhalb eines klar bestimmten Werkkomplexes durch Ortswechsel, aber auch durch den Wechsel von Inhalten oder Formaten wurde von den beteiligten Kunstschaffenden je unterschiedlich angegangen. Da die Performance nach wie vor auf eine vergängliche, wenn auch wiederholbare Handlung setzt, war das transformierbare Raumdispositiv eine wichtige Untersuchungsanlage, welche narrative und kontextbezogene Elemente des Ausstellungsraums miteinbezog.

So erarbeitete zum Beispiel die Künstlerin Katja Schenker, die in ihren Performances Körperkraft, Material und physikalische Kräfte geschickt kombiniert, in einer Live-Situation im Kunstverein Konstanz aus einer auf einem im Verhältnis zum Raum winzigen Kubus zusammengepressten Papierfläche von 134 Quadratmetern eine raumfüllende Landschaft. Sie zog in einer performativen Aktion das stark zerknüllte Papier vor Publikum auseinander. Was in einer Performance für das Publikum sichtbar waren, war die Handlung der Künstlerin und die Fragilität des Materials Papier: zwei Elemente, die ausschlaggebend dafür waren, wie die Form des erst zusammengepressten Ballens sich im Raum ausdehnen würde. Das Resultat war anschliessend als Installation mit dem Titel *moll* für einen Monat im Ausstellungsraum zu sehen. Die Papierinstallation wurde während der Finissage in einem performativen Akt abgebaut, in verschiedene Teile getrennt, wovon ein Teil weiter nach Sierre reiste und dort in einer Bibliothek wieder aufgebaut wurde.[2] Der interessanteste Teil dieser Arbeit war jedoch für das Publikum vorerst nicht sichtbar: der Vorgang des Pressens der 134 Quadratmeter grossen Papierfläche auf einen Kubus von 1,6 × 1,8 × 0,7 Metern. Für diesen Vorgang, der nicht im Ausstellungskontext stattfand, wurde eine Turnhalle organisiert, in der die Künstlerin zusammen mit ihrem Team von Helfern die Papierfläche von allen vier Seiten her bearbeitete und allein mit Körperkraft zusammenzupressen versuchte.[3]

Andere Kunstschaffende, wie die Tanz-Performerin Dorothea Rust oder der Konzeptkünstler Berclaz de Sierre, waren mit einem Fundus an Material unterwegs, den sie in den je wechselnden räumlichen Situationen neu installierten und performten. Bei Dorothea Rust bestand dieser Fundus aus Schuhen, Taschen, Kletterseilen, Teppichen,

Haken, Äpfeln, Papierseiten, die sie für ihre Tanzperformances im Kunstraum K3 in Zürich und in Sierre verwendete. Im K3 war der Prozess der De-Installation für das Publikum sichtbar, während man in Sierre in einer Live-Performance der Künstlerin zu verschiedenen Installationsteilen im Park des Schlosses geführt wurde. Die Sichtbarkeit des Installationsprozesses machten die beiden Kunstschaffenden Valerian Maly/Klara Schilliger wie auch Janusz Baldyga zum zentralen Teil der Performancehandlung, die im Fall von Maly/Schilliger zwei Wochen in Anspruch nahm und in einer Schaufenstersituation im Kunstraum Marks Blond Project von aussen durch das Publikum permanent beobachtbar war.

1 www.installaction.com

2 Katja Schenker, *Arbeiten an der Erdoberfläche*. Nürnberg, Verlag für moderne Kunst Nürnberg, 2011.

3 Heute besteht von diesem Teil der Performance ein Video.

Janusz Baldyga, PL

Janusz Baldyga aus Warschau (geboren 1954 in Lublin) begann seine künstlerische Karriere als Performer im Aktionstheater, das im Polen der 1970er Jahre eine wichtige soziokulturelle Funktion hatte. Mitbegründer und Mitglied der Künstlergruppe Pracownia (1976–1981), zusammen mit Jerzy Onuch und Łukasz Szajna (1976 1979), Mitbegründer der Pracownia Gallery in Warschau, Mitglied der Akademia Ruchu (Movement Academy) seit 1979. Heute ist er als Performer und Plastiker tätig, wobei seine Objekte oft ihren Anfang in einer Performance nehmen, indem er beispielsweise Tische mit einem Tuch bedeckt und in pausenlosem Umgehen mit einer Schnur umwickelt. Oder er balanciert auf einem Holzbrett, das er zugleich Schritt um Schritt zu brechen vermag, was schlussendlich ein ringförmiges Objekt ergibt. Während des Projekts *Bauch des Wals* hat er zwei Performances aufgeführt, in Konstanz und in Sierre. In der *Double Flag Performance* in Sierre verschob er auf dem Tennisplatz mit Hilfe verschiedener Halter aus Eisen und seiner eigenen Körperkraft ein 2 × 3 Meter grosses Holzbrett vom Boden in die Vertikale, das so als Installation für den Rest des Symposiums stehen blieb.

Christophe Fellay, CH

Christoph Fellay ist Schlagzeuger und zeitgenössischer Komponist (geboren 1966). Als Musiker ist er vor allem im Bereich Sound-Installation und Soundscape aktiv. Er hat beispielsweise als Stipendiat in San Francisco einen grossen Soundscape vor Ort entwickelt und installiert. Zudem interpretiert er sein Instrument, das Schlagzeug, zunehmend als räumliche Skulptur, die mit Hilfe von räumlichen Positionierungen einen Raumklang in der Architektur erzeugt. Dazu nimmt er oft auch elektronische Erweiterungen seines Instruments mit Samplern und Lautsprechern vor.

Das künstlerische Projekt für *Bauch des Wals,* präsentiert im Kunstraum Marks Blond in Bern, ging von der Idee aus, den Besucher des Projektraums mit der Stadt und ihren Geräuschen in Verbindung zu setzen. Für ein Soundscape wurden reale Geräusche in der Spychergasse gesammelt, die über ein an der Schaufensterscheibe des Raums angebrachtes Mikrophon verstärkt und in den Raum zurückgespielt wurden. Der Projektraum wurde so zu einem Klangraum, der die Stadt wie einen lebendigen Körper wahrnehmen liess: real oder imaginiert. Der Aussenraum wiederum bildete den erweiterten Wahrnehmungsraum für die Geräusche der Gasse und des Verkehrs. Zudem brachte Christophe Fellay in Bern und Sierre Konzeptmusik mit verschiedenen Trommeln, Schlagzeug, Schlaginstrumenten und Live-Elektronik zur Aufführung.

Simon Kindle, FL/ Sophie Hofer / Katrin Keller, CH

Kindle, geboren 1983 in Vaduz, arbeitet nach seinem Studium der bildenden Kunst an der Hochschule Luzern – Design & Kunst vor allem im Bereich Installation, Szenographie und Performance. Die Aktion *Vaduz, my pleasure – es ist uns ein Vergnügen (+[pozitif, -iv])* bestand aus der Situierung eines Performanceobjekts, in dem der Künstler selbst Platz fand, vor dem Kunstraum Vaduz, einer Rede von Sophie Hofer und der Möglichkeit der Interaktion durch das Publikum, das den Künstler im Performanceobjekt in Schwingung versetzen konnte. Das Objekt war so Skulptur geworden; die Rede war eine Einweihungsrede der Skulptur im öffentlichen Raum. Das Städtle Vaduz, das bereits mit Skulpturen übermöbliert ist, erhielt so ein weiteres Exponat, wenn auch nur temporär. Für seine Arbeit in Sierre hatte Simon Kindle seine Kollegin Katrin Keller eingeladen. Die beiden Performer beobachteten und reflektierten – schwarz gekleidet und mit seltsamen Kothurnen beschuht – das Symposium zwei Tage lang, ohne ein Wort zu sprechen. Das Schweigen des Marcel Duchamp wurde stark überbewertet, die Referenz an Joseph Beuys und damit verbunden an Duchamp war bewusst gesucht. Zudem stellte sich die Frage, ob das gezielte und für alle sichtbare Beobachten als stumme Handlung von zwei Personen die Atmosphäre bzw. die Essenz eines Symposiums beeinflussen würde. Hat es nicht? Hat es doch?

Pe Lang, CH

Geboren 1974, Klang-Performer. Der Künstler arbeitet mit Klang-Installationen, Performance und Komposition. Dafür fokussiert er oft minimale kinetische Systeme, einfachste elektronische Mittel, die mit verschiedenen Materialien kombiniert werden. So entstehen ungewöhnliche Klangquellen. In seinen Arbeiten ist ein aufs Minimum reduzierter Materialgebrauch vorherrschend (Uhrgläser, Batterien, Elektrodraht etc.). Er bringt diese Materalen mit einfachen Koppelungen und Schaltungen zum Klingen.

Lang realisierte zahlreiche Kompositionen und Klang-Performances, z. B. für Transmediale Berlin, Elektra Montreal, Sonic Arts Amsterdam, Dissonanze Roma, isea Singapore oder Bitforms Gallery New York. Er erhielt zahlreiche Preise und Werkbeiträge für seine Arbeit (Bundesamt für Kultur, Swiss Art Award, artists-in-lab).

Für das Projekt *Bauch des Wals* konzipierte Pe Lang eine Live-Sound-Performance im K3 in Zürich, und für das Château Mercier in Sierre liess er auf einer Plastikmembran mit Vertiefungen über eine elektrisch gesteuerte Vibration kleine Kugeln rotieren, die ein für die Besucher des öffentlichen Parks irritierendes Geräusch erzeugten.

Davor Ljubičić, DE

Der in Bosnien aufgewachsene Künstler (geboren 1958, Studium an der Akademie der Bildenden Künste in Sarajevo 1980–1984) lebt seit 1992, dem Jahr seiner Flucht aus Banja Luka im Jugoslawien-Krieg, in Deutschland. Er kommt von einer expressiven, raumgreifenden Malerei – vor allem mit Graphit oder Graphitpulver –, die oft in performativen Malsettings entstand. In

seinen aktuellen Installationen arbeitet er auch mit gefundenen Materialien, einfacher Elektronik, Spiegeln und Sound-Elementen, die er in seine Malerei einfügt oder in räumlichen Situationen installiert.

Für den Kunstraum K3 in Zürich hat der Künstler ein Objekt mit einem Tisch, zwei gefundenen Milchkannen und einer Sound-Installation realisiert: *O.T. (TWINS)*, Video-Objekt, 2008/09. Der Sound rührte von Kratzgeräuschen mit seinen Fingernägeln an den Milchkannen her. Die Milchkannen haben wiederum eine eigene Geschichte: Er hatte sie aus einem Nachlass von Freunden, die ihren Haushalt wegen Scheidung auflösten, übernommen. Für Sierre hat der Künstler im Turmaufgang die Zeichnungsperformance und Installation *O.T.C. ora et labora* (2010/11) inszeniert. Grossformatige Graphitzeichnungen hingen im Raum; eine in den Raum projizierte Videoaufzeichnung – wiederum mit irritierenden Kratzgeräuschen – zeigte den Künstler beim Zeichnen mit einem an ein schweres Metallkreuz befestigten Stück Graphit.

Valerian Maly / Klara Schilliger, CH

Die in Bern lebenden Künstler Klara Schilliger, geboren 1953 in Sursee, und Valerian Maly, geboren 1959 in Tübingen, arbeiten seit 1984 gemeinsam in den Bereichen Performance Art und Installation. Für einige spezifische Werke (meist mit direktem Einbezug des Publikums) verwenden sie den Begriff der ‹InstallAction›. Die intermediären Installationen und Performances sind oft ortsbezogene Interventionen, denen projektbezogene Recherchen vorausgehen. Maly / Schilliger weisen eine rege Ausstellungs- und Performancetätigkeit in etablierten Instituten der Kunstszene ebenso wie an innovativen Offspaces und Festivals in Europa, den USA und Asien auf. 2008 erhielten sie den Kunstpreis der Stadt Bern.

Im Rahmen der Ausstellung *A travers le champs* im Goms im Oberwallis (2008) führten Klara Schilliger und Valerian Maly eine zweiteilige Aktion durch. Für *In Gold geritzte Ranken* wurde eine InstallAction von 2008/09 in der spätgotischen Pfarrkirche von Münster erarbeitet, die dem Hochaltar des Ortes gewidmet war. Die zweiteilige Arbeit umfasste einerseits die Initiierung und Herausgabe eines Kunstführers (zu Ostern 2009, rechtzeitig zum 500-Jahr-Jubiläum der Weihung des Hochaltars), andererseits eine raumgreifende Installation mit variablen Objekten im Kirchenraum selbst, die schon auf das Erscheinen des Kunstführer hinwies. Zwischen Aktion und Objekt pendeln sich somit ihre Arbeiten ein, was der eigens kreierte Begriff InstallAction treffend umreisst. Sie benutzen Strukturen und Systeme, um installativ etwas zu bauen, was über einen längeren Zeitraum hinweg bestehen bleibt; und Action verweist auf Aktion, die temporär etwas bewirkt und auch hinterlässt.

Für die Projektstation von *Bauch des Wals* im Berner Offspace Marks Blond erarbeiteten sie eine neue Installation mit Performance, die sich um den biblischen Text der Jonas-Geschichte dreht. Mit Zeichenkohle, die aus Rebreisern vom Weinberg um das Schloss Mercier nach einem alten Rezept des Renaissancemalers Cennino Cennini (um 1370–1440, Florenz) hergestellt wurde, schrieben die zwei Kunstschaffenden in einer zwei Wochen dauernden Aktion im Marks Blond die biblische Geschichte von Jonah und dem Wal in Hebräisch, Arabisch und Deutsch Wort für Wort auf die Wände des Kunstraums. Verschiedene Lesungen aus der Bibel auf Hebräisch, Arabisch und Deutsch nach der interlinearen Bibelübersetzung (auch in Sierre) begleiteten die Aktion.

Victorine Müller, CH

Bei Victorine Müllers Performances und Installationen spielen der Körper und das Licht in seiner suggestiven Wirkung eine zentrale Rolle. Androgyne Fabelwesen zwischen Traum und Sinnlichkeit werden von der Künstlerin thematisiert. Mit ihren Werken schafft sie zeitgemässe Darstellungen der menschlichen Figur, die sie in oder zwischen grosse transparente Hüllen oder Raumelemente positioniert. Die dabei entstehenden Hüllen haben oft einen objekthaften Charakter. In den letzten Jahren hat Müller die Skulpturen und Zeichnungen auch losgelöst von ihren Performances in musealen Räumen gezeigt, zuletzt im Weiertal bei Winterthur (2013), in der Kirche Saint-Merri Paris (2012), in der Kunsthalle Wil (2011), in der Konkordienkirche Mannheim (2010), im Kunstmuseum Solothurn (2008), im project space der Kunsthalle Wien (2008) sowie im Centre PasquArt Biel (2007). Die grossformatigen transparenten Objekte werden im Ausstellungsraum vor allem durch Theaterlicht in Szene gesetzt, was ihre Körperlichkeit verändert.

Für den Kunstraum Vaduz erarbeitete Victorine Müller im Rahmen des Projekts *Bauch des Wals* mit Lichtobjekten und opaken Figuren aus Pappmaché eine neue Installation mit dem Titel *Pressentiment* (2010). In Sierre installierte sie den *Erdling*, eine transparente walförmige Skulptur, mit Lichteffekten auf der Terrasse des Schlosses.

Boris Nieslony, DE

Geboren 1945 in Grimma, verbrachte Boris Nieslony seine Kindheit und Jugend in Heimen. Zum Künstler wurde er durch eine Aktion: Ab dem 2. Oktober 1966 lebte er neun Monate lang innerhalb eines Kreidekreises auf dem Georgsplatz in Hannover. Von 1969 bis 1974 studierte Nieslony Malerei in Berlin, doch wechselte er dann zur Performance nach Hamburg. Nach dem Studium führte er grosse performative Aktionen im Künstlerhaus Hamburg und im Künstlerhaus Stuttgart (1980, *Das Konzil,* an dem für 30 Tage insgesamt 70 Künstler beteiligt waren) durch. Zugleich baute er Performance-Netzwerke auf. 1985 kam es zur Gründung der Performancegruppe *Black Market International*, die ursprünglich sieben Künstler umfasste. 1986 gründete er die *Art Service Association* für Performer und Theoretiker (ASA).

Nieslony versteht seine Arbeit gleichermassen formal wie thematisch und inhaltlich orientiert. Ein wesentliches Thema ist die Kunst der Begegnung. In diesem Sinne – nicht nur in Kontrast zum klassischen Kunstmarkt – gehören Begegnungen und die Zusammenarbeit mit anderen Künstlern zu seinem Werk. Aus Gründungen und Mitgründungen des Künstlers entstanden viele, teils langlebige Initiativen, Gruppen und Projekte. Hierzu zählen seit 1995 die Serie der *Performance Konferenzen*, die Theorie und Praxis verbindet, wie auch das Performancearchiv *Die Schwarze Lade*. Im Rahmen des Projekts *Bauch des Wals* war er Gast und Beobachter des Symposiums. Er führte im Billardzimmer des Schloss Mercier eine Performance auf: Eine Stunde lang lag er auf dem Billardtisch in seitlicher Lage und legte sich Sonnenblumenkerne ins Ohr, die neben ihm auf dem grünen Velours aufgehäuft waren.

Denis Romanovski, SE

Für den 1970 in Minsk geborenen, heute in Stockholm lebenden Künstler ist Performance vor allem eine gesellschaftliche Handlung. Der früher als Spitzensportler (Langlauf) aktive Romanovski thematisiert dabei vor allem Fragen der Event- und Medienkultur. So hat er als Langlaufmarathon-Teilnehmer am Wasa-Lauf seine direkten körperlichen Erlebnisse in einer Live-Schaltung zu einem Kunstpublikum nach Stockholm transportiert. Sein besonderes Interesse gilt dem Phänomen Karaoke, das nicht nur als Live-Performance eine künstlerische Plattform darstellt, sondern ihn auch als installatives Element fasziniert.

Für das Projekt *Bauch des Wals* baute er ein leeres Aquarium mit der Aufschrift *NO FISH HERE* (2011) im Teich des Parks auf und… begann zu angeln.

Dorothea Rust, CH

Das Projekt der erst als Tanzperformerin, später als Künstlerin ausgebildeten Dorothea Rust interessiert vor allem durch ihre raumgreifenden Körperaktionen, die auf dem Medium Tanz basieren, aber auch Materialen, Gesten und Objekte. Sie ist mit einem Fundus an Materialien und Objekten unterwegs – Teppichen, Rucksäcken, Fischerstiefeln, Giesskanne, Seilen, Zetteln mit Wörtern, Äpfeln, aber auch mit Bewegungen und gesungenen Tönen –, mit denen sie jeweils ortsspezifische Installationen oder Situationen performativ erarbeitet. Im Kunstraum K3 in Zürich verstellte sie eine offene Raumsituation mit ihren Seilen, Objekten und Äpfeln. *Newtons Äpfel* (2010/11) brachte ihren Fundus gegen die Schwerkraft zum Schweben. Zudem warf sie bei der Finissage etwa 6000 Briefumschläge aus dem Fenster in den Hof, die alle an sie adressiert waren und authentische Postsendungen an die Künstlerin darstellten. Nach Sierre brachte sie die Äpfel und ein paar Objekte mit, die sie im Park verteilte. In einer Performance mit dem Publikum liess sie sich mit verbundenen Augen durch das Publikum zu den verschiedenen Orten, wo die Objekte installiert waren, mit Worten dirigieren.

Katja Schenker, CH

Die Performancekünstlerin Katja Schenker ist in letzter Zeit vor allem durch ortsspezifische Installationen und materialbetonte Performances aufgefallen. Ihre Arbeiten mit Stoff, Schläuchen, Fallschirmseide, Asphalt, Beton, Backsteinen und anderen Materialien machen eine einfache körperliche Handlung zur Ausgangslage. Die Werke bleiben aber auch als Objekte nach der Performance, nach der Aktion zurück. In Bern hat sie im Hof der Verwaltung der schweizerischen Landestopografie einen Platz von Hand asphaltiert und mit Sträuchern bepflanzt. Von Hand terrassierte Löcher in der Erde, selbst hergestellte Konglomeratgesteine, doppelte Böden: Die Künstlerin erarbeitet mit ihren Materialien und ihrer eigenen Körperkraft grossformatige, eher architektonisch anmutende Flächen in Innen- und Aussenräumen. Eigentliche Topografien. Für das Projekt *Bauch des Wals* im Kunstverein Konstanz entwickelte sie eine neue Performance mit Papier, das von der Grösse her sieben mal die Bodenfläche des grossen Oberlichtsaals umfasste, also 134 m², und vor der Ausstellung in einer Turnhalle mit zahlreichen Helfern (aber ohne Maschinen) auf das Volumen von 1,6 × 1,8 × 0,7 m zusammengepresst worden war. Bei der Eröffnung der Ausstellung stand in der Mitte des Raums ein kleiner, unscheinbarer weisser Ballen, umfasst von straff gezurrten Schnüren. Die Künstlerin zerrte und faltete diesen Ballen während der Eröffnung auseinander. Sie zog das zerknüllte Papier in alle Ecken des Raums und schuf so gleichzeitig eine bizarre, im hellen Licht des Raums an einen Gletscher erinnernde Papierlandschaft.

Ein Teil des Papiers reiste nach Sierre weiter in die Bibliothek des Schloss Mercier.

Stuart Sherman, USA

Die Präsentation eines berühmten Performanceobjekts von Stuart Sherman (1945/2001, USA) war in Zusammenarbeit mit dem Theaterfachmann Klaus Hersche im K3 in Zürich zu sehen. Stuart Sherman galt als innovativer Performancekünstler und Autor, der auch Drehbücher für Theater, Film und Video schrieb. Seine Performances, die vor allem ab den 1970er Jahren entstanden, nannte er *spectacles;* es waren präzise geplante, stupend rhythmisierte Abläufe und Demonstrationen zu bestimmten Alltagsobjekten, die der Künstler auf einem einfachen Klapptischchen – oft in Parks, an Strassenecken aufgestellt – präsentierte und mit absurden Sprachgesten, Wort- und Textfetzen begleitete. Es konnten aber auch Theaterstoffe sein, die er mit den Utensilien auf dem Tisch aufführte: *Faust, Hamlet, Ödipus* als One-Man-Show. Seine *spectacles* filmte er mit Videokameras; die Filme werden heute im Museum of Modern Art in New York aufbewahrt, sein Archiv in der Fales Library der New York University.

Im K3 war sein Performance-Klapptisch mit verschiedenen Utensilien samt Koffer zu sehen. Klaus Hersche (früher Leiter des Festivals Belluard in Freiburg, CH) zeichnete anhand von Filmmaterial und eigenen Erinnerungen an den

Künstler Stuart Sherman die Arbeit mit dem Performance-Tisch nach. Der Klapptisch war im Jahr 2000 bei Hersche geblieben, nachdem Sherman eine Performance beim Belluard Bollwerk Festival realisiert hatte und dann auf Reisen ging. Den Tisch liess er bei Hersche zurück, weil er nicht wusste, wann er wieder eine feste Wohnung haben würde. 2001 starb er an AIDS.

Berclaz de Sierre, CH

Berclaz de Sierre, geboren am 15. April 1986 in Paris, lebt in Siders und ist ein konzeptuell arbeitender Künstler, der sich vor allem mit dem Thema der Namensidentität auseinandersetzt. Dabei spielt seine eigene biografische Erfahrung eine zentrale Rolle. Als er sein Studium der Kunst in Genf 1998 beendet hatte, verbot ihm ein Namensvetter – der ebenfalls Künstler ist –, seinen eigenen Namen zu verwenden. Berclaz de Sierre benutzt seither diesen Künstlernamen als sein Label. In seiner Arbeit spielen fortan Namensvetter eine zentrale Rolle. Er sucht beispielsweise solche von bedeutenden, aber bereits verstorbenen Künstlern, z. B. von Leonardo da Vinci, Sandro Botticelli, Arnold Böcklin, Paul Klee, Albert Anker oder Jean Tinguely. Er stöbert per Telefonbuch oder Internet nach ihnen und besucht sie an ihrem Wohnort, wo er sie um ein Interview, eine Videoaufzeichnung und ein Fotoporträt bittet. Die Geschichten, die er dabei erlebt, haben ihren eigenen Stellenwert. Zudem interessieren ihn seit einiger Zeit auch Namen von Produkten (Möbel, Kleider, Schuhe, Accessoires). Er bestellt aus Versandkatalogen Kleidung, Möbelstücke, Werkzeuge oder andere Einrichtungsgegenstände, die Namen von berühmten Kulturschaffenden und Stars tragen. Aus diesen Objekten kombiniert er Räume, Einrichtungen für Ausstellungsräume, Installationen. Für das Projekt *Bauch des Wals* hat er im K3 einen *Gilbert & George*-Raum mit Möbeln, Teppichen und Taschen eingerichtet. In Konstanz war er mit Matratze *Konstanz* und Bettwäsche *Bodensee* unterwegs, und in Sierre führte er Kleidungsstücke und Unterwäsche mit dem Label *Gilbert* oder *George* auf der Treppe in der Halle im Schloss Mercier vor.

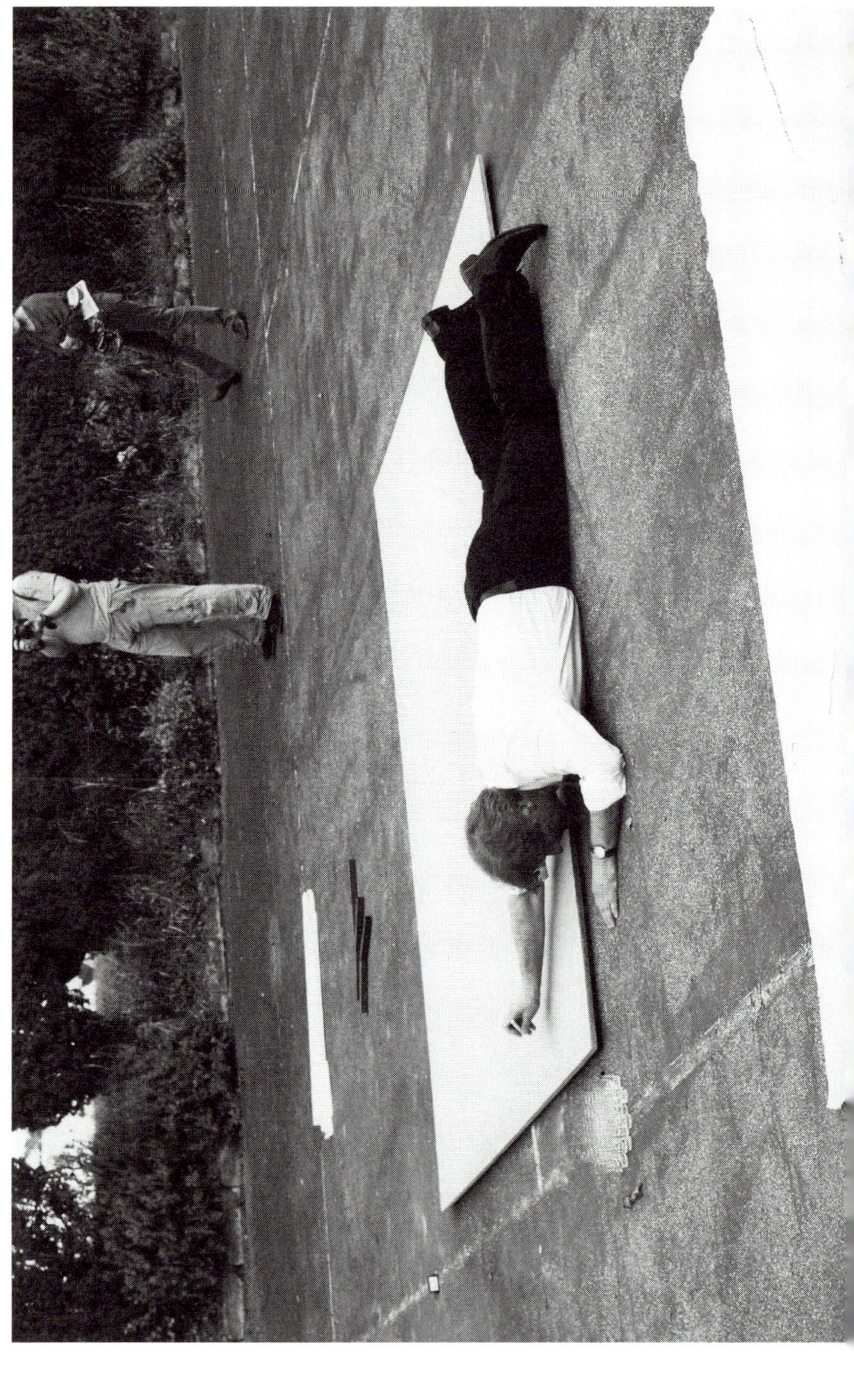

Janusz Baldyga

8.4.2011, Sierre
Janusz Baldyga auf dem Tennisplatz von Schloss Mercier mit der Performance/
Installation *Flag performance*. ©Sibylle Omlin

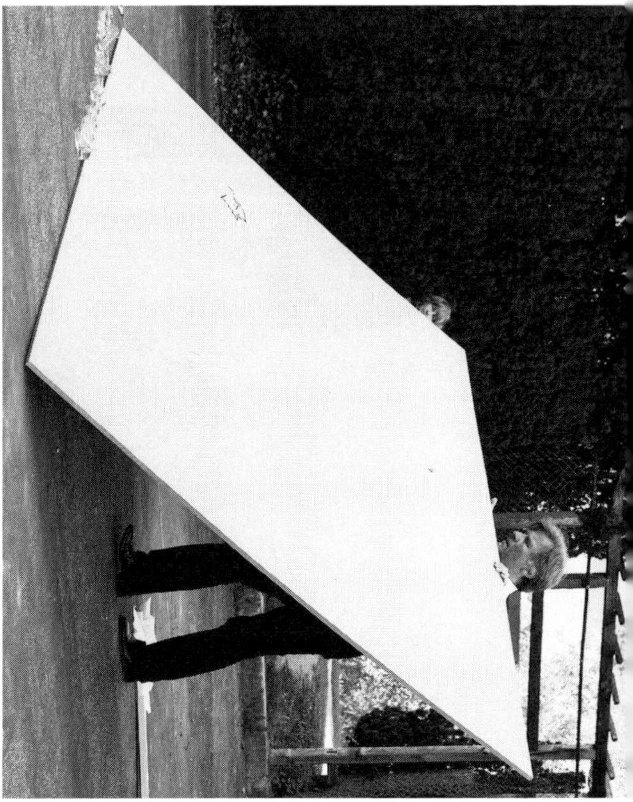

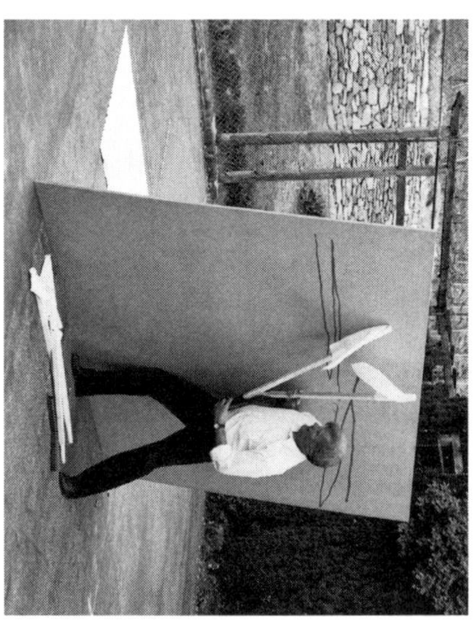

Janusz Baldyga

8.4.2011, Sierre
Janusz Baldyga and the performance/installation *Flag performance*
on the tennis court of Mercier Castle. ©Davor Ljubičić/Sibylle Omlin

Jarusz Baldyga

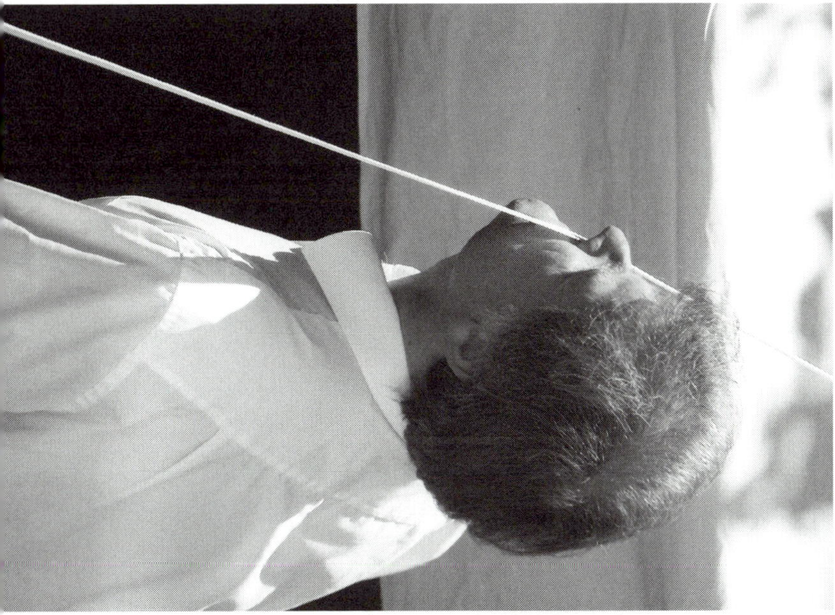

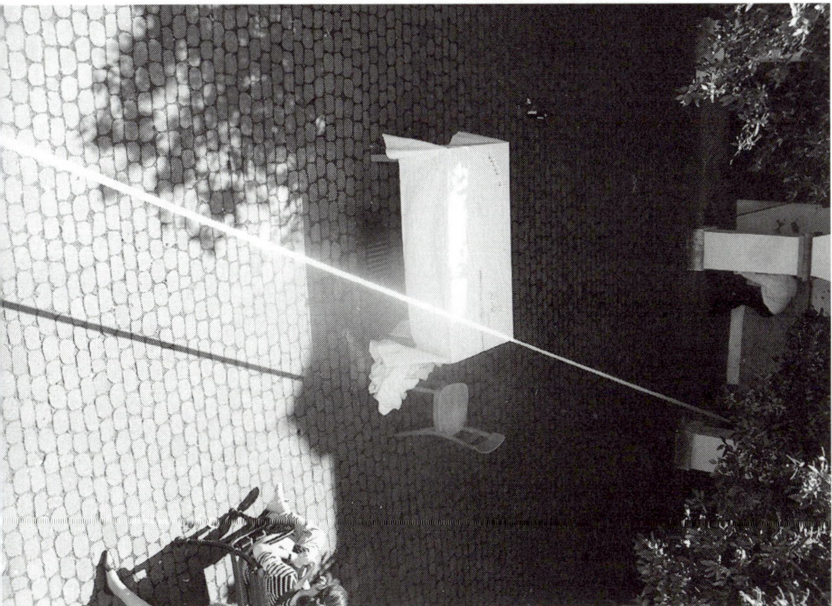

3.4.2011, Constance
Janusz Baldyga is performing *Market Place* in the courtyard
of the Kunstverein Constance. ©Stefan Postius/Sibylle Omlin

1.10.2010, Zürich
Berclaz de Sierre *Gilbert and George Tour I* im Ausstellungsraum K3,
Vernissage. ©Ingrid Kaeser

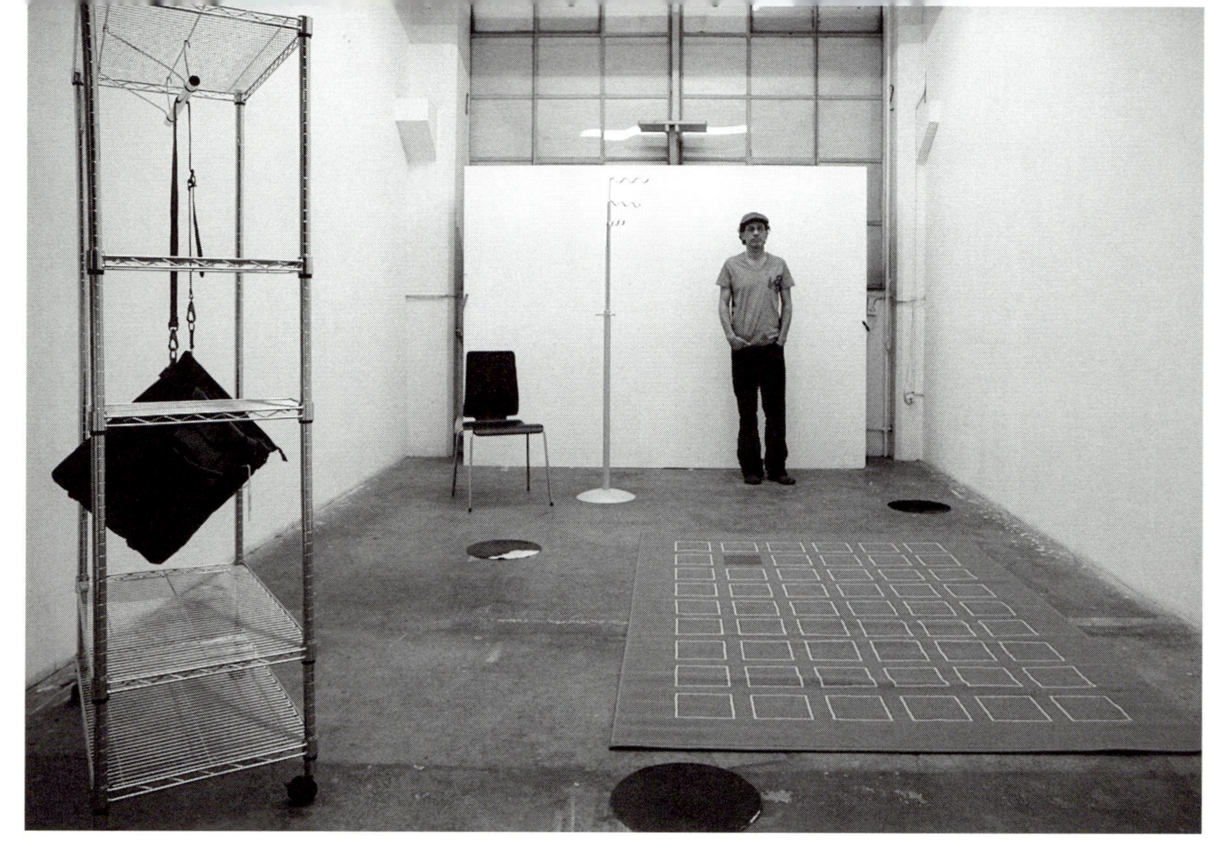

1.10.2010, Zurich,
Berclaz de Sierre *Gilbert and George Tour I*
at K3 exhibition space, opening. ©Ingrid Kaeser

Berclaz de Sierre

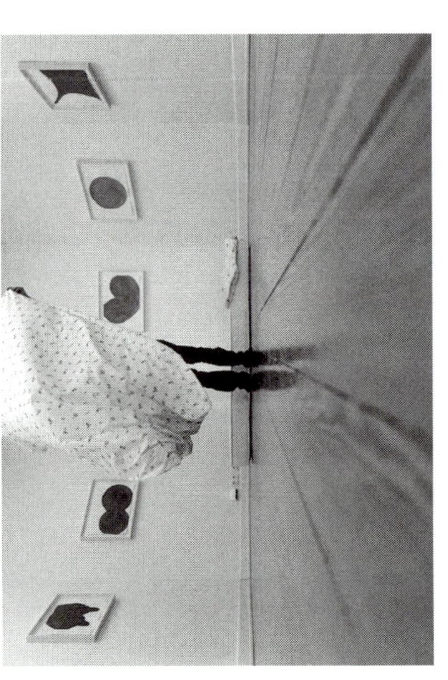
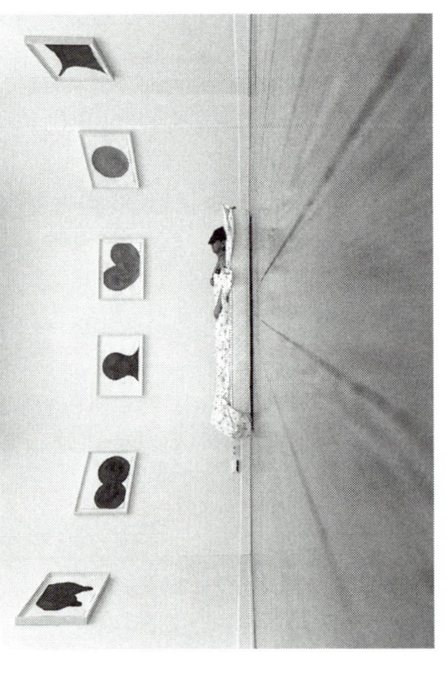
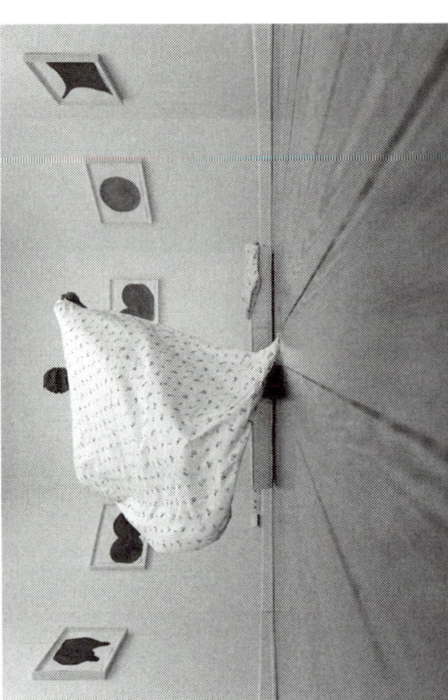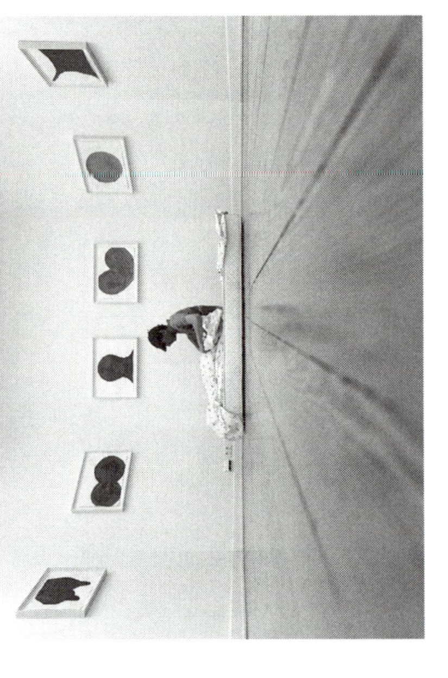

Berclaz de Sierre

3.4.2011, Konstanz
Berclaz de Sierre *Gilbert and George Tour II* im Kunstverein Konstanz,
Kabinett (im Hintergrund Zeichnungen von Katja Schenker), Finissage.
©Stefan Postius

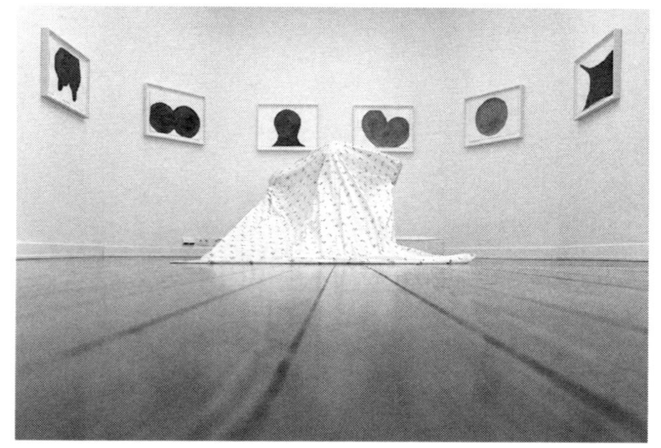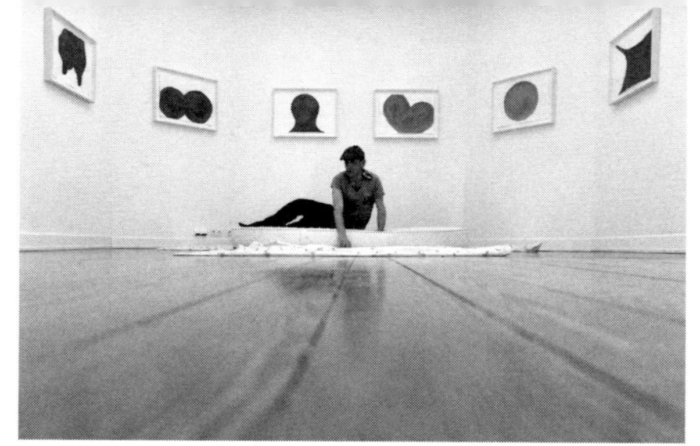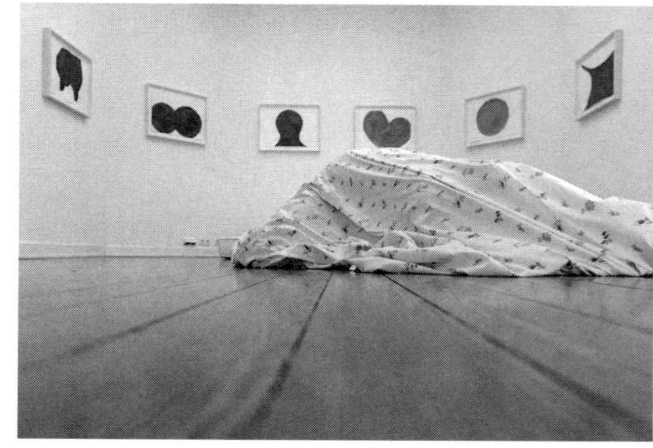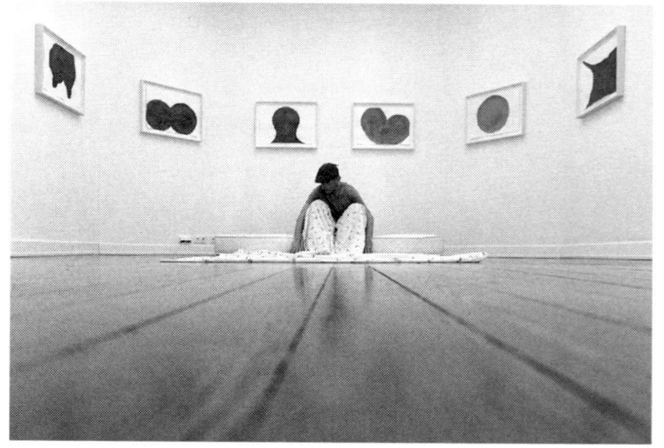

3.4.2011, Constance
Berclaz de Sierre *Gilbert and George Tour II* at Kunstverein Konstanz,
drawing room (background drawings from Katja Schenker),
closing day. ©Stefan Postius

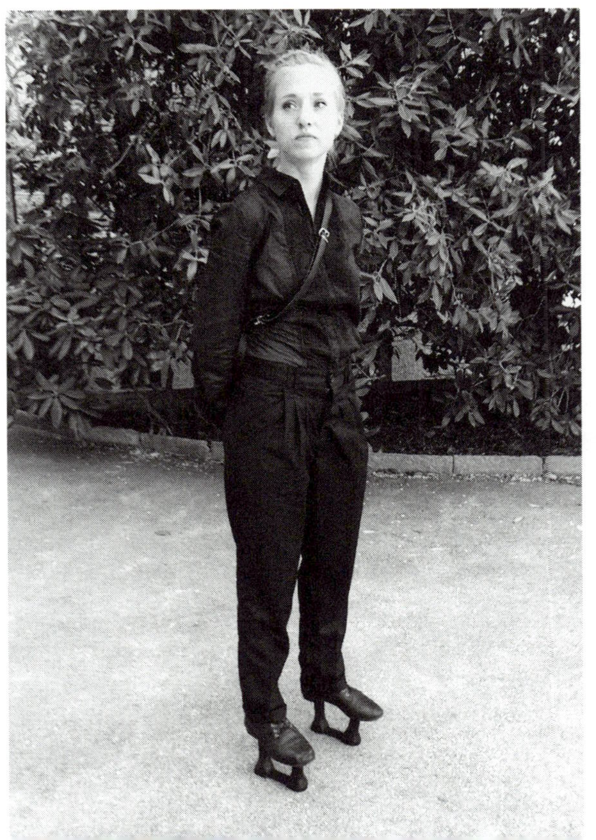

9.4.2011, Sierre
Katrin Keller bei ihrer *long duration performance* mit Simon Kindle
während des zweitägigen Symposiums *Perform the exhibition space*
im Schloss Mercier in Sierre. ©Davor Ljubičić

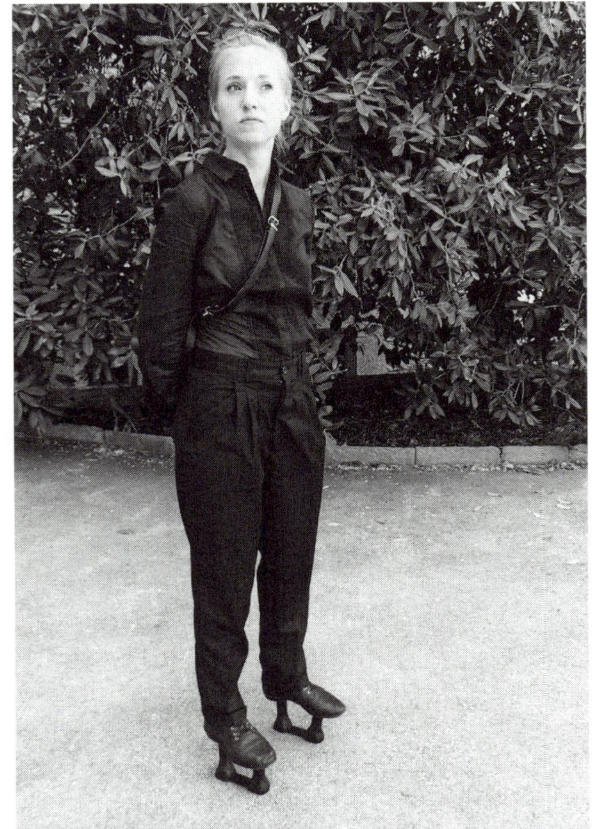

9.4.2011, Sierre
Katrin Keller during her *long duration performance*
with Simon Kindle at the symposium *Perform the exhibition space*
in Mercier Castle. ©Davor Ljubičić

Boris Nieslony

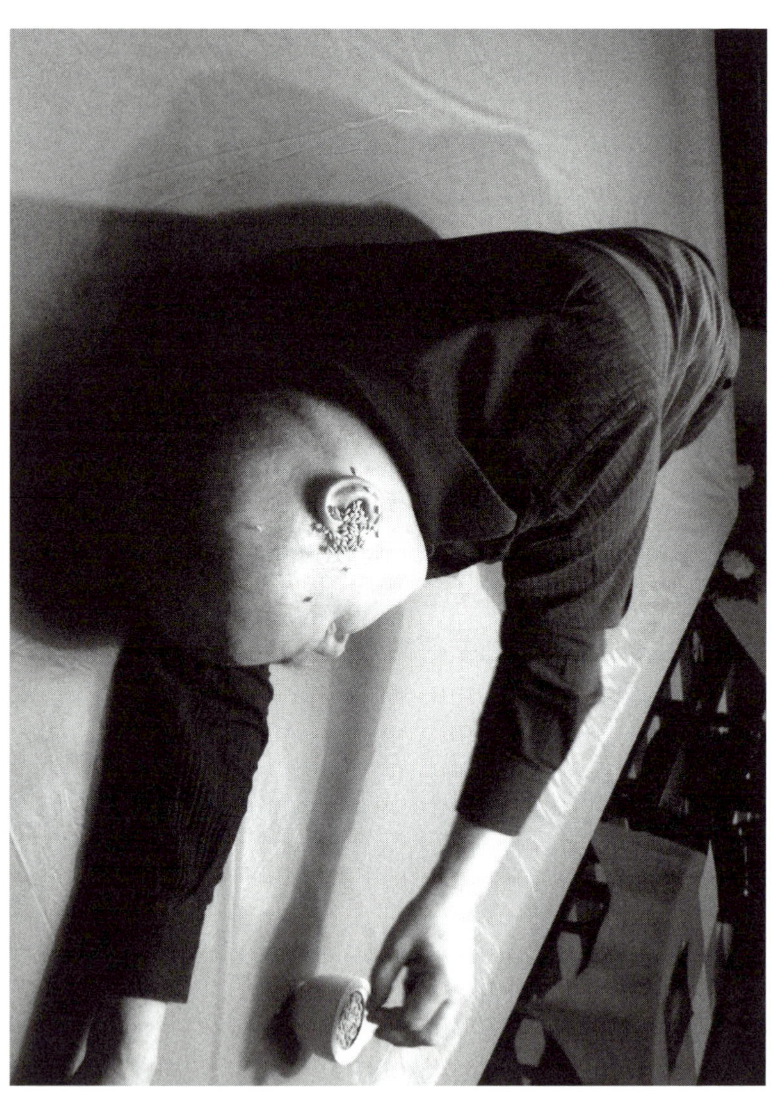

9.4.2011, Sierre
Boris Nieslony is performig on a billard table at Mercier Castle,
moving sunflower cernels from a cup beside him to his ear.
© Sibylle Omlin

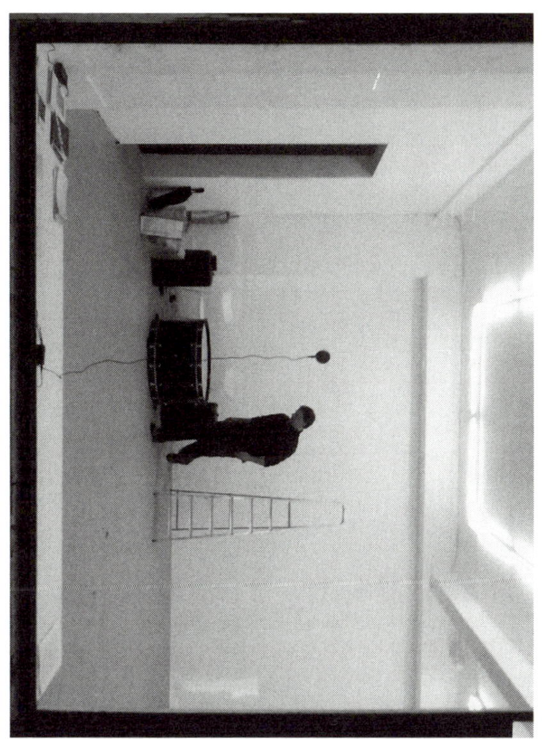

11.11.2010, Bern
Christophe Fellay installiert den Soundscape *Spychergasse 8*
im Kunstraum Marks Blond. © Sibylle Omlin

Christophe Fellay

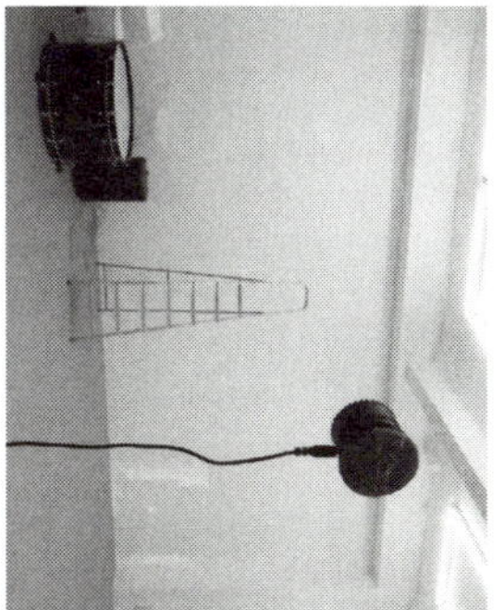

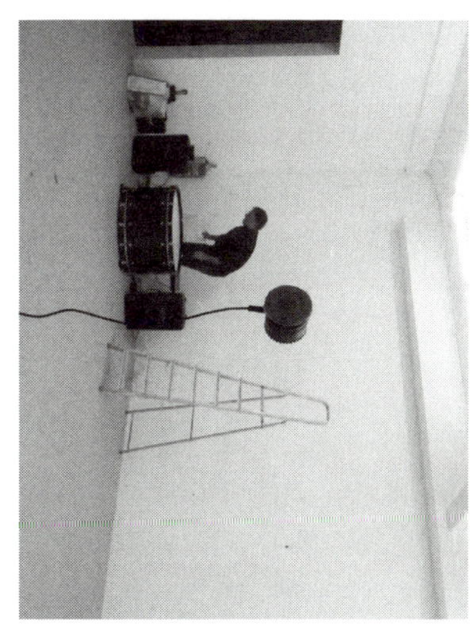

11.11.2010, Bern
Christophe Fellay installing the soundscape *Spychergasse 8*
at Marks Blond contemporary art space. © Sibylle Omlin

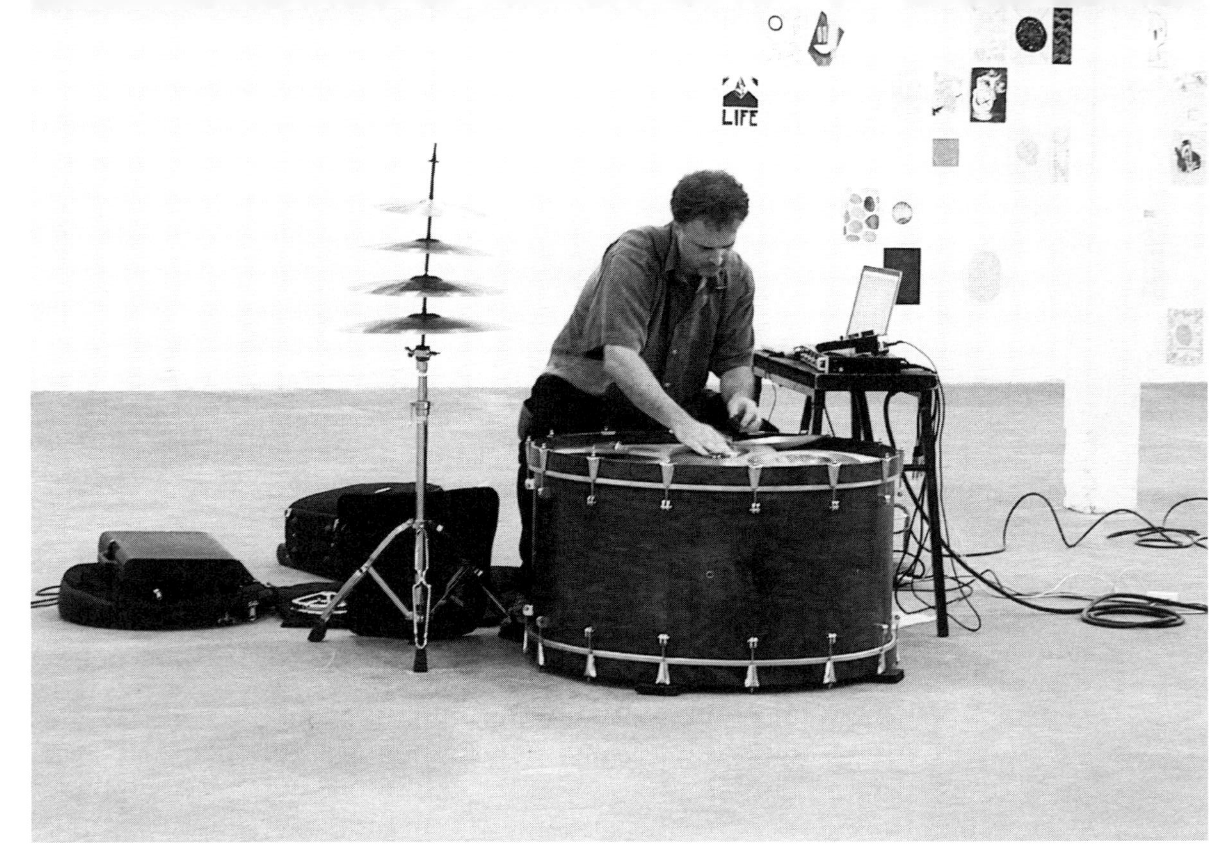

9.4.2011, Sierre
USEGO: Konzert von Christophe Fellay im Rahmen des Symposiums
Perform the exhibition space. © Claire Liengme

9.4.2011, Sierre
USEGO: concert of Christophe Fellay at the symposium
Perform the exhibition space in Sierre. ©Claire Liengme

Christophe Fellay

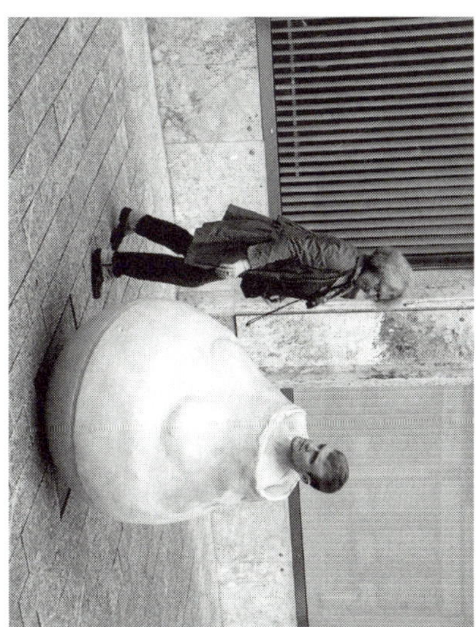

Simon Kindle/Sophie Hofer

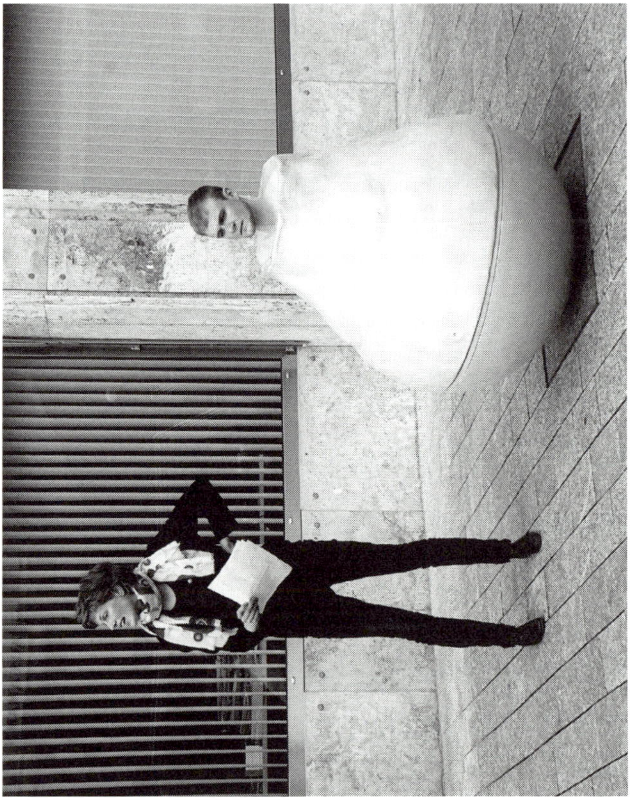

22.6.2010, Vaduz
Simon Kindle/Sophie Hofer bei der Performance *Vaduz, my pleasure*
im Städle vor dem Kunstraum Engländerbau. © Evelyne Bermann

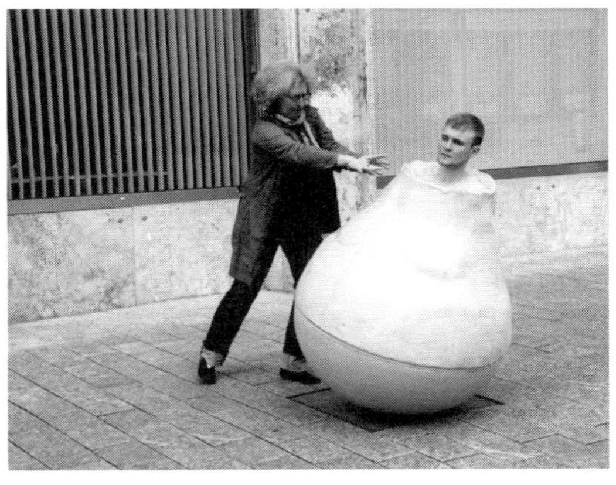

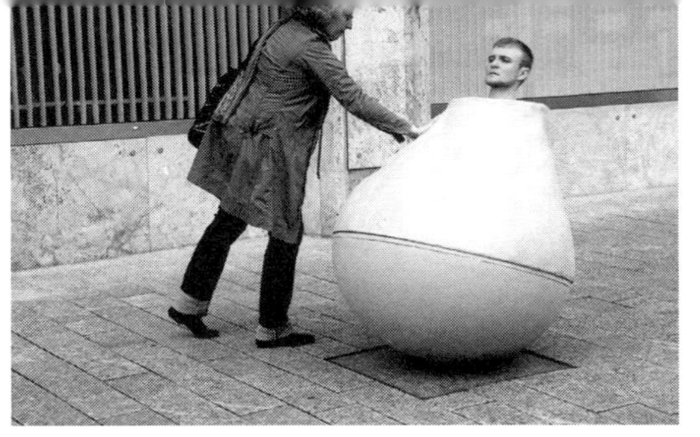

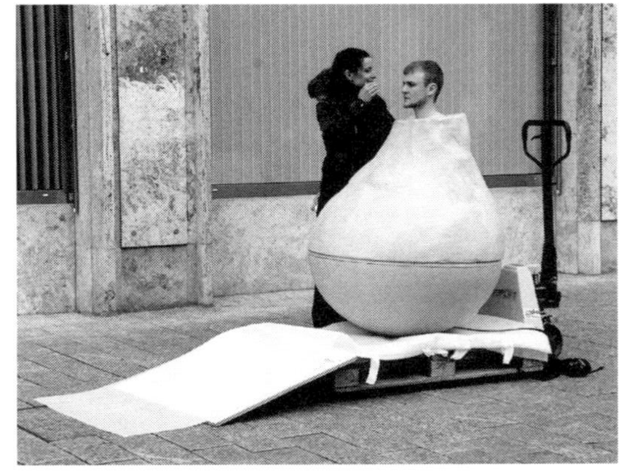

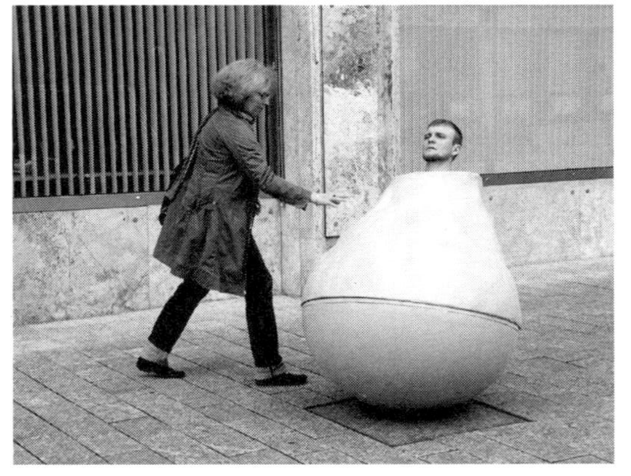

22.6.2010, Vaduz
Simon Kindle/Sophie Hofer during their performance *Vaduz, my pleasure*
at Städle in front of Kunstraum Engländerbau. ©Evelyne Bermann

Simon Kindle/Sophie Hofer

15.10.2010, Zürich
Untitled II, Performance im K3 von Pe Lang, Instrumente.
Konzept: Pe Lang und Marianthi Papalexandri-Alexandri. ©Ingrid Kaeser

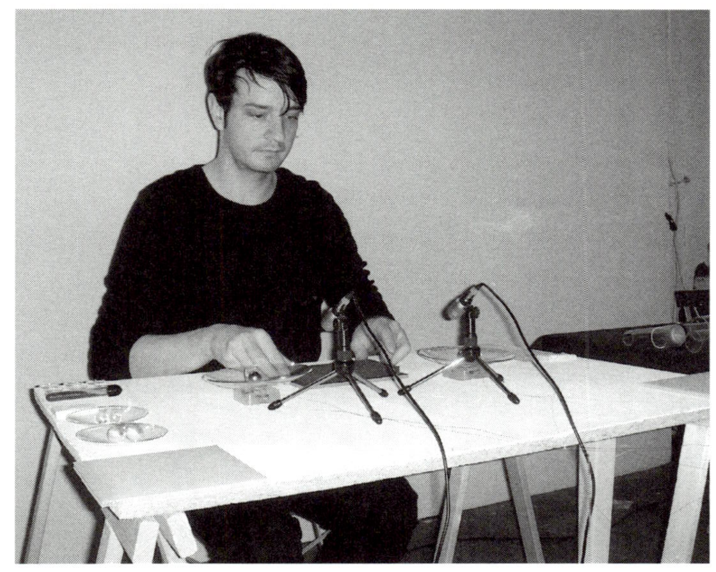

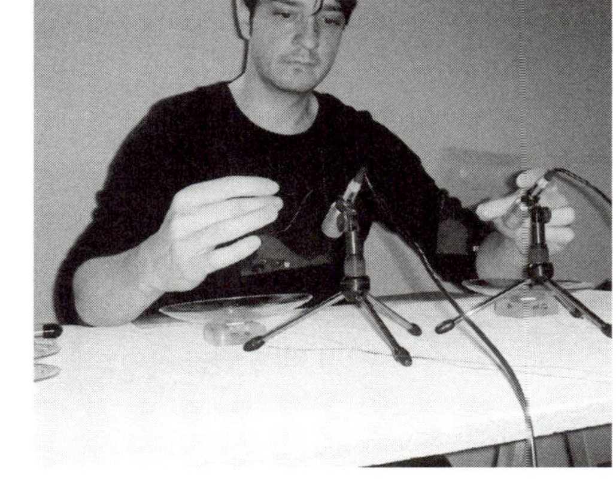

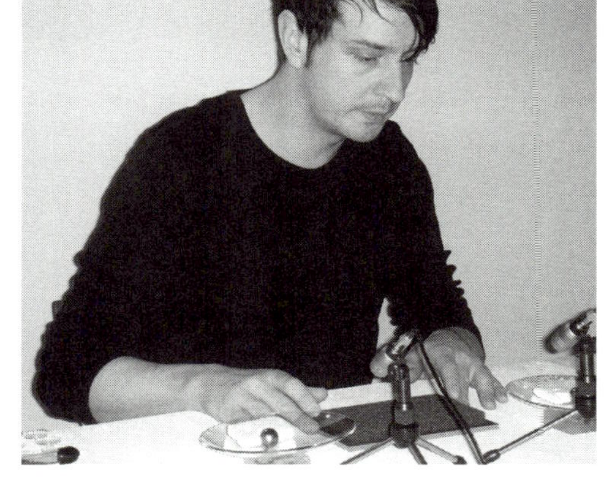

15.10.2010, Zurich
Untitled II, performance at K3 art space by Pe Lang, instruments,
concept: Pe Lang and Marianthi Papalexandri-Alexandri. ©Ingrid Kaeser

8.–10.4.2011, Sierre
Pe Langs Installation von vibrierenden Metallkügelchen in einem
Plastik-Board im Park von Schloss Mercier. © Davor Ljubičić

Pe Lang

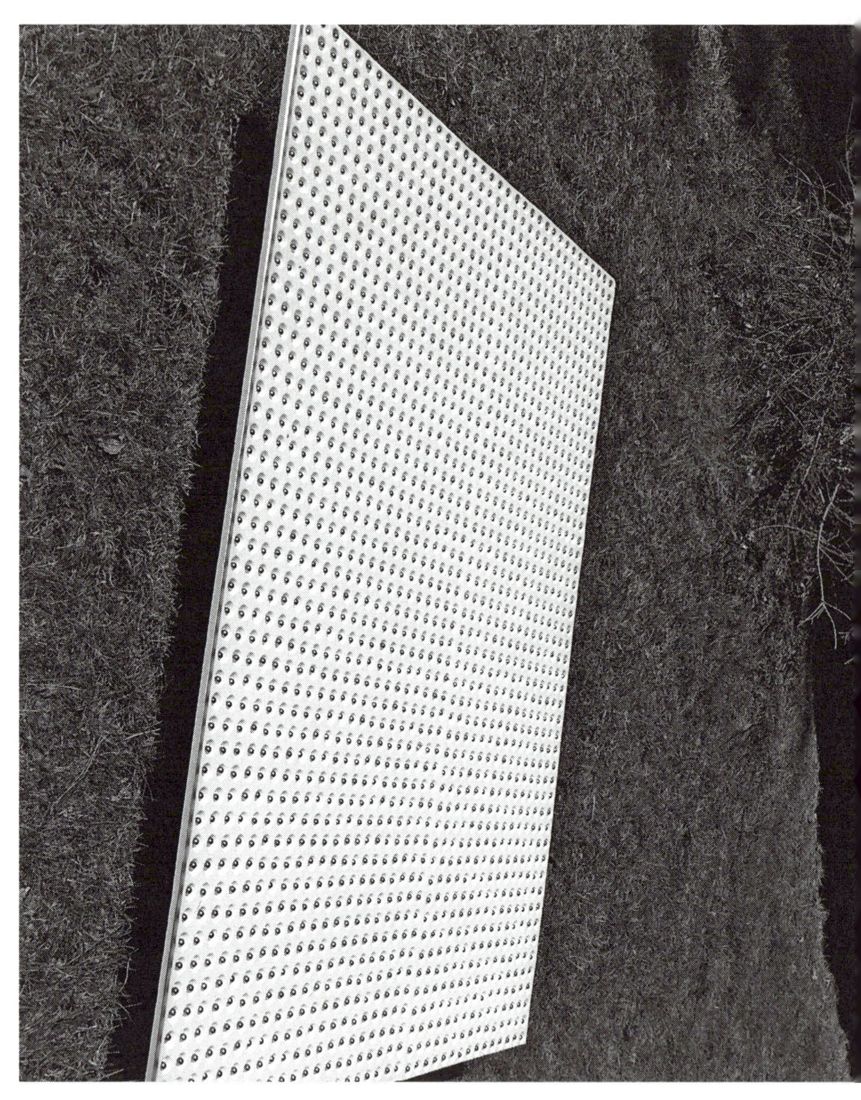

8.–10.4.2011, Sierre
Pe Lang, installation of vibrant metal balls on a plastic board
on the park of Mercier Castle. ©Davor Ljubičić